Regimes in Tropical Africa

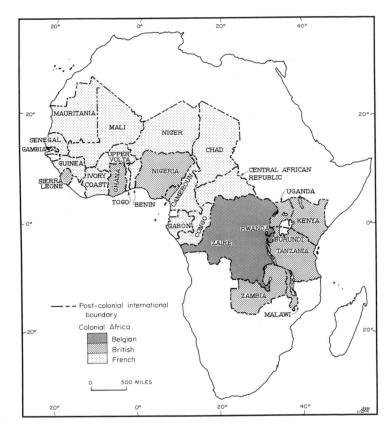

MAURITANIA
MALI
NIGER
CHAD
SENEGAL
GAMBIA
GUINEA
UPPER VOLTA
NIGERIA
CENTRAL AFRICAN REPUBLIC
SIERRA LEONE
IVORY COAST
GHANA
CAMEROUN
UGANDA
TOGO BENIN
GABON
CONGO
RWANDA
KENYA
BURUNDI
TANZANIA
ZAIRE
ZAMBIA
MALAWI

Post-colonial international boundary

Colonial Africa
Belgian
British
French

0   500 MILES

Callier

Regimes in Tropical Africa

Changing Forms of Supremacy, 1945-1975

RUTH BERINS COLLIER

University of California Press

Berkeley / Los Angeles / London

University of California Press
Berkeley and Los Angeles, California

University of California Press, Ltd.
London, England

© 1982 by
The Regents of the University of California

1 2 3 4 5 6 7 8 9

Library of Congress Cataloging in Publication Data

Collier, Ruth Berins.
    Regimes in Tropical Africa.

    Bibliography: p.
    Includes index.
    1. Africa, Sub-Saharan—Politics and government—1884–1960.
2. Africa, Sub-Saharan—Politics and government—1960
3. Nationalism—Africa, Sub-Saharan. I. Title.
DT352.7.C64   320.967   80–28445
ISBN 0–520–04313–8

For my parents
Esther Meyers Berins and Maurice H. Berins

Contents

Tables and Figures

Figures

Acknowledgments

I have incurred a number of debts in the course of writing this book. Donald Morrison, Mary Welfling, and Robert Jackman were most generous in their willingness to share data with me. I am grateful to those who read and commented on earlier versions of the manuscript: Aristide Zolberg, Philippe Schmitter, Sidney Verba, Richard Stryker, Sheldon Gellar, Raymond Hopkins, and Marc Ross. Special thanks are due to Robert Bates and Nelson Kasfir, whose detailed comments and encouragement were particularly helpful. Christopher Achen gave valued advice on methodological problems. Benjamin Most, Richard Miller, and Pamela Stefanowicz provided much appreciated research assistance.

I would also like to express appreciation to the International Development Institute and the Department of Political Science at Indiana University, the Center of International Studies at Princeton University, and the Institute of International Studies at the University of California, Berkeley, for providing indispensable institutional support. Particular thanks are due to Carl G. Rosberg, Director of the Berkeley Institute, and to its staff of skilled typists. Material previously published in "Parties, Coups, and Authoritarian Rule: Patterns of Political Change in Tropical Africa" is reprinted from *Comparative Political Studies* 11, no. 1 (April 1978): 62–93, by permission of the publisher, Sage Publications, Inc.

Last, but not least, I would like to thank my husband David, a political scientist in his own right, who encouraged, put up with, pitched in, and did all the kinds of things for which spouses have been made famous in end-of-book acknowledgments. I deeply appreciate the loving support he has given me in his roles as husband and critic.

1. Introduction

The end of World War II ushered in a period of changing forms of political supremacy across tropical Africa. Colonial rule, based on foreign military-bureaucratic domination, began to give way to a new mode of political domination. This process of decolonization was characterized by the introduction into the African colonies of many of the democratic institutions of the European colonial powers. Elections were held, the right to vote was extended until it became universal, political parties appeared on the scene to contest these elections, and the powers of government increasingly resided in an elected parliament and prime minister rather than with the colonial rulers. The new order, of course, was like the old in many important respects, particularly in the control of the economy, which in most cases was to remain unchanged after formal political independence as well. Nevertheless, this attempt to transfer democratic institutions to Africa meant a change in the personae of the ruling elite and an experiment in a different mode of political supremacy.

The new mode, which was theoretically based on popular sovereignty and electoral support rather than on coercion, posed both opportunities and risks to the new indigenous elite, in that a newly enfranchised electorate represented a potential source of political support but also a political resource that could be mobilized by rival elite groups. Across the continent, some nationalist movements were able to move into the new institutional context and harness this new source of political supremacy more successfully than others, and these differences had important consequences for subsequent patterns of political change. In almost all cases, however, the

new order was not sufficiently congruent with the needs or preferences of the emerging political elite, who after independence moved
quite rapidly and deliberately to dismantle these democratic institutions. There followed a period of political jockeying and institutional experimentation as political elites sought to establish various
types of authoritarian regimes which would allow them to consolidate power and prolong their rule.

A fundamental issue in this period of regime change in Africa thus
involved the formation of a new ruling elite or political class and the
new institutions and structures through which it tried to rule. Despite the existence of striking continuity, in most cases, between
certain aspects of colonial and independent (neocolonial) patterns
of rule, one should not lose sight of the problems that arose in the
transfer of power to an indigenous political class—a kind of over-
simplification that is likely to occur in formulations of this process
that emphasize the seemingly facile substitutions of new (Black)
faces in old (White) roles. There was no well-established political
class waiting in the wings for the opportunity to take over the reins
of power, nor did self-government and independence involve the
replacement of colonial rulers position for position in similar role
structures. Rather, political roles and structures were being changed
and created anew, a new political game was being introduced, and
in this context a new political class was created that sought some
basis for rule. The process of regime change, from the introduction
of democratic institutions to their abandonment and the establishment of authoritarian regimes, must thus be seen in terms of the
emergence of a new dominant class and, in turn, the attempts of
that class to consolidate its position. As Richard Sklar (1979) has
argued, class formation based on the exercise of political power is
one of the most important political and social processes occurring
across Africa, and the authoritarian regime is a major mechanism of
class consolidation.

This book is concerned with the ways in which the introduction
of electoral politics during the period of decolonization facilitated
or hampered the emergence of a cohesive political elite. It analyzes
the experience of the African political elite with these electoral
institutions, the steps political leaders took to adjust, transform,
and dismantle them, and the new structures of authoritarian rule set
up in their place.

The analysis seeks to delineate patterns within the rapid and seemingly chaotic sequences of change that have characterized African political regimes since independence and to address the question of why, and in which countries, certain patterns have been followed. Somewhat more specifically, the book explores differences among countries in the initial experience with electoral politics and the implications of those differences for the emergence of different types of regime and different patterns of regime change in the post-independence period. Furthermore, it attempts to understand the various types of regime that characterize independent Africa in terms of the tendency toward the types of supremacy or rule that they represent. The study is based on a comparative examination of the twenty-six Black African countries[1] that went through this process of decolonization after World War II and became independent in the late 1950s and early 1960s: the former colonies and trust territories of French West Africa, French Equatorial Africa, British West Africa, British East Africa, Malawi and Zambia in British Central Africa, and Belgian Africa.[2]

1. These are Burundi, Cameroun, Central African Republic, Chad, Congo (Brazzaville), Congo (later Zaire), Dahomey (later Benin), Gabon, The Gambia, Ghana, Guinea, Ivory Coast, Kenya, Malawi, Mali, Mauritania, Niger, Nigeria, Rwanda, Senegal, Sierra Leone, Tanzania (formerly Tanganyika, until the merger with Zanzibar in 1964), Togo, Uganda, Upper Volta, and Zambia.

Because a central goal of this book is to explore patterns of continuity and change in African countries from the period of decolonization through the post-independence period, I felt it was important to use a single name for each unit (colony/country) throughout the entire time period considered. I have therefore, with considerable twinges of discomfort, used the post-independence names when referring to the colonial period, even in cases in which the colonial name was different. The major exception is the reference to the pre-independence trust territory of Ruanda-Urundi, which became independent as the two separate countries of Rwanda and Burundi. In general, then, the names used throughout the book are the current names of the countries. In two countries, however, the current names were adopted so recently that I have, except for the most recent period, employed the name used for these countries during most of the post-independence period under consideration: Congo (Kinshasa), which was renamed "Zaire" in 1971, and Dahomey, which was renamed "Benin" in 1975. (To distinguish the two Congos, I refer, when necessary, to Congo-Brazzaville or Congo-Zaire.) Finally, it may be noted that "Tanzania" refers in the period before 1964 only to the mainland of Tanganyika, "Nigeria" includes only after unification in 1961 what had been Northern Cameroons before independence, and "Cameroun" refers to the French trust territory during the colonial period and to the union of this territory with the British trust territory of Southern Cameroons during the post-independence period.

2. This case base of twenty-six places the study at an intermediate level of comparative analysis which makes it possible to bring together two approaches to comparison that are valuable to combine: the selective use of statistical comparison, and the use of qualitative evidence and systematic qualitative comparison. Twenty-

This first chapter introduces three interrelated themes around which the study revolves: the analysis of national political regimes in tropical Africa, the consequences of the introduction of mass political participation, and the role of elections in the rise and functioning of authoritarian regimes. In order to provide a basis for understanding the emergence of the new political elite in Africa, Chapter 2 goes back to the period of decolonization to analyze the set of rules that defined a new political game, based on universal suffrage and competitive elections, which led to the creation of an indigenous political elite that would inherit the new state. Chapter 3 seeks to explain differences among colonies in the degree to which a relatively cohesive or divided political elite emerged through this new political game. Chapter 4 then argues that these differences had important implications for the ways in which the multi-party competitive institutions introduced during decolonization were dismantled as the dominant political elite or elite faction sought to consolidate and entrench its position. These differences likewise help to account for the distinct forms of authoritarian regimes that were set up, particularly the one-party regime and the military regime. Chapter 5 goes on to suggest the ways in which different post-independence regimes may serve to consolidate the position of the dominant elite: their potential for functioning as a legitimacy apparatus and the way in which they are designed to enlist at least the passive support of the masses and to manage the limited pluralism that characterizes authoritarian regimes. The concluding chapter synthesizes the analysis by identifying modal patterns of regime change in tropical Africa.

A final introductory point should be made about the time period covered in the analysis. The study focuses specifically on the experience with decolonization and the immediate post-independence period in Africa, and hence on a particular historical conjuncture: the period in which national elites came to assume power, created new political institutions, and initially attempted to consolidate

---

six cases hardly provide, of course, an adequate basis for elaborate multivariate analysis, and especially in the parts of the analysis that focus on patterns within colonial subgroups, statistical comparison is used primarily to reinforce arguments made on the basis of qualitative evidence. The approach to this type of "small N" analysis is thus similar to that advocated by Gurr (1972: 38–39): "As a rule of thumb, at least 10 and preferably 20 [cases] are needed for any kind of informative statistical generalization. If fewer than 10 cases can be identified and studied, statistical . . . correlations are only embellishments on, and not substitutes for, narrative comparison and generalization."

their dominance. The post-independence period considered here is thus the approximately fifteen years before 1975. The decision to focus on this period was made not only out of an arbitrary preference for multiples of five, but, more importantly, because of the nature of the analytic model employed—one which does not consider variables that can be applied at any point in time but considers instead a specific historical moment. The "independent" variables in this analysis involve specific events in the period of decolonization. It seems likely that as these events recede into the past, their explanatory or causal importance will dissipate to some degree. This is not to say that the earlier events will become "irrelevant." It is likely that their effects, the chain of events considered here as post-independence outcomes, will, along with additional factors, shape the pattern of subsequent developments. To analyze those subsequent developments, however, will require a broader analytic model. Therefore, the "immediate post-independence period" in which the discrete events of decolonization can be expected to have a direct effect must be limited, and thus the 1975 cutoff point has been chosen. This immediate post-independence period is not, of course, bounded by a sharp break or a single year that pertains to all countries. As of 1980, indeed, the patterns delineated in this study continue to hold up well. Political developments since 1975 are discussed in Chapter 6.

Regime

The analysis of national political regimes[3] in African studies has gone through various phases. The kaleidoscopic pattern of events in the years immediately before and after independence led many scholars to focus on regimes. Dramatic changes took place as electoral institutions were introduced, one-party regimes were formed, and military governments came to power. Many analysts sought to assess and explain these events. There followed, however, a period of scholarly disillusionment with the study of regime, with the major exception of the on-going concern of some scholars with the causes of military intervention and with types of military rule.[4] This

3. As indicated below, I define *regime* as the structure of formal, legitimate power.

4. See, for instance, Bienen (1968 and 1978), Lee (1969), Welch (1970b), First (1972), Bebler (1973), and Decalo (1976b), as well as numerous articles and monographs on specific African cases and comparative analyses not limited to Africa.

tendency to turn attention away from the study of regime was in part a reaction to the argument that many of the concepts with which regime had been analyzed were not appropriate.[5] For instance, earlier analyses placed substantial emphasis on the role of different party systems as an important aspect of differences in regime, employing such familiar distinctions as those between "mass," "mobilizing," or "revolutionary-centralizing" parties on the one hand and "patron," "elite," or "pragmatic-pluralist" parties on the other. When it was discovered that these distinctions failed to provide accurate descriptions and exaggerated the contrasts among civilian regimes, there followed a period in which differences among regimes tended to be minimized to the point of being considered virtually irrelevant. This conclusion was reinforced by the suggestion that there was little difference between civilian and military regimes in terms, for example, of performance and internal cohesion (Zolberg, 1968a: 94; Dowse, 1969: 213; McKinlay and Cohan, 1975 and 1976; Decalo, 1976b; Jackman, 1976).

At about the same time that interest in these party/regime distinctions waned, new perspectives which captured the interest of many analysts tended to treat regime as epiphenomenal. Within the Marxist tradition, these concerns can be referred to as the political-economy perspective; within the development tradition, these concerns can be called the constraints-on-development perspective. For the former, what is often stressed is that the important "stuff" of politics is the broad type of political and economic domination: late-developing countries following dependent capitalist strategies of economic growth will have similar types of economic and class domination. For the latter, it is argued that because of the similar cultural, multi-ethnic, historical, and economic context of African countries, few options are open to many countries on the continent: all types of regimes would be similarly constrained by these harsh realities.

While these arguments make important points, the neglect of regime is, I believe, a mistake. The dependency framework, which has been one of the most influential of these new perspectives, has called attention to some crucially important features of the political

---

5. See Bienen (1967 and 1970) and Zolberg (1966a). The impact on the study of regime is discussed further in Collier (1978: 66).

economy of Africa and other late-developing areas. Yet an exclusive focus on the issues centrally raised by some forms of dependency analysis can lead to a neglect of national or domestic politics. Fernando Henrique Cardoso, one of the most important analysts of dependency issues, has for years stressed the importance of careful analysis of the domestic political context (1969: 162–63; 1973: 143), and he and other scholars have recently underlined the importance of treating domestic politics as a central issue in analyses of Latin American political economy (Cardoso, 1979; Corradi, 1978; O'Donnell, 1979). In the field of African politics a similar call for reorientation toward the importance of internal factors and the independent role of indigenous classes has been made by Sklar (1979) and Leys (1978). Once this role is recognized, the regime and the political mechanisms through which indigenous classes pursue their interests become important.

The study of politics must take place on two levels. These have usefully been distinguished by Cardoso (1979) as the "state" and the "regime." What are these two levels? For Cardoso, the "state" refers to the pact of domination—the class relationships, the distribution of economic and political resources, and broad policy outlines and priorities that flow from the overall type of economic system. The other level, that of "regime," refers to the mode of domination, to the political relationships and mechanisms that support a system of class domination and economic policy priorities.

Cardoso argues that there is no automatic relationship between state and regime. Rather, a given type of economic system and the pattern of class relations that accompanies it can coexist with and be maintained by any of a variety of types of regime. This is quite clear for the countries of Africa. Across the continent, regimes vary from country to country and over time within countries. With the regime changes that have been taking place since the end of the 1970s, particularly the re-introduction of multi-party politics in Nigeria and Ghana and the new form of one-party dominant regime introduced in Senegal, this variability appears to be increasing. Yet these variations and changes within countries do not seem to correspond to differences and changes in the interplay of the basic economic and social forces. Rather, the multiple varieties can each be explained in terms of, or as supporting or being consistent with, a similar pact of domination.

The fact that similar systems of economic and political domination on a general level may be consistent with or supported by different kinds of regime should not lead to the conclusion that regime is unimportant. Within the context of a Marxist analysis that recognizes the importance of the economic base, Gramsci has been perhaps the most important theorist to emphasize the autonomy of the superstructure or the realm of the political (Gramsci, 1971: 407; Boggs, 1971: 81, 95–97; Joll, 1978: 112–13; Merrington, 1978: 152). For Gramsci, "the concrete meaning of politics . . . was its function as an agency for enlisting mass energies in the struggle for ideological hegemony" (Boggs, 1971: 34), and it is from this point of view that it is useful to approach the question of regime. A study of regime is therefore important in answering the question of how a given type of social system is supported. What are the mechanisms of support and compliance? What is the nature of the legitimation of the state? In Sklar's (1979) terms, what are the political structures set up by the emerging dominant class to further the process of class consolidation?

The importance of regime has also been reflected in the fact that regime has been a matter of great concern to political actors in Africa, who have often found it important to change the regime frequently. Although as a general rule a given type of regime is neither necessary for nor inevitably inconsistent with a given pattern of societal allocations, in specific circumstances regime changes do occur in order to change the basic policy orientation of the state (or to preserve it when it appears threatened). Regime change also occurs in response to issues of regional or ethnic distribution and in response to issues of legitimacy and support. Without addressing the question of regime, one cannot grasp political process.

In describing politics in Africa, then, it is not sufficient to describe Africa's position in and the nature of its incorporation into the world capitalist system or the relations of production in the economic base. It is also important to evaluate the way in which and the degree of success or failure with which the political elite is attempting to consolidate its class position and establish potentially hegemonic structures that to some degree incorporate the mass of the population into the system as a support group or, more minimally, neutralize them as a potential opposition. It is precisely this type of analysis that Gramsci employed to understand the potential for class conflict and revolutionary action in different societies (see Boggs, 1971: 101–4). This is the question of regime.

Because this book is concerned with analyzing regimes and regime change, it is important to discuss the concept of regime and the issue of its relationship to other components of the political system, particularly the state. Cardoso's distinction is very suggestive and provides a convenient point of entry to this discussion. Modifying and elaborating this distinction somewhat, I find it helpful to refer to the state, as a first approximation, as the public sector. As such, however, it is more than the aggregate of specific institutions—it is an analytic abstraction (Edelman, 1967: 1; O'Donnell, 1979: 286–87). It is the public mechanisms and institutions of collective goal attainment or of the authoritative allocation of values. Since the state pursues goals and allocates values for the collectivity, and since a given pattern of allocations favors certain interests at the expense of others, the state is, as Weber no less than Marx put it, "a relation of men dominating men" or "organized domination." Since it makes binding decisions for the whole collectivity, it requires compliance. It makes decisions and extracts compliance through its various components: the public administration, legal order, coercive apparatus, and political institutions.

We can thus think of the state in two distinct analytic categories: the structures and mechanisms of decision-making and the structures and mechanisms of decision-compliance. This second category can be separated into coercive mechanisms and legitimating mechanisms. As many analysts have asserted, the preferred and more secure basis for compliance is acceptance of the decision by the people. Acceptance is based on the attribution of legitimacy to decisions and the decision-making process. To the extent that there is no legitimacy, compliance is dependent upon coercion.

This brings us to the definition of *regime*. Leaving aside the coercive arm of the state, we can think of the two analytic categories of the state as the decision-making structures and the legitimating structures.[6] Following Lasswell and Kaplan (1950: 130ff.), we may say that the regime is the authority structure or the structure of formal, legitimate power. In this sense, it may be thought of as the legitimating structure of the state.[7] It should be stressed that this

6. Cf. the two tasks or functions assigned to the state—the accumulation function and the legitimacy function—by analysts such as Habermas (1975), O'Connor (1973), and Wolfe (1977).

7. The regime, of course, is not the only source of legitimacy, nor is it a necessary one. The regime, rather, is one possible source of legitimacy—it is the institutional apparatus through which the state may attempt to establish legitimacy. This appara-

conception of regime distinguishes it analytically from the decision-making structure. This corresponds to the distinction that Lasswell and Kaplan have referred to as the pattern of effective power versus the pattern of formal power. The word *formal* is used to refer to the fact that the regime is the pattern or structure that is described in the political formula, which is the part of the political myth describing the legitimate structure of power. *Formal* is thus used to convey two ideas: first, the idea of authority or legitimacy; and, second, the idea of symbolic status—that is to say, the regime may be fictive (Lasswell and Kaplan, 1950: 132).

For instance, the political myth may, as is common in the modern world, state that legitimate decisions should stem from the people. The political formula in turn may call for voting in elections. Voting, however, is a formal practice that "may or may not actually constitute the making of a decision" (Lasswell and Kaplan, 1950: 130). And so it is with the other components of regime. It is perfectly clear that most African legislatures do not play the role formally assigned to them. The regime as the authority structure may coincide with the decision-making structure, or it may not. Even if it does not, however, the regime may play an important role which affects legitimacy, coercion, and governmental capacity.

In terms of the above conceptualization, then, the state is the set of public institutions concerned with making and enforcing decisions for the collectivity. The regime is a part of the state, the legitimating apparatus. It is the structure of formal legitimate authority—which in addition may or may not constitute the decision-making apparatus. States can differ with respect to the class that controls them and the consequent pattern of collective goals pursued, and with respect to the structure of the regime, the fictiveness of the regime (or the extent to which it coincides with the decision-making structure), and the degree of legitimacy generated by the regime (that is, the extent to which the regime provides legitimacy for the collective decision-making process).

The perspective presented here, like that of Cardoso, is that a

---

tus may be minimal or it may be relatively elaborate; furthermore, it may be more or less successful in actually evoking or establishing legitimacy. Thus, a state could lack an effective institutional legitimacy apparatus and yet be regarded as legitimate by those who approve its particular policies, respond to a charismatic leader, etc., or it could lack legitimacy, relying almost exclusively on coercion.

given pattern of collective goals or allocations does not necessarily require a specific type of regime. The classical Marxist argument is that patterns of allocations are determined by the productive forces and the relations of production. While we may view the state on this general and abstract level as being at least in part the superstructural expression of the economic base, the economic base does not take us so far in providing an explanation for regime. This is not to say that the range of regime possibilities is not severely constrained by economic and class considerations, nor is it to deny that some cases of regime change in Africa may have been prompted quite directly by these considerations. Rather, we may adopt Althusser's position (1971: 135; 1969: 111; see also Geras, 1978: 253; and Przeworski, 1980: 1–3) that though the base may be determinant "in the last instance," each level (base and superstructure) has its own substantially autonomous history. As Cavarozzi (1975: 33–37) has suggested, two levels of conflict are reflected within the state. The first, which is ultimately predominant, is class conflict. The second is political conflict over incumbency. This latter has been particularly evident in Africa where the state is an arena of class formation as much as it is one of class conflict. As a result, political conflict in Africa has often appeared to involve "non-ideological" conflict among regional or ethnic groups or among political factions. Cavarozzi goes on to stress that political dynamics on this second level must be understood in terms of processes inherent to the internal logic of the political sphere and the relatively autonomous generation of political projects.

It is from this perspective that this book will examine the patterns of regime change that have occurred in Africa in the post-independence period. During that period, a variety of types of regime were established in independent Africa. If fundamental differences in the economic base do not account for the differences in regime, how are these differences to be explained? It is the thesis of this study that part of the explanation concerns the degree of cohesion of the political class that emerged out of the way in which political institutions were transferred from the European democracies to the African colonies and the experiences each of the colonies had with electoral politics during the decade and a half of decolonization. In making this argument, this study revives certain concerns that have recently been relatively dormant in African political analysis, and it attempts to demonstrate that such factors as mass mobilization and electoral participation, types of party system, and types of colonial rule possess explanatory power.

Mass Participation

A central feature of the regime changes that occurred during the period of decolonization in Africa was the rapid introduction of mass electoral participation, ultimately in the form of a completely unrestricted universal suffrage. This rapid introduction of mass participation, in roughly a decade and a half, is a distinctive fact of African political history. Before 1945, the few elections that had been held in Africa were based on a highly restricted elite franchise in the major cities. By 1960, elections based on universal suffrage had occurred in almost all the African colonies under consideration here. This sudden entry of the African masses into political life contrasts strikingly with what has occurred in most other parts of the world. In most countries of Europe, the growth of mass participation in politics and the broadening of the franchise occurred over a much longer period, and in some countries in Latin America, literacy requirements continue to disenfranchise the masses, even though elections were introduced a century and a half ago. The question thus arises: what was the impact of this rapid entry of the masses onto the political scene in Africa? In order to introduce the issues that arise in addressing this question, it is useful to explore briefly some broader comparative perspectives on the impact of the introduction of mass suffrage.

This analytically unique period of the initial incorporation of the masses into participation in national political life has been a major concern of analysts of social change in all areas of the world. For Bendix (1964), it was a central aspect of nation-building; for Marshall (1965) it was a political requirement of capitalist industrialization; and for the participants in the Committee on Political Development of the Social Science Research Council, it was one of the major "crises" of political development (Binder et al., 1971; Grew, 1978).

Early scholarly concern with this theme centered upon the experience of the democratic countries of Europe, where mass incorporation took the form of the extension of citizenship—of political rights, primarily in the form of suffrage, as well as of civil rights (to use Marshall's terminology).[8] In many European countries, political incorporation of the lower classes through the extension of universal manhood suffrage did not upset the existing distribution of economic or power resources but, rather, supported existing social and economic relations. This compatibility of the extension of political rights to the lower classes with the existing distribution of resources represented a kind of paradox. It ran counter to the expectations of many analysts who assumed that this extension of political participation would result in successful demands for major redistribution throughout society. As Marshall (1965: 92–93) puzzled: how is it possible that the two opposing principles of citizenship, which is a system of equality, and capitalism, which is a system not of equality but of inequality, were reconciled and became allies, rather than antagonists?

The question was one that confronted Marx as an observer of the events in Europe. Prior to the introduction of universal suffrage, Marx had emphasized the system of voting privileges as a mechanism of class domination (Wesolowski, 1967: 80–81). As long as the suffrage was restricted to property-holders, the system of democratic elections was quite obviously a mechanism of direct rule and domination of the property-owning class. However, the extension of mass political rights in the form of universal suffrage proved not to be antithetical to the interests of the dominant classes. Marx explained this system-supportive nature of mass suffrage in terms of what might be called "ideological domination" (Wesolowski, 1967: 81) through which, without ideology and representatives of their own, the lower classes voted for bourgeois representatives to parliament. This argument was elaborated by Gramsci in his concept of hegemony, a situation in which class rule is based on the diffusion throughout society of the values of the dominant class, whose ideology provides the framework for identifying problems,

8. For Marshall (1965: 78) civil rights were composed of "the rights necessary for individual freedom—liberty of the person, freedom of speech, thought and faith, the right to own property and to conclude valid contracts, and the right to justice." Political rights referred to "the right to participate in the exercise of political power, as a member of a body invested with political authority or as an elector of the members of such a body." Marshall was also concerned with a third component of citizenship, which he called "social rights." These last, which came into existence primarily in the twentieth century, included "the whole range from the right to a modicum of economic welfare and security to the right to share to the full in the social heritage and to live the life of a civilized being according to the standards prevailing in the society."

proposing solutions, and, more generally, posing social and political questions. In this view, electoral participation is akin to what has more recently been called *mobilized participation,* which reflects the ability of the elites to persuade and influence the masses, in contradistinction to *autonomous participation,* which reflects the interests and more spontaneously derived opinions of the participants. While the latter involves articulation of the interests of the participant, the former is better understood in terms of the initiating role not of the participant but of political leaders who, as political entrepreneurs or constituency creators, mobilize new groups into politics in an attempt to create an effective power base (Huntington and Nelson, 1976: 33; see also Parry, 1972b; and Hermet, 1978).

This view of the role of elections in liberal democratic regimes is not limited to Marxist analysts but, as Hermet (1978: 2) has pointed out, has much in common with the skepticism about elections expressed by such observers as Mosca and Schumpeter. Many analysts of Western democracies have suggested that the franchise was extended and the lower classes were politically incorporated, not so much in response to demands from below, but at least equally on elite initiative when the ruling groups or elite factions saw the possibility of generating additional support for pursuing their own ends.[9]

Within Europe, perhaps the most famous case of the extension of universal manhood suffrage to generate support occurred in France under Napoleon III. In 1851, unable to succeed himself as constitutional president of the Republic, Napoleon III executed a coup d'état. He tried to legitimate and garner support for the coup by restoring universal manhood suffrage (which he had helped the Assembly repeal the year before) and by holding a plebiscite. In this plebiscite, he was elected president for a ten-year term, officially winning 92 percent of the vote (Palmer, 1960: 477). In elections under the Second Empire, official candidates were announced by the Emperor, and all the resources and powers of the government were used to ensure their success. Most of these candidates did in fact win; many were unopposed. In the elections of 1852 and 1857, the official candidates received 83 percent and 84.6 percent, respectively, of the vote (Zeldin, 1958: esp. 10, 41, 74, 78–91).

---

9. In his comparative analysis of European democracies, Therborn (1977) argues that while there was popular pressure for an expanded franchise, this was not a decisive factor.

This use of electoral participation as a support mechanism was widely noted throughout Europe. It was particularly influential with Bismarck (Pflanze, 1963: 223, 226–28) and could not have escaped the attention of Disraeli. Both of these leaders, in the following decade, oversaw a dramatic extension of the suffrage, which was again system-supporting. In Germany, this extension of the suffrage had the effect of strengthening the conservative forces (Bendix, 1964: 98). Among the mass electorate, particularly the peasantry, Bismarck found a new source of support for the monarchy and was able to exploit the support of the lower classes against the bourgeoisie (Pflanze, 1963: 222ff.). Similarly, in England, the Reform Bill of 1867 was "meant to perpetuate the control of the propertied classes and form a 'bulwark against democracy'" (Thomas, 1978: 71). In sponsoring the reform bill, Disraeli's major motivation was to seize the political initiative for a movement that had considerable popular support and, in so doing, to keep the opposition divided and thus retain power. His specific perceptions and anticipations about the electoral propensities of those newly enfranchised by the Reform Bill are hard to reconstruct, but it seems clear that he was aware that the clientelist control and system of "influence" over the lower classes (see Clark, 1965: 210–11) would safeguard the traditionally Conservative areas, and all in all the effect of the Reform Bill was to enfranchise a class that tended to vote Conservative. Following further liberalizing amendments, the Conservatives in 1874 won their first clear victory in thirty-three years. In England, as in France and Germany, then, "the enfranchisement of new classes proved compatible with the retention of much political power in old hands" (Thomas, 1978: 72). Rokkan summarized this situation:

[T]he decision to extend the vote was not uniformly a response to pressures from below, it was as often the results of contests for influence at the top and of deliberate moves to broaden the bases for an integrated national power structure. The French Revolution had sown its plebiscitarian seed and the success of Napoleon III had a distinct impact on political minds in Western Europe. By a much debated historical coincidence, the two great Conservative leaders Disraeli and Bismarck proceeded in 1867 within months of each other to extend the suffrage further than their Liberal antagonists had wanted. In both cases these leaps in the dark were motivated by a profound belief that the entry of the working classes into the electorate would strengthen the unity and stability of the nation-state. (1970: 31)

The use of the vote to gain support is reflected in the fact that throughout Europe liberals and those who championed the cause of working-class political power were often opposed to the extension of the franchise at the same time that conservatives were advocating it:

> [L]iberals favored the *régime censitaire* [which restricted the suffrage to taxpayers] and feared the possibilities of electoral manipulation inherent in the extension of the suffrage to the economically dependent. Conservatives, once they recognized the importance of the vote as a basis of local power, tended to favor the enfranchisement of the "lower orders": they had good reason to expect that, at least on the patriarchal estates in the country-side, those in positions of dependence would naturally vote for the local notables. (Bendix, 1964: 97)

A similar pattern of extending the franchise for political support has been found in the United States. Schattschneider maintains that in the United States some of the most important steps in the expansion of the electorate have occurred not in response to demands from below but when a political party has needed additional support and has gone to the masses to find it. In treating the vote as a means of getting support, rather than as a means of mass interest-articulation, parties look for those voters who are most easily solicited. These are previously uninvolved, nonparticipant, new voters. Schattschneider (1942: 48) adds: "To assert that an indignant people wrested the right to vote from a reluctant government is a humorous inversion of the truth, an invention of persuasive politicians who told the fable to the historians."

The experience of the North Atlantic democracies thus indicated that political incorporation of the masses through the extension of political rights represented a potential source of mass political power, but its effective exercise demanded "experience, organization and a change of ideas" (Marshall, 1965: 105). As Engels stated: ". . . the possessing class rules directly through the medium of universal suffrage. As long as the oppressed class . . . is not yet ripe to emancipate itself, it will in its majority regard the existing order of society as the only one possible and, politically, will form the tail of the capitalist class . . ." (Engels, 1959: 393–94). Or, as John Stuart Mill argued when confronted with the idea that the extension of political rights in England would make workers "masters of the situation": "They may be able to decide whether a Whig or a Tory shall be elected—they may be masters of so small a matter as that" (quoted in Thomas, 1978: 72). Finally, analyzing mass participation in liberal democratic elections as "electoral putsches" of the bourgeoisie (Hermet, 1978: 2), Gramsci stated: "What votes do measure is precisely the effectiveness and the capacity of active minorities, elites, leadership, etc. to expand their own views, to persuade others" (translated by Przeworski, 1975: 66).

Within the North Atlantic context, then, the introduction of mass electoral participation seemed to be a system-supporting mechanism that did not threaten the existing distribution of resources. This is not to say that mass enfranchisement meant *no* changes in existing patterns of allocations but rather that, at least initially, it meant relatively minor changes of distribution in favor of the participant masses and posed little fundamental threat to the underlying pattern of economic and class relationships. Instead, the introduction of mass electoral participation represented the development of a new political resource with which the old political battles among elites continued to be fought.

Following World War II, a new set of assessments concerning the role of political participation began to predominate, particularly with reference to political contexts that differed substantially from that of the older European democracies. Much of this analysis centered on the consequences of the introduction of mass participation in the new states.[10] Among scholars who analyzed these

---

10. It may be noted that these discussions, particularly regarding the new states, do not limit the idea of political participation to electoral participation. In fact, there has been a recent resurgence of interest in the concept of participation which has included a number of attempts to redefine its boundaries, its dimensions, and its types or modes (see, for instance, Parry, 1972b; Huntington and Nelson, 1976; Verba, Nie, and Kim, 1971; Kasfir, 1976b). In the present study I am not attempting to assess mass participation in Africa in all its diverse forms. Rather, I am concerned with one form of political participation, voting, an act which would be included in almost any definition of political participation (see Parry, 1972b: 3). However, in order for voting in all types of elections (e.g., in controlled or noncompetitive elections) to be included in definitions of political participation, the concept of participation must not be limited to attempts to influence government, especially on the part of the participant. Two distinctions are involved here. The first concerns who is attempting to influence government—the participant, or a third party who is responsible for stimulating the participant act. This is the distinction made by Huntington and Nelson (1976) between autonomous and mobilized participation. The second distinction, which cuts across the first, is between participation as an input and participation as an output, in Easton's (1965) terms. I do not want to limit the present use of the term *participation* to inputs to—demands on or attempts to influence—government or the political system, whether autonomous or mobilized. Participation can also be an output—a government policy which has the goal of

cases, incorporation of the masses into participation in national political life was seen as a central aspect of political development and modernization (Eisenstadt, 1964: 577; Rustow, 1967: 5; Black, 1967: 93; Huntington, 1969: 93; Binder et al., 1971). Yet at the same time, many analyses of the new states emphasized effects of the introduction of mass political participation quite the opposite of those observed in Europe. In Europe the result was often system-supporting; in the new states the result was said to be disruptive of the existing system, leading to excessive popular demands and instability. How is this presumed difference between the effects of mass incorporation in the new and old states to be explained?

Implicitly or explicitly, many analysts saw this difference as a result of the role of institutional transfer as a source of political change. This perspective was critical of the tendency to focus exclusively on internal causes of change within countries and suggested instead that political change involves a long and complex history of the transfer of ideas, techniques, and institutions among countries (see Bendix, 1967: 330). Whereas the former tends to predict similarities among countries (such as the functional-prerequisites approach to development, which sees political outcomes as a result of the attainment of certain levels of social and economic modernization in each country), the latter, with its emphasis on the various

---

generating political support. This understanding of *participation* is particularly important in the case of voting, because in probably all cases voting has at least some mobilizational aspects, since one votes for a platform defined by someone else (or for a set of "representative" acts determined by someone else); of the modes of participation defined by Verba, Nie, and Kim (1971), voting is associated with the least amount of initiative on the part of the participant. More importantly, voting, even in those cases when it can be characterized in part as an input or an attempt to influence government, can also be viewed as a mechanism for the generation of support or legitimacy. In general, one can characterize pre-independence electoral participation in Africa as mobilized-input participation, in which the African elite went to the masses to seek their support for self-government, for office, and then for independence. Most post-independence electoral participation, as we shall see later, can be characterized as mobilized-output participation, which is associated not with demand-making or even with the seeking of political office, but with the generation of support. We will return to these themes later. The point I want to stress here is that in this analysis I am not using voting as an indicator of political participation in general. Rather, I am specifically interested in voting as a particular form of participation. Furthermore, electoral participation in Africa is interesting not as a mechanism of mass interest-articulation or voter influence but, in the period of decolonization, as part of a set of rules for structuring elite competition and as a resource or liability for political leaders and, in the post-independence period, as a potential source of mobilized support for political elites and the state.

contexts into which an institution can be transferred, is a useful starting point for trying to explain differences in political outcomes. Three aspects of this context have been important in systematic analyses: rate, timing, and sequence.

Rate refers to the "speed" with which a given institution is introduced. A later-developing country can quickly adopt the latest form of an institution or technique without having to "invent" it anew. Highly capital-intensive technology can be quickly introduced in a country that has previously been pre-industrial. These opportunities of late-developers led an early observer to stress the advantages of backwardness (Veblen, 1961) and have led more recent and less sanguine observers to emphasize the disadvantages of such technology transfers and to call instead for "appropriate technologies." Similarly, a country can rapidly evolve from a point of never having had elections to full universal suffrage through a process of "borrowing." With respect to mass participation, Weiner has summarized the arguments made by many authors:

> [A] very rapid large-scale increase in political participation often creates a crisis situation because it frightens the existing elite so that it responds with repression; [because] it strains the resources of the state, particularly of newly formed political systems with limited administrative capabilities and financial resources; and because there is a tendency for new participants, who have not been socialized into a civic order with established rules for influencing public authority, to use violence and civil disobedience. (1971: 193*n*)

Timing refers to the broad historical era in which an innovation is transferred or in which a country develops. Depending on timing, countries are constrained and influenced by different sets of international norms, different political ideologies, and different international political and economic environments.[11] In the twentieth century, for instance, the notion of popular sovereignty has become almost universally accepted, and the pressures to legitimate a regime on the basis of some form of mass participation are greater than they were a century ago. The timing variable distinguishes, for example, between countries that modernized before versus after the emergence of Marxism as a major political ideology; before versus

11. A focus on the effects of timing is similar to what Tilly (1975: 624) has called historical theories—"those which account for the characteristics of any particular government through its individual relationship to some historical transformation affecting the world as a whole."

after the Russian, Chinese, or Cuban revolutions; and before versus after the emergence of ideologies and organizational techniques which form the basis for modern labor movements. The issue of timing has received the greatest attention in the distinction between early modernizers and successive waves of later modernizers and the way in which the presence of earlier, more powerful modernizers fundamentally changes the parameters of modernization of those that follow, as both the tradition of research exemplified by Gerschenkron (1966) and the dependency framework have emphasized.

Sequence refers to the order in which an innovation is introduced relative to *other* aspects of change *within* a given country. The general pattern is for late-modernizers to adopt new innovations (such as universal suffrage, capital-intensive technologies, and state welfare programs [Collier and Messick, 1975]) at lower levels of social and economic modernization than did early modernizers.

Many of the hypotheses about the effects of mass participation in the new states have referred to these issues of rate, sequence, and timing. In general, it has been asserted that when mass participation is introduced quickly; earlier relative to economic and social development and to certain other political changes (such as the development of centralized authority and an effective centralized government, the emergence of institutionalized political parties, and the establishment of national identity); and in the context of the ideologies, norms, and political models available in the mid-twentieth century, the impact will be antithetical to the existing distribution of economic and power resources. The effects most often mentioned are generation of popular demands beyond the ability (or desire) of the elite to respond to them; inability to consolidate power, establish strong institutions, and pursue national goals; political instability; exacerbation of ethnic and local rivalries; and reactive, repressive authoritarian rule.[12]

Thus, two quite different views of the effect of the introduction

12. A sampling of the sources in which these hypotheses are found includes: Huntington (1969: esp. 4–5, 198, 398), Emerson (1960: 221–22), Weiner (1971: esp. 181, 195), Rustow (1967: 125–28), Nordlinger (1968), Myrdal (1968: 119, 769, 774), Lipset (1959b: 75, 83–84), Organski (1965: 219), Lerner (1964: 21), De Schweinitz (1970: 530–31), Dahl (1971: 36–39, 74), Wallerstein (1961: 86–87), Lemarchand (1964: 560), Johnson (1964: 98–99), Needler (1968: 95), Zolberg (1966a: 75), Flanigan and Fogelman (1971: 484), Kraus (1971), and Lofchie (1971a).

of mass participation emerge from the literature. The first view emphasizes its compatibility with the distribution of economic and political resources and the degree to which it strengthens the state and the elite groups who oversee it. The second emphasizes the problems that are likely to ensue for the maintenance of central authority and the continuing supremacy of the ruling groups. Which of these two views is more relevant for understanding the situation in Africa? Did the introduction of mass participation in Africa represent a political resource that could successfully be exploited by elites and used to their advantage, or did it represent the real or potential granting of political power to popular groups who would oppose and threaten the position of those elites?

The conventional wisdom in analyses of the African experience has expressed two contrasting views about the introduction of mass participation. On the one hand, that electoral participation in the period of decolonization was mobilized from above is widely noted, and the roles of patron-client relationships, of traditional authority, and of outright electoral manipulation have been recognized. On the other hand, it is commonly argued that the introduction of mass politics in Africa was destabilizing, rather than supportive of the existing order, in that it led to "excessive" demands for redistribution based on class and/or ethnicity, and that this effect accounts for the "departicipation" (Kasfir, 1976b) which African countries have undergone since independence.

A major concern of this book is to describe the rate and sequence of the introduction of mass electoral participation in Africa and to assess the extent to which it was supportive or destabilizing. More specifically, it will explore the extent to which new elites moving into position to assume control of the state were able to use an expanding franchise to enhance their power and dominance, or on the contrary, the degree to which it inhibited the formation of a dominant elite coalition which could control the state. It will be argued that the effects of the pre-independence experience were not uniform across the African countries. Rather, under certain circumstances the introduction of mass electoral politics facilitated the formation of a relatively dominant and cohesive ruling elite and increased its political resources, while under other circumstances, it worked to hinder the formation of a relatively united ruling elite and the ability of the elite to establish supremacy.

Elections and Authoritarian Regimes

After independence in Africa, the democratic institutions introduced during the period of decolonization were quite rapidly and deliberately dismantled and authoritarian regimes were established. Across the African cases, there was some variation in the ways in which democratic regimes were abandoned and in the types of authoritarian regimes that were set up. A principal goal of this book is describing and explaining this variation. In pursuing this concern, two phases of the relationship between elections and authoritarian rule will be explored. The first is the way in which the relatively brief experience with competitive elections during the period of decolonization affected the patterns of regime breakdown or evolution and the role of immediate post-independence electoral policy in the establishment of authoritarian rule. The second is the roles of different types of controlled elections under authoritarian regimes. It will be suggested that these differing uses of controlled elections provide a useful basis for distinguishing among types of authoritarian rule.

The study of regime change in Africa is thus the study of the collapse of the "tutelary" democratic regimes introduced during decolonization and the emergence of various types of authoritarian regimes. What is the nature of these changes, and how are the different types of regimes to be distinguished? Given the conceptualization of regimes put forth above, types of regimes may be distinguished according to their authority structures or their formal mechanisms of legitimation. In the twentieth century claims to legitimacy have almost universally been made with reference to rule by the people, a fact which directs our attention to the question of institutionalized mechanisms of mass political participation. Within this framework, one may refer to democratic regimes as those that hold liberal, or what Hermet calls "classical," elections. These are characterized by freedom of voters (universal suffrage, equal weighting of votes, secret ballots with freedom from external pressure, and accurate counting of the ballots), "genuine" competition, and the real possibility of replacing officeholders with opposition candidates as an outcome of balloting (Hermet, 1978: 3).[13] For

---

13. I do not want to enter the theoretical discussion of the definition of democracy, but I do want to have a criterion for making certain kinds of distinctions that will arise in the course of this study. This simple definition seems to correspond to

present purposes, the salient feature of authoritarian regimes is that they do not hold classical elections. What, then, is substituted? What institutionalized mechanisms of legitimation are provided, if any? The answer to this question, which provides a basis for distinguishing subtypes of authoritarian regimes, often involves some form of controlled election.[14] Linz (1975: 179–80, 278) has suggested that one of the most important criteria for distinguishing types of authoritarian regimes is the degree and type of popular participation and mobilization. Furthermore, he argues, it is important to consider the forms of controlled and noncompetitive elections: "The opportunity for popular participation, even if controlled, channelled, manipulated, and under co-opted leadership, makes such regimes different" (Linz, 1972: 31). Analysis of elec-

---

what comparative analysts as well as ordinary speakers commonly have in mind when referring to democratic regimes. As Duverger (1951: 353) has suggested: "The simplest and most realistic definition of democracy is the following: a regime in which those who govern are chosen by those who are governed, by means of free and open elections." In his review of definitions of democracy Sartori (1968: 112) has observed that when it is used as a *descriptive* term, the standard definitions most often provided refer to "concepts of representation, majority rule, opposition, competition, alternative government, control, and the like," that is, formal institutional arrangements rather than references to "the people." The definition being proposed here is also similar to that put forth by Therborn (1977: 4).

14. As will become clear in Chapter 5, a consequence of this conceptualization of authoritarian regimes is to include Tanzania with what might be regarded as strange bedfellows. The more egalitarian pattern of collective goals in Tanzania is quite distinct from that in most of the rest of Africa, and the leadership of that country seems more interested in genuine mass participation, both as a goal and as a means to socialist development, than elsewhere (Barker and Saul, 1974; Barkan, 1979a: 28–29). Nevertheless, participation and pluralism are in fact limited in Tanzania in many of the same ways as in other African countries (Barkan, 1979a: 29; Hall and Lucas, 1979: 186): though the pattern of collective goals may be unique in tropical Africa, the regime is not. Thus, the Tanzanian regime is a similar mechanism for limiting participation and pluralism, though the challenge to the leadership may be from the right rather than from the left. Though in some ways the authoritarian category groups disparate cases, this grouping of regimes points to similar techniques of control and legitimation, of the limitation of certain kinds of political participation, and of the concentration of power, regardless of whether the leadership is "benevolent" or "self-interested," in Saul's (1972: 116) terminology.

Put more generally, the present means of distinguishing among types of regime does not consider the substantive content of public policy nor does it specify in whose interest policies are pursued; that is, it avoids specifying the class content of supremacy. There is a parallel here with a point made earlier: just as different regimes can support and maintain similar patterns of allocations or collective goals, so there is the possibility that quite different collective goals can be supported by similar regimes.

toral devices such as these will play a central role in the discussion of post-independence authoritarian regimes.

In analyzing the place of elections in African politics, it is useful to think in terms of two dialectically interrelated aspects of the role of elections in the larger political process (see Saul, 1972). These two aspects parallel the contrasting interpretations of the impact of mass political participation discussed in the previous section. The first aspect is control by voters of leaders and government, most typically in the form of democratic accountability. The second is control by the political elite of the participants; from this point of view, elections aid the political elite in enhancing its power and reinforcing supremacy. Conventionally, elections have been treated in terms of the first of these aspects, as mechanisms of popular representation and democratic accountability. To the extent that elections have deviated from the classical model, they have often been regarded either as insignificant or as a sham. More recently, however, attention has been given to other aspects of elections, particularly their role in reinforcing supremacy. This role has been recognized by students of classical and nonclassical elections alike. In an American government primer, for example, Lowi (1976) has analyzed classical elections in the United States as techniques to "maintain conquest." He suggests that these elections do not function as a mechanism for popular control of government and public policy. On the contrary, it is rarely possible on the basis of election results to make any clear inference about voter preferences on issues (Lowi, 1976: 243). Rather, he argues, elections have the purpose of providing consent and thus of generating legitimacy for whatever decisions are made (Lowi, 1976: 257–58; see also Edelman, 1967; Katznelson and Kesselman, 1975; and Ginsberg and Weissberg, 1978).

In addition to serving as legitimating mechanisms, elections may contribute to supremacy by serving as mechanisms for concentrating power and decreasing the heterogeneity, present in civil society, of those with input to the decision-making process. Such elections are a technique for insulating the decision-making and policy-formation processes from opposing interests and pressures in civil society. They are not simply a mechanism of representation but a mechanism to limit pluralism and distort "pure" representation. Some electoral systems, of course, do this more than others; but in his study of different electoral systems, Rae (1967: 134–35) concludes that if any finding can be elevated to the status of a "law," it is that all electoral systems, including extant systems of proportional representation, function to concentrate power by strengthening the strongest and eliminating the weakest. Electoral systems, he adds, must be regarded as political instruments. It may be noted that this limitation of pluralism and the insulation of the decision-making process have also been noted by authors who have approached the issue from another point of view: not from the perspective of maintaining or consolidating supremacy but from the perspective of governmental capacity. What is involved here is the idea that, as Lowi (1976: 258) has asserted, the demands of "government" are inconsistent with the demands of representation, or as Milnor (1969: 2) has put it: "The end product of pure representation is an elite able to disagree on almost anything." These arguments all assume that pure representation is obstructive and will incapacitate the government, an assumption which, as Rae (1967: 137) suggests, must be explored empirically for each case. It is clear, however, that electoral systems do function, to varying degrees, to limit pluralism and thus to insulate and facilitate decision-making for the collectivity by the social groups which control the state. [15]

The degree to which elections function to reinforce supremacy in the above ways depends, of course, on the specific electoral system. Furthermore, the role of elections in legitimation and their role in

15. This rethinking of the role of elections as a mechanism for achieving or consolidating political supremacy rather than exclusively as a mechanism of representation corresponds to a similar reassessment that has occurred concerning the role of interest groups. Whereas an early emphasis of many analysts was on the role of interest groups in demand-making and in representing a particular constituency on the "input" side of politics, a central thrust of recent literature is to call attention to the ways in which the state creates, subsidizes, and regulates groups, in part in order to control the groups themselves and the publics they presumably represent (Schmitter, 1974; O'Donnell, 1977; Collier and Collier, 1977 and 1979). Given that interest groups play a role both in demand-making and in serving as mechanisms of state control, Schmitter (1977) has argued that the traditional topic of interest "representation" should be redefined as involving interest "intermediation." Thus, both in the field of interest politics (the functional sphere) and in electoral politics (the territorial sphere) there is a reorientation away from the idea of representational structures pure and simple toward structures that serve as a mediating link between the state and civil society, through which, at least in part, the state attempts to control mass publics. From this perspective, interest-group pluralism versus corporatism, on the one hand, and classical versus controlled elections, on the other, are seen not as totally different structures but as points along a continuum.

concentrating power do not necessarily reinforce each other. Arrayed on a continuum, classical elections—particularly those with systems of proportional representation—can be located at or near one end, limiting pluralism and concentrating power less and probably (though not necessarily) having as a result more potential for eliciting legitimacy and consent. Various types of controlled elections, such as the one-party elections that characterize independent Africa, can be located at or near the other end of the continuum, concentrating power and limiting pluralism more and probably having less potential for generating legitimacy.[16]

Sensitivity to this issue of the varying contribution of elections to reinforcing supremacy helps to guide the discussion of the place of elections in the rise of authoritarian regimes in Africa. The introduction of classical elections during the period of decolonization set into motion in many of these countries forces that led sooner or later to the abandonment of elections or to their transformation into some form of controlled election. Given the very low incidence of democratic regimes in the world, the high correspondence between the existence of democratic regimes and relatively early capitalist development, the preconditions for democracy that have been suggested in studies of this topic, and the hasty construction of democratic institutions in Africa during the brief period of decolonization, it hardly seems necessary to dwell here on the question of why democratic regimes did not flourish in Africa (see Bretton, 1966; Andreski, 1968; First, 1972). Of greater interest is the way in which the experiences of various colonies with classical elections led to different patterns of regime breakdown or regime change. Particularly relevant here, it will be shown, was the experience of African political elites with classical elections as a mechanism for managing pluralism, adjusting competing elite claims, and producing a more or less cohesive political elite; that is to say, the degree to which

16. It is clear from this discussion that I agree with Linz's contention that authoritarian regimes are commonly instituted with the purpose of limiting pluralism. Unlike Linz, however, I would not make the issue of the degree of limitation of pluralism the basis for distinguishing between authoritarian and other types of regimes, particularly democratic regimes; instead, I share the preference of Oppenheim (1975: 305) for limited definitions that do "not make true 'by definition' what had better be left open to empirical investigation," and his consequent adoption of an institutional definition of regime which leaves open the possibility, for instance, that "democracy in an institutional sense is compatible with various distributions of political power, ranging from a single power elite through a multiplicity of countervailing power groups to genuine polyarchy" (306).

competitive elections reinforced or undermined supremacy influenced the pattern of regime evolution and the types of authoritarian regimes that emerged.

In analyzing the effect of the introduction of multi-party competitive elections in Africa in this way, certain traits of civil society must also be kept in mind. Though to varying degrees different electoral arrangements act as gatekeepers, disallowing the expression of certain interests through a particular channel, the degree of pluralism that "gets through" the gate is dependent not only on the restrictiveness of the electoral arrangements but also on the degree of homogeneity and hegemony in civil society. Within this context, it will be shown that differences in colonial rule (differences that can be summarized as direct versus indirect rule) produced somewhat different degrees of heterogeneity, which found expression in political cleavages. Furthermore, the different metropoles introduced somewhat different electoral systems. These contrasts in colonial rule and electoral systems led to a cumulative pattern of differences, the outcome of which meant that in French Africa, for instance, there was a greater likelihood that a somewhat more cohesive and less fractionalized political elite would emerge out of the electoral process and assume control of the new independent states; whereas in British Africa, especially in the nonsettler, nonmulti-racial areas, the indigenous political elite was more likely to be characterized by greater pluralism and political fractionalization.

From these different situations, authoritarian regimes of varying types emerged in somewhat different ways. In some cases, a one-party authoritarian regime emerged from the dynamics of the competitive electoral experience itself. In other cases, new rulers moved more deliberately to eliminate political opposition and competitive party politics and to institute an authoritarian regime. In yet other cases, there was no move on the part of the post-independence civilian political elite to dismantle democratic structures, yet the regime broke down. This study will explore the ways in which these different patterns appeared.

This perspective on the role of elections in reinforcing supremacy also provides a starting point for analyzing the continuing use of elections in many countries after authoritarian rule has been established. Once classical elections, the hallmark of democratic regimes, had been abandoned in Africa, the authoritarian regimes that were set up exhibited quite different electoral arrangements. In some cases the electoral arena was shut down completely; in other cases, differing types of controlled elections were instituted. The latter outcome occurred in virtually all civilian regimes, indicating a striking reluctance to dispense with elections entirely. Why did the new civilian political elite find it important to retain some type of election, particularly in a situation in which they felt it necessary to control and manipulate the election substantially?

The decision to hold elections in one form or another must be viewed as a policy choice by the political elite—in Wriggins's (1969) terms, as part of a strategy for staying in power, specifically a strategy for aggregating power, building a support coalition, and establishing legitimacy. The analysis will explore the forms that this policy choice took—including the alternative decisions to eliminate elections completely, to hold one-party elections that offer no choice among candidates, and to retain some element of competition and voter choice within the one-party framework—and the ways in which these regime choices appeared to serve the needs of the governing elite. The study thus explores the various approaches to reinforcing supremacy that have been employed in the post-independence period in tropical Africa.

2. The Transfer of Elections and Mass Suffrage to Africa

At the level of regime, the most important change during the period of decolonization was the transfer to the African colonies of many of the democratic institutions of the European colonial powers. Two aspects of this process serve as the point of entry into the larger argument of this book concerning the factors that shaped post-independence patterns of regime change. The first, with which this chapter is concerned, is the introduction of elections—particularly the rate and sequence of this introduction and of the expansion of the franchise and the level of mass electoral participation that was attained by independence. The second, which will be discussed in Chapter 3, is the party system, particularly the degree of party dominance or fractionalization that emerged out of this new context of competitive electoral politics, and the degree of cohesion of the political elite that the party system reflected.

Before analyzing the introduction of elections and the expansion of electoral participation in Africa, however, it is appropriate to discuss briefly the reasons for the transfer of European democratic institutions. As Wasserman (1976: 174) has suggested, decolonization consisted of two apparently contradictory processes. The first, the more discontinuous and visible, was the withdrawal of direct colonial authority by the metropole. This process involved a dramatic change of regime—a change in political institutions and in patterns of recruitment into decision-making roles. This was the process of democratization. Wasserman argues that this first process must be understood in terms of the second, which was characterized by continuity and consisted of the preservation of the colonial political economy and the integration of an indigenous elite into positions of authority in a way that would protect the economic and strategic interests of the metropole. This formulation echoes an earlier formulation of Nettl and Robertson (1968) concerning the contradictions within the process of decolonization (see also Kilson, 1966: 171 and Post, 1968b: 191). Viewing independence from the point of view of the transfer or inheritance of property rights, they suggested: "Inheritance implies continuity in the sense that certain rights to possession are transferred; consequently the object possessed itself remains intact. But it is also discontinuous in that it involves a complete change of ownership. This means that one and the same situation combines strong positive elements of association as well as strongly negative elements of dissociation" (Nettl and Robertson, 1968: 72). As they go on to show, the structure of the situation itself tends to encourage the inheritance elite to favor association and continuity rather than dissociation and dramatic change (see also Gellar, 1973: 395ff.). Much has been made of this basic continuity of political economy from the colonial to the post-colonial period, that is, of the pattern of neocolonialism that characterizes most of independent Africa. Political independence in most places in tropical Africa has been accompanied by little change in the ownership of the means of production, the control of the economy, the structure of the economy, and the patterns of allocations.

Yet, although the two processes, one discontinuous and the other continuous, tended to occur together, the first, or the specific choice of the form it took, was not necessarily the means of achieving the second; put another way, assuming that the metropole had a fundamental interest in maintaining the basic structure of the colonial political economy, that interest is insufficient to explain the introduction of democratic institutions as part of the process of decolonization.

To a substantial extent, of course, the introduction of democratic institutions did advance fundamental metropolitan interests. Democratization introduced metropolitan institutions and ideologies to Africa, and it can be seen as part of an effort both to socialize the indigenous elite and to "fill political space" with Western institutions in order to keep the post-colonial states within the Western orbit. Furthermore, as Bayart (1978: 71) has pointed out, "from the standpoint of the colonial power, elections defined and delimited the legal and legitimate political arena outside of which no political gains were to be made," and it was an arena the metropole was substantially able to control and manipulate. The introduction of democratic institutions was thus a mechanism by which the colonial powers created "an African 'elite' and . . . reached an understanding with it about independence" (Markovitz, 1977: 179). Various types of nationalist movements reflected different class and social bases, but the general pattern of the move to independence was one of the creation of an "organizational bourgeoisie" which came to power and gained independence as a result of "'an arrangement' between colonial and African establishments that recognized each other and proposed no radical alteration of previous arrangements" (Markovitz, 1977: 179). In this way, elections and democratization clearly advanced the political-economic interests of the metropole as it retreated from outright colonial control.

The relationship between the metropole and democratic institutions, however, is complex. Democratic regimes will not by themselves assure the preservation of metropolitan interests. In fact, there are on record many cases of the Western capitalist core moving against democratic regimes when they failed (or even threatened to fail) to assure the continuity of a given political-economic pattern. This has occurred particularly, perhaps, when the United States has intervened against democratic regimes in Latin America or, more recently, has supported and aided the military overthrow of democratic regimes and their replacement with what have turned out to be harshly repressive authoritarian regimes based on the exclusion of the popular sectors from political and economic participation (O'Donnell, 1978; Collier, forthcoming).[1] In the Third World, then, authoritarian rather than democratic regimes often seem most supportive of dependent capitalism and the capitalist core. In Africa there are the cases of Touré, Keita, Nkrumah, and Nyerere, all of whom came to power through the democratic political game set up in the course of decolonization but did not play the "proper" role of a loyal inheritance elite. Elsewhere, where the outcome was more congruent with the political-economic interests

1. While classical Marxist scholarship saw liberal democracy as "bourgeois" democracy—a regime (or form of state) through which capital rules (see Chapter 1), more recent strands of Marxist analysis have pointed to contradictions between capitalism and democracy (Bowles and Gintis, 1980; Wolfe, 1977; and cf. the more general literature on the contradictions between legitimacy and accumulation, e.g., Habermas, 1975; O'Connor, 1973). These analyses have focused on advanced capitalist societies; the Latin American literature explores some of these contradictions for earlier stages of dependent capitalist industrialization.

of the departing colonial powers, this outcome was attributable not simply to the "automatic" recruitment to positions of power of reliable and sympathetic members of the indigenous elite through the rules of the democratic game being introduced. Rather, those very rules had to be bent, that very game had to be manipulated as the metropole intervened in elections, aided parties it considered to be supportive of its interests, and harassed and even banned those parties that threatened them. The democratic game could not automatically and unattended assure the right outcome from the point of view of the metropole. Why, then, was democracy introduced?

All this is not to suggest that a democratic Africa simply contradicted fundamental metropolitan interests, but, rather, that the pursuit of those interests is not a sufficient explanation of the introduction of democracy. Nevertheless, in a brief review of the reasons, it is well to start with the way in which democratization was consistent with and advanced metropolitan political-economic and strategic interests. As mentioned above, the maintenance of close political and economic ties was an objective for the metropoles, and this motivation was clearly one of the reasons for the transfer of Western institutions. In the post-war period, when the colonial relationship began to be altered, the colonies came to be seen as political units with a new relationship to the metropole but still attached to it, either in a commonwealth of independent countries or in a community of associated entities. Such a redefinition of the relationship was premised on the idea of greater similarity and the trappings of greater equality among the entities. From the point of view of the metropole, then, decolonization took the form of democratization at least partly in an attempt to perpetuate the earlier relationship through a newly redefined political association with the colonies. There were, however, other quite different reasons as well.

Ideological pressures within the metropole also played an important role in the democratization of the colonies. Anti-colonial sentiment on the part of the parties of the left in France and the Labour Party of Britain led them to advocate introduction of democratic institutions in Africa, for these were viewed as essential components of equality (Morgenthau, 1964: 33; Young, 1970a: 465–66). To this could be added a tactical factor, concerning the need to find a way in which the metropole could exit gracefully and still save face. This point has been emphasized by Young (1965: 35–36), who argues that the transfer of European institutions to

Africa helped the European powers to maintain their self-respect as they withdrew from imperial greatness. He quotes Mackenzie's remark that there is "a sentiment among Europeans that if they are to go, it must be with honour, honour defined by European standards of good government and democracy."

The transfer of European democratic institutions to Africa did not, of course, only involve imposition of a political regime by a colonial power. While there was substantial variation from colony to colony and among groups within each colony, the demands of African nationalists were an important factor—sometimes the most important factor—in the introduction of these political reforms. Again, the reasons can be seen as both political and ideological. First, the introduction of democratic institutions, and particularly of universal suffrage, created a political resource for those indigenous elites who were in a position to take advantage of it. On the one hand, it was a resource to be used against colonial rule, since democratic institutions, the political formula of rule by the people, and popular support provided the basis for a kind of political legitimacy which undermined any justification of colonial rule and which caught the colonial powers in an ideological contradiction (Emerson, 1960: 242–43). On the other hand, universal democratic suffrage introduced a new political resource into the politics of factional rivalries among the indigenous elite. It was thus demanded by younger nationalists who sought to supplant older, more conservative groups in positions of influence. In short, democratization was an important political resource in the demand for independence.

Finally, there is an ideological factor. The normative preference of the African elite for democracy reflected their schooling by Western teachers, often in Europe or the United States, and the socialization that derived from this education and from the colonial experience itself. The context of colonialism, of inequality, of beliefs about "advanced" versus "primitive," of rulers versus ruled, defined European ways, habits, attitudes, values, and practices as superior, while African traditions were considered inferior or "uncivilized." Within this context, metropolitan political institutions had considerable prestige among the Africans. What Périn has said about the Belgian Congo is probably also true for the rest of Africa: "The political regime of Belgium has shown itself to be endowed with a rather surprising prestige, even amongst certain Congolese leaders least suspect of indulgence toward the colonizing nation" (quoted in Young, 1965: 176).

Thus, the transfer of European political institutions to Africa seemed appropriate both to the departing colonial powers and to the successor elite as an exit and an entrance device, respectively. The introduction of European democratic institutions was appropriate for the transfer of political power and for the transition from colonial to independent status. It was less appropriate for the consolidation of power by the victorious nationalist faction following independence; as a result, these institutions were rather hastily abandoned. The introduction of democratic institutions was also clearly unnecessary for the perpetuation of the colonial political economy, as is attested by the continuity of this political economy under the authoritarian regimes that have come to characterize independent Africa. At the specific historical moment of decolonization, however, there was a congruence of interest of the colonial and metropolitan sides in the transfer of Europe's own political institutions and particularly universal suffrage.

Introduction of Elections in Africa

Before 1945, very few elections had been held in any African colony at the territorial level,[2] and those that did occur involved in important measure a franchise restricted to European residents.

2. The limitation of this discussion to elections at the territorial (as opposed to local) level is primarily a practical one. Only very sketchy and incomplete data are available for municipal or local elections. References to the setting up of local councils with at least some elected members can be found, but it is difficult to determine how many elections were actually held subsequently, how many people voted, and even the precise localities in which these elections were held. Even if this information were available, the problem of aggregating it in a way that is meaningfully descriptive at the territorial level, which is the level of the present analysis, would be very difficult. This is particularly true in the British areas of indirect rule, where the institutions of local government were often the traditional ones and varied widely from area to area.

It may further be pointed out that the reform of local government (or the introduction of a metropolitan-like system of representation at the local level) did not, in most instances, pre-date the introduction of elections on the territorial level, so that the focus on the territorial level does not produce significant distortions in the time period involved. The major exceptions are the municipal councils set up earlier in some African cities. These municipal councils, however, seem to have involved very little electoral participation. It has been reported that in Ghana (the Gold Coast)

Among the British colonies, the vote was extended to European settlers in Kenya in 1920 and in Zambia in 1924 and to a small number of Africans residing in the capital city or a few other municipalities in British West Africa, also in the mid-1920s. In French Africa, the vote was granted in 1848 in Senegal to French citizens, a category which included natives of France and of the four "overseas communes" established in Senegal. In addition, a very limited franchise was introduced in 1925 in Dahomey, Ivory Coast, Guinea, and Mali; and in 1936 in the four colonies of French Equatorial Africa.

After 1945, extensions in the suffrage came quickly throughout colonial Africa. By independence, which was achieved between 1957 and 1965, the colonial powers had provided for at least one election based on universal suffrage, the "independence election," in all the countries considered in this study except Tanzania.[3] In analyzing the introduction of elections and universal suffrage in Africa, it is useful to consider the colonies of the three metropoles separately, since the different patterns reflect colonial policy.

French Colonies

In French Africa, evolution of elections and the franchise was similar for all of the colonies, as policy was made for them as a group, or occasionally as two groups corresponding to the two

---

in 1922, only 46 of 1,117 registered actually voted in the municipal elections in Accra; none voted out of 717 registered in Cape Coast; and only 2 out of 299 in Sekondi (Buell, 1965: 833). The situation is not much different in other cities of British West Africa: in Freetown, Sierra Leone, there were only 674 registered voters in 1924 (Buell, 1965: 882); and in Lagos, Nigeria, only 12 percent of the 2,231 registered (or about 260 people) voted in the town council election of 1923 (Buell, 1965: 661). In French Africa, before World War II, five municipal councils were set up in the four colonies of AEF, but membership on these was by appointment (Thompson and Adloff, 1960: 52). In AOF, twenty-three municipal councils were set up before World War II, fourteen of which were in Senegal and only nine in the seven other colonies of the Federation (Suret-Canale, 1971: 330). Some of these (the "second degree" communes) had councils elected by a restricted suffrage; the others, however (the "first degree" communes), had appointed councils.

3. In the Congo (Zaire) and the Northern Region of Nigeria the pre-independence election was based on manhood, not universal suffrage. Sierra Leone did not have a comparable independence election within a year or two prior to independence. There, the comparable election, based on universal suffrage, took place a year after independence. It is this election which is used as the basis for scoring in this analysis. See Appendix I.

federations of French West Africa (AOF) and French Equatorial Africa (AEF).[4] Only Senegal had a distinctive colonial administrative history. There, French citizenship was extended to the natives of the four communes early on. The French citizens of Senegal (natives either of France or of the communes) elected a deputy to the French National Assembly in Paris from 1848 until the post-World War II reforms, with the exception of the period during the Second Empire. In addition, starting in 1879, they elected a Conseil Général of Senegal. In 1939, noncitizens of Senegal sat on the council and were elected by noncitizens who had completed military service (Robinson, 1955: 49).

Outside Senegal, each colony had an advisory administrative council. After 1925, three elected members were added to official members on the councils in Dahomey, Ivory Coast, Guinea, and Mali. These elected members were noncitizens who were elected on a very limited franchise, restricted geographically to the most advanced regions of the colonies (French West Africa, 1925: 341). In fact, most of the electorate was concentrated in the large cities, particularly, of course, the capital cities (see Zolberg, 1964: 50). It has been reported that only one-tenth of one percent of the population voted in these elections in AEF in 1936 (Suret-Canale, 1971: 330). No similar figures are readily available for elections in the other colonies, but Robinson (1955: 163) reports that the limited franchise of 1946 represented a large increase in the number enfranchised, so the number was surely very small.

Before World War II, the only other elections above the local level in French Africa were for representatives to the Conseil Supérieur, an advisory council to the Minister of Colonies in Paris. Only French citizens were allowed to vote in these elections, and by 1936 only 2,136 Africans throughout French Africa had been granted citizenship outside the four communes of Senegal (Cowan, 1958: 40).

After World War II, change in the franchise proceeded rapidly. The 1944 Brazzaville Conference resulted in a number of recom-

4. The colonies in AOF were: Dahomey, Guinea, Ivory Coast, Mali, Mauritania, Niger, Senegal, and Upper Volta. Those in AEF were: CAR, Chad, Congo, and Gabon. Though the two French trust territories were not formally included in the two French colonial federations, the political changes and reforms in Togo and Cameroun closely paralleled those in AOF and AEF, respectively, and for the present purposes they are grouped with them.

mendations about the future relationship between France and her colonies. According to these recommendations, the colonies were to be integrated with France into a single political unit. This meant that "the eventual formation, even in the distant future, of self-government in the colonies" was dismissed as a possibility (Morgenthau, 1964: 38). Moreover, as part of France, the colonies would be governed by the French Constitution rather than their own constitutions, and they would therefore participate in French political institutions. As a result, in 1945, Africans voting on two rolls (an upper roll of those with the status of "citizen" and a lower roll of African "subjects") elected delegates to the French Constituent Assembly. The Conference also recommended the creation of territorial assemblies, eventually to be elected by universal suffrage, as well as the democratization of local and regional councils. Most of the recommendations were not implemented until 1957, but the groundwork had been laid, and starting in 1945 and 1946 Africans did participate in direct elections to the French Constituent Assemblies, the French National Assembly, and the new territorial assembly of each colony. They also voted in the referenda on the constitutions, although participation was limited to the first college or upper roll of voters.

Under the 1946 Constitution, a restricted franchise operated on the basis of a two-college system for elections to the territorial assembly of each colony and for the indirect elections to the Conseil Général of the two federations, French West Africa and French Equatorial Africa. The one exception was Senegal, which had a single electoral roll. The two-college system was maintained for AEF and Cameroun at the level of elections to the French National Assembly, but a single college system was established for AOF. The chronology of the steps broadening the franchise and eliminating the dual-college system has been summarized by Ruth Schachter Morgenthau:

> In 1946 the criteria for the vote were individual identity or importance in the society: for example, notables; members or former members of local assemblies, co-operatives, unions; holders of French decorations; regular wage earners in establishments recognized by law; ministers of religion; veterans; owners of legally registered property; holders of hunting or driver's licenses. A 1947 law added "all those who can prove they can read and write in French or Arabic." The electoral law for the 1951 National Assembly included a new criterion: status within the family,

such as heads of families who pay tax, and mothers of two children living or dead in the service of France. The 1955 municipal law made the franchise universal in the cities, and finally in 1956 the Loi-Cadre allowed every citizen over 21 to vote. The 1952 law for the territorial assemblies reduced the number of seats reserved to the first college, and the Loi-Cadre eliminated it altogether. (1964: 55–56)

British Colonies

The introduction of elections in the British colonies took place within the context of an evolving legislative council in each colony. Sitting on the council were both "official" members (i.e., senior government officials who sat ex-officio and who were Europeans), and "unofficial" members, representing local, but not necessarily indigenous, interests. Unofficial seats were first introduced as a way of representing and protecting European settler or commercial interests; eventually, African interests were recognized and given formal representation on the council, though at first Europeans were sometimes nominated to "represent African interests." While the officials formed a majority in the beginning of the evolution of the system, the unofficial members held an increasing proportion of the seats as the system evolved.

The method of selection also underwent a gradual evolution. In the beginning, unofficial seats were filled by appointment. The electoral principle was gradually introduced in each colony, and unofficial seats were increasingly filled by election rather than nomination. Elections themselves were introduced in stages, with some form of indirect election, often by local governmental bodies which were not themselves elected, frequently preceding direct elections, which took place on the basis of an ever-widening franchise. A third and simultaneous aspect of the evolution of the legislative council was the expanding geographical territory to which it referred. Initially it was an institution that corresponded only to the Crown Colony, but it was gradually extended to encompass the Protectorate governments as well. It was not unusual for geographical areas within the same territory to be at different "stages" at any given time. The final stage of the evolutionary process was a democratically elected legislative council, elected on a universal franchise, with powers of self-government and encompassing the political units that subsequently became independent nations.

In contrast to French colonial policy, British colonial policy was made separately for each colony, depending on whether the British believed that the colony was "ready" for a particular change. A major factor was the presence (generally in East and Central Africa) or absence (generally in West Africa) of European settlers in the colony. As a result of this "pragmatic" approach to colonial policy, the timing and to some extent the sequence of the different steps in the evolution of the legislative council varied among the British colonies. Table 1 indicates the dates at which each of the British colonies reached certain major stages in this evolutionary process. The difference between the British colonies in East and Central Africa and those in West Africa is evident. In general, there was a more gradual progression through these stages in West Africa. Elected seats in the legislative council were introduced in the mid-1920s,

Table 1. *Major Dates in the Introduction of Electoral Politics in British Colonies*

	First election to legislative council	First African elected to legislative council	First territory-wide election	First election with universal suffrage
West Africa				
Gambia	1947	1947	1954	1960
Ghana	1925	1925	1951[a]	1956
Nigeria	1923	1923	1951[b]	1959[c]
Sierra Leone	1924	1924	1957[d]	1962
East and Central Africa				
Kenya	1920	1957	1957	1963
Malawi	1956	1961[e]	1961[e]	1964[f]
Tanzania	1958	1958	1958	1962
Uganda	1958	1958[g]	1958[g]	1962
Zambia	1924	1959[h]	1959[h]	1964

Sources: The data for West Africa come primarily from Price (1967) and Jordan (1969). The East African data come from a wide variety of country monographs and colonial documents which are listed in the bibliography.

[a]Indirect election through local government body in Northern Territories.

[b]Regional elections.

[c]Manhood suffrage in the Northern Region.

[d]Direct elections in 1957 in the Colony, indirect by local government bodies in the Protectorate.

[e]Indirect elections in 1956.

[f]All constituencies were uncontested and no voting took place.

[g]Previous indirect elections through local government bodies.

[h]Indirect elections in 1948 and 1954 by African Representative Council.

and Africans ran for those seats on a restricted franchise, generally limited to the more developed coastal towns. New constitutions introduced after World War II instituted an unofficial majority.[5] By the beginning of the 1950s, elections were held throughout the territories and were no longer limited to coastal towns, though in the new areas the elections were often indirect, which tended to mean that power was retained by the traditional authorities. The period of the 1950s was one of extending the franchise and evolving toward a system of direct election for the whole territory.

The pattern in East and Central Africa was somewhat different, although it also took place within the context of an evolving legislative council. In Kenya and Zambia, which had the largest concentrations of European settlers, the first elections to the legislative council took place in the 1920s, but these involved only Europeans. The first African was not elected until 1957 in Kenya and 1959 in Zambia.[6] Universal suffrage was granted in these countries in 1963 and 1964, respectively. Elsewhere, the first elections, which in these cases did involve Africans, did not occur until the mid-1950s; universal suffrage was not introduced until 1962 in Tanzania and Uganda and 1964 in Malawi. Given this late start, African electoral experience in the pre-independence period in East and Central Africa was very short indeed.

The differences among British colonies were further complicated by the wide variety of electoral arrangements employed. First, indirect elections were held in three ways: (1) indirect election by a nonelected body, e.g., a local government body; (2) indirect election by an already constituted elected body, again, usually a local government body; or (3) a multi-stage indirect election in which delegates were elected to an electoral college. Second, there were arrangements whereby seats were reserved for a particular category of people, generally for chiefs (in West Africa) or for racial or communal minority groups (in East and Central Africa): (1) election of reserved seats by a special roll of voters, i.e., by chiefs or by a racial or communal roll; (2) a multi-stage election in which a special roll

5. Sierra Leone's post-war constitution was not implemented until 1951; as a result, her evolution lagged behind that of Ghana and Nigeria, as did the evolution of The Gambia.
6. In 1948 and 1954 in Zambia, Africans were "selected for appointment" by the African Representative Council, with the final power of appointment residing with the governor.

(generally a communal group) selected its candidates for reserved seats, who were then voted upon by all the voters in the final election; and (3) election of seats reserved for candidates of a given communal group for whom there were no special channels of nomination.

To get a better idea of the variation in the rate of introduction of universal suffrage and in the use of these electoral arrangements, let us look more closely at the experience of two colonies, one in West Africa and one in East Africa. The first is Ghana (the Gold Coast), which had a relatively gradual evolution of elections to the legislative council and greater experience with universal suffrage before independence and where chiefs had fairly great influence. The second is Tanzania (Tanganyika), where elections were introduced rapidly, where there had been no experience with universal suffrage before independence, and where multi-racial politics—that is, institutional arrangements guaranteeing the (over)representation of non-African communal groups—was introduced.

Until 1874, Ghana was administered jointly with Sierra Leone. The first legislative council was set up in 1850 and included an African. After 1874, the council usually included Africans. In 1925, membership was extended to include elected Africans: six provincial members elected through the Joint Provincial Council and three municipal members directly elected from Accra, Cape Coast, and Sekondi. The 1946 Constitution united the colony and Ashanti under a single legislative council and provided for an unofficial majority. Direct election was still limited to a few members, elected on a restricted franchise in the coastal towns. The 1951 constitutional changes instituted a council with five directly elected municipal seats, thirty-three rural seats indirectly elected in a two-stage system, nineteen elected from the Northern Territories by the Northern Territorial Council sitting as an electoral college, eighteen additional territorial seats chosen by groups of chiefs, six representatives of the European Chambers of Commerce and Mines, and three official members. The suffrage was extended to all rate-payers, although this was applicable only to the five municipal seats, where direct elections had previously been held, and to the thirty-three indirectly elected rural seats. In 1954, all seats were directly elected on a wide franchise that included all who paid the basic rate. Before independence, in the 1956 election, this last requirement was dropped and full universal suffrage was introduced.

In Tanzania (Tanganyika), the legislative council was established in 1926 and was composed of thirteen officials and ten appointed unofficial members (seven Europeans and three Asians). In 1945, the first African was appointed. The council was expanded to sixty-one in 1955, including thirty unofficial members, ten appointed from each race. These thirty unofficial members were elected for the first time in a two-part election held in 1958–59. The principle of racial parity was upheld under a system whereby all races voted for all thirty seats. The franchise was restricted on the basis of economic and educational qualifications, which meant that all Europeans, most Asians, and only a very limited percentage of the Africans were granted the vote. Nevertheless, Africans comprised a majority of the electorate (Bienen, 1967: 53). In 1960, an unofficial majority was instituted on the council and the franchise was substantially widened, although no election based on universal suffrage was held before independence.

Belgian Colonies

In Belgium, as in France, no thought was given to eventual democratization until after World War II (Young, 1965: 36). Once the notion of decolonization had been accepted, it was generally assumed in Belgium that there was sufficient time to proceed with democratic reforms very gradually, "building from the ground up" (Young, 1965: 36, 41). Accordingly, democratization in both the Congo (Zaire) and the trust territory of Ruanda-Urundi (which became independent as the two countries of Rwanda and Burundi) involved a system of indirect election through local government bodies and a very late appearance of a legislative body at the territorial level.

In the Congo, the first important reforms came in 1957, when a two-tiered system of urban government, involving indirect elections, was announced. The lower tier consisted of a number of communal councils which elected the urban council on the upper tier. Although all communes were represented on an equal basis, parity between European and African representation was guaranteed by the inclusion of a number of European interest-group representatives. For elections to the communal council, the franchise was extended to males twenty-five years of age and older. The new system was applied in three cities on a trial basis in 1957 and was extended to four others the following year. The 1957 reforms also included introduction of elections—either direct or indirect, depending on local circumstances—in rural administration. This was implemented at the initiative of the localities over the next three years. The 1959 reforms provided for three-tiered indirect elections to the legislative council, which was eventually to be the upper legislative chamber. At the bottom of this system, voters would elect territorial and communal councils directly. The middle tier consisted of a provincial council. Elections based on adult male suffrage were held in 1959, but were widely boycotted, and in most of Leopoldville province the territorial councils were never constituted. The final pre-independence reforms called for direct election to the House of Representatives and indirect election to the Senate. The franchise for the elections of 1960 still did not extend the vote to women. As in Belgium, voting was made compulsory.

In Ruanda-Urundi introduction of democratic reforms came somewhat earlier than in the Congo, because of its status as a trust territory under the United Nations. Under the League of Nations, there had been talk of a democratic evolution of the territory. In fact, however, Belgium was convinced it should "maintain and consolidate the traditional cadre of the Tutsi directing class because of their qualities, their undeniable intellectual superiority, and their potential for leadership" (Belgian Government Report, quoted in Webster, 1966: 20). The U.N. Trusteeship Agreement of 1947 adopted the goal of establishing representative institutions. In 1952, a multi-tiered system of indirectly elected councils was introduced. At the bottom was the subchiefdom council, elected by notables, who were themselves appointed. Elections were held under this system in 1953. According to the 1956 reforms, the notables forming the electoral colleges of the subchiefdom were to be chosen by a secret ballot of the adult male population. In 1957 the General Council of Ruanda-Urundi was set up. All members, including nine official members, were appointed by the governor, except for four: two chosen by each of the two superior councils of Ruanda and Urundi from among their membership. In 1959 a two-tiered system was introduced. The subchiefdoms were enlarged into communes, each of which was to have a council directly elected by male suffrage. These councils would elect representatives from among their membership to a state council, which would also include a few appointed members and which would legislate with the Mwami, the traditional king, in an increasing number of policy areas. In 1960 these communal elections were held. In 1961, only a year before independence, the first legislative elections were held and universal suffrage was introduced.

Rate

The difference between rates of expansion of electoral participation in the French and the British colonies are summarized in Tables 2 and 3. Table 2 shows the number of territory-wide elections[7] prior to the introduction of universal suffrage and the number of elections with universal suffrage prior to independence. It can be seen that the French colonies had more experience with

Table 2. *Rate of Introduction of Electoral Participation:*
Numbers of Elections

	Number of territory-wide elections before the introduction of universal suffrage	Number of pre-independence elections with universal suffrage
British Colonies		
Gambia	1	2
Ghana	2	1
Kenya	2	1
Malawi	1	1[a]
Nigeria	3[b]	1[c]
Sierra Leone	1	1[d]
Tanzania	2	0
Uganda	2	1
Zambia	2	1
French Colonies	7	2[e]

[a]No polling actually took place because none of the constituencies was contested.
[b]Including regional elections.
[c]Manhood suffrage in the Northern Region.
[d]As noted in text, this election followed independence.
[e]Guinea and Gabon each had one. This figure does not include the 1958 referendum.

7. For the French colonies, the first territory-wide election is considered to be the first election to the territorial assembly, which was held in 1946. For British Africa, territory-wide election refers to one in which there was voting throughout most of the territory, that is, the election must not have been restricted to a relatively small geographic area; and indirect elections based on selection by an already constituted body are not included, but indirect elections based on a multi-tiered system with popular voting at the base level are.

Table 3. *Rate of Expansion of Electoral Participation in Africa:*
Number of Years until Introduction of Universal Suffrage

	(A) From first election to legislative council	(B) From election of first African	(C) From first territory-wide election
British West Africa			
Gambia	13	13	6
Ghana	31	31	5
Nigeria	33	33	8
Sierra Leone	37	37	5
British East and Central Africa			
Kenya	43	6	6
Malawi	8	3	3
Tanzania	4	4	4
Uganda	4	4	4
Zambia	40	5	5
French Africa			
Senegal	78	78	11
Dahomey, Guinea, Ivory Coast, Mali	32	32	11
Mauritania, Niger, Upper Volta	11	11	11
French Equatorial Africa	20	20	11

limited-suffrage and universal-suffrage elections before independence. They had seven direct elections prior to the introduction of
universal suffrage, whereas the British colonies had two at most.
Africans in the French colonies voted on the basis of universal
suffrage three times prior to independence, whereas in the British
colonies they generally voted on this basis only once. Experience
with elections was substantially greater in French Africa than anywhere else in tropical Africa. As Morgenthau put it:

> French Africans went to the polls numerous times to elect representatives
> to fill the many posts the new October 1946 Constitution opened to
> Africans. Between 1945 and 1958, West African voters took part in four
> referenda. They voted in direct elections to the *Constituante* and Na-
> tional Assembly at least five times, and directly elected territorial coun-
> cillors to territorial assemblies three times. [There were in addition at

least eight indirect elections.] . . . Frequent elections maintained an almost continuous climate of electioneering in [French] Africa. (Morgenthau, 1964: 54–55)

Table 3 shows the number of years between the first election to the territorial assembly and the final introduction of universal suffrage. Because of the evolving nature of the legislative council under British colonial rule, the year of the first election has been defined in three different ways: the year in which a member was first elected to the legislative council (column A), the year in which the first African was elected to the legislative council (column B), and the year of the first territory-wide election to the legislative council (column C). For French Africa, the first election has been defined as the first election to the Conseil Général in Senegal and to the administrative councils for the rest of French Africa (columns A and B).

Table 3 clearly reveals the difference between the British policy in West Africa and in East Africa. In West Africa, the first election of an African occurred long before the introduction of universal suffrage (see columns A and B). In East and Central Africa, the pattern of electoral evolution was heavily influenced by the presence of British settlers. This affected colonial policy concerning the introduction of electoral participation for the region as a whole—even where there were relatively few settlers, as in Uganda and Malawi—because of the special relationships among these colonies,[8] and presumably because of a potential reference group or demonstration effect, which would have heightened demands in the settler colonies for the extension of any rights granted to Africans in neighboring colonies, thus jeopardizing the privileged position of the larger settler communities. Electoral participation for European settlers was introduced in East and Central Africa quite early (see column A for Zambia and Kenya, the only colonies with sizable settler populations), but for Africans it was introduced late, in order to protect settler interests. The contrast with British policy in West Africa can be seen by comparing East and Central Africa with West Africa in column B. It may be noted, however, that though the British began to introduce democratic reform quite early in West Africa, only a

8. The Central African Federation that tied Malawi (Nyasaland) and Zambia (Northern Rhodesia) to Rhodesia (Southern Rhodesia) already existed, and proposals had been made for integrating the three East African colonies—Uganda, Kenya and Tanzania. Multi-racial politics (in institutional form) were introduced in Malawi but not in Uganda.

very short time elapsed between the introduction of territory-wide elections and the introduction of universal suffrage (see column C). Indeed, it is comparable to the speed of introduction in East and Central Africa, where Africans began to participate in elections relatively late.

The more gradual introduction of universal suffrage in French Africa, noted in Table 2 in terms of number of elections, is also evident in Table 3 in terms of the number of years from the first territory-wide election to universal suffrage. It is clear that British East and Central Africa experienced the most rapid evolution to universal suffrage from the time of the first election of an African; the distinction between British West Africa and French Africa is less pronounced.

It is difficult to include Belgian Africa in these comparisons because of the relatively late introduction of an elected assembly at the territorial level, combined with the more widespread use of indirect, multi-tiered elections. While in one sense three elections were scheduled in the Congo, the 1957 indirect election did not culminate in an election to a territorial assembly, nor did the 1959 election, due to widespread boycotting. It can thus be said that before independence there was only one territory-wide election in the Congo that was comparable to those held elsewhere. Of the four elections in Ruanda-Urundi, only three involved a popular franchise, and only two of these culminated in a legislative body. Thus, if elections not culminating in a territorial assembly are excluded, as local government elections have been excluded elsewhere, the number of elections in Belgian Africa is similar to that in British Africa.

The similarity between Belgian and British Africa can also be seen in the rapid rate of introduction of universal suffrage. In terms of the number of years from the first election to a territorial assembly to the introduction of universal suffrage—a figure which for Belgian Africa represents the shortest rather than the longest calculation—both Belgian colonies had an extremely fast rate. Ruanda-Urundi had just one (indirect) election only a year before the introduction of universal suffrage. In the Congo the first election to a territorial assembly was based on universal suffrage (if the failed election of the year before is excluded). The Belgian colonies are unique, however, in that elections were held at the local or communal level before they were introduced at the territorial level. Even if these elections are included in calculating the base year, thus making the most gradual possible interpretation of the introduction of universal suffrage, the result is five years for Ruanda-Urundi and only three for the Congo, figures comparable to those in column C of Table 3 for British Africa.

Level of Participation

Another important aspect of expansion of electoral participation—and one which had consequences for the course of post-independence politics—is the level of mass participation that was actually achieved in pre-independence elections. Because figures or estimates of the total population are available for all countries (Morrison et al., 1972: 480–83), the proportion of total population, rather than of adult population, is used to assess the level of participation. Table 4 presents the proportion of the population voting in territory-wide elections in the pre-independence period. It can be seen that by the late 1950s, French Africa had achieved quite high levels of voting. The turnout was particularly great for the 1958 referendum, although these results were probably inflated (Zolberg, 1966a: 79; de Lusignan, 1969: 21), and most of the French colonies did not maintain that rate of turnout for their independence election, which occurred the following year. Nevertheless, by the end of the 1950s, over 20 percent of the population was generally participating in elections in French Africa.

Relatively high levels of participation were attained even more quickly in Belgian Africa, where voting was compulsory. In the Congo over 20 percent of the population participated in the first territory-wide direct election in 1960. Burundi and particularly Rwanda attained even higher levels in their first territory-wide election—26 percent and 46 percent, respectively—although they had had longer experience with indirect elections (dating back to 1953).

In British Africa, the pre-independence rates of participation were somewhat lower: four colonies (The Gambia, Sierra Leone, Kenya, and Uganda) reached 20 percent by the independence election (in Sierra Leone, the comparable election actually took place a year after independence—see note 3 above). In these comparisons it should be borne in mind that two British colonies, Tanzania and Nigeria, had not yet attained full universal suffrage. In Tanzania, however, only 12 percent of the population voted in a presidential election based on universal suffrage held two years later, indicating that though the low figures for 1960 reflect the restricted suffrage at the time, the level of voting was relatively low quite apart from that limitation. On the other hand, in Nigeria, where universal suffrage was not extended to the Northern Region, the rate of electoral participation was quite high among those eligible to vote and may well have reached the 20 percent level with full suffrage in the North.

From this data, another index of the rate of expansion of electoral participation may be derived: the number of years that elapsed between the first election and the year in which the level of participation first reached 20 percent of the population, a level at which most of the colonies can be scored (see Table 5). The four British colonies that did reach the 20 percent level of participation (including Sierra Leone) did so quite quickly in comparison to French Africa, although not in comparison to Belgian Africa. Tanzania and Zambia did not reach that level before independence, but they nevertheless attained that level somewhat more quickly than did French Africa. The remaining three countries of ex-British Africa, Ghana, Nigeria, and Malawi, did not attain the 20 percent level. In Ghana, often seen as a case of high level of mobilization, the official returns of the 1960 presidential election, which are generally regarded as suspiciously high (Austin, 1964: 39), record a turnout of only 17.6 percent of the population.

Comparison with European Democracies

Many hypotheses about the effects of electoral participation in the Third World (see Chapter 1) involve an explicit or implicit comparison with those countries in Europe that have become stable democracies. These hypotheses focus on the more rapid introduction of participation in the Third World and on differences in social and economic context. Few attempts have been made, however, to examine the extent of these differences.

A summary of three main steps in the evolution of electoral participation in Europe is presented in Table 6. It should be noted that this table, which is derived from Rokkan (1970: 84–85), underestimates the period over which the suffrage evolved, because column A presents the date Rokkan calls the "major postrevolutionary reorganization"; actually, in many cases electoral

Table 4. *Percent of Total Population Voting in Pre-Independence Territory-wide Elections**

	1946	'47	'48	'49	'50	'51	'52	'53	'54	'55	'56	'57	'58	'59	'60	'61	'62	'63	'64
British West Africa																			
Gambia																	37		
Ghana									12		11								
Nigeria																			
Sierra Leone												8		16			30[a]		
British East and Central Africa																			
Kenya												1				11		22	
Malawi																3			0
Tanzania													0.3[b]		1		12[a]		
Uganda																16	27		
Zambia														0.3[c]			4		18
French West Africa																			
Dahomey	2					9					10	16	23	20					
Guinea	4					9					21	22	42						
Ivory Coast	5					4					20	27	51	45					
Mali	3					10	7				12	19	25	18					
Mauritania	1					6					14	30	36	38					
Niger	1					3					13	14	19	12[d]					
Senegal	5	4				12					17	21	31	28					
Togo						2.5[c]	4.3[c]				15		24	22					
Upper Volta			3			7	12				17	25	36	23					

	1946	'47	'48	'49	'50	'51	'52	'53	'54	'55	'56	'57	'58	'59	'60	'61	'62	'63	'64
French Equatorial Africa																			
Cameroun							8.3												
CAR	2					7					9		44	16					
Chad	0.7					6					11		26	8					
Congo	2					8					22		47	19					
Gabon	3					7					13	34	48	34					
Belgian Africa																			
Burundi								0.3								26			
Rwanda								0.6								46			
Zaire															20				

*Including elections to territorial assembly or legislative council and to French National Assembly and referenda.
a Post-independence election.
b This represents half of the constituencies. Elections in the others were held in 1959, but most were uncontested.
c Percent registered.
d Election held in 1958.

Table 5. *Number of Years from First Election to Year in Which 20 Percent of Population Voted* (Pre-Independence)*

French Africa	From 1946 election
West Africa	
Dahomey	12
Guinea	10
Ivory Coast	10
Mali	12
Mauritania	11
Niger	(19)
Senegal	11
Togo	12
Upper Volta	11
Equatorial Africa	
Cameroun	
CAR	12
Chad	12
Congo	10
Gabon	11

British Africa	From first election	From election of first African	From first territory-wide election
West Africa			
Gambia[a]	by 15	by 15	by 8
Ghana	—	—	—
Nigeria	—	—	—
Sierra Leone[b]	38	38	5
East and Central Africa			
Kenya	43	6	6
Malawi	—	—	—
Tanzania	(7)	(7)	(7)
Uganda	4	4	4
Zambia	(44)	(9)	(9)

Belgian Africa	From first indirect election	From first direct election
Burundi	3	0
Rwanda	8	0
Zaire	3	0

*Years in parentheses refer to post-independence elections. Twenty percent participation was not reached before independence in these countries.

[a]No data available before 1962 election.

[b]Election one year after independence.

Table 6. *Rate of Expansion of the Franchise in Democratic Europe*

	(A) Year of "post- revolutionary reorganization"	(B) Date of manhood suffrage	(C) Date of universal suffrage	(D) B − A	(E) C − A
Belgium	1831	1919[a]	1949	88	118
Denmark	1849	1849	1915	0	66
Finland	1906	1906	1906	0	0
France	1789	1793/1848/1851	1945	4/59/62	156
Iceland	1874	1920	1920	46	46
Ireland	1801	1918	1923	117	122
Luxembourg	1848	1919	1919	71	71
Netherlands	1848	1918	1922	68	72
Norway	1814	1898	1915	84	101
Sweden	1866	1920	1920	54	54
Switzerland	1848	1848	—	0	
United Kingdom		1918	1929		

Source: These data are derived primarily from Rokkan (1970: 84–85).
  [a]Manhood suffrage with plural votes since 1893.

participation was introduced prior to this date. This is particularly important to remember with respect to Finland and Switzerland, which, according to Table 6, proceeded very quickly to manhood suffrage. Finland had held direct elections to the Four-Estate Diet beginning in 1809, and Switzerland had a long history of elections to city councils and cantonal assemblies prior to political unification of the territory. A comparison of column D of Table 6 to column B of Table 3 shows clearly that electoral participation was introduced more gradually in Europe than in Africa. The difference is even greater if the base year used for Africa is the first territory-wide election (see column C of Table 3). With the exceptions of Denmark, the initial attempt in France, and the cases of Finland and Switzerland mentioned above, the extension of the franchise is more gradual for all European cases than it is for any of the African cases.

The same pattern can be seen with respect to the rates of voting (see Table 7). A comparison between the first column of Table 7 and Table 5 reveals clearly the contrast between African and European experiences. Unfortunately, good data is not readily available for the years before 1918/19 for Denmark, Finland, and France, the countries with the fastest rate of constitutional evolution. In Finland, however, there was evidently a rapid increase in electoral participation, with 30 percent of the population voting within, at most, thirteen years of the post-revolutionary reorganization. De-

Table 7. *Rate of Growth of Electoral Participation in Democratic Europe* (percentage of total population)*

	20	30	40	50
Belgium	1919(88)	†	†	1949(118)
Denmark	1918(69)[a]	1920(71)	1929(80)	1947(98)
Finland	nd	1919(13)[a]	1945(39)	1962(56)
France	1919(130)[a]	†	1945(156)	1956(167)
Iceland	nd	nd	nd	1946(72)[a]
Ireland	nd	1918(117)[a]	1927(126)	‡
Netherlands	1918(70)	†	1922(74)	1946(98)
Norway	1918(104)	1921(107)	1930(116)	1936(122)
Sweden	1921(55)	1928(62)	1932(66)	1952(86)
Switzerland	1928(80)	‡	‡	‡
United Kingdom[b]	1918(86)	1922(100)	†	1929(107)

Source: Based on information from Rokkan (1970: 84–85); Rokkan and Meyriat (1969); and Banks (1971).

*Table shows the year in which each level of electoral participation was reached and, in parentheses, the number of years elapsed since the year of "post-revolutionary reorganization" (from Rokkan, 1970).

nd = No data available.

†This level of participation was skipped.

‡This level of participation was not reached before the mid-1900s.

[a]Level reached at least by year indicated. Earlier data not provided.

[b]Years calculated from 1832 Reform Bill.

spite this lack of data, it is clear that, with these three possible exceptions, growth of participation in Europe was far more gradual than in Africa. It should be noted that if it had been possible to make this comparison on the basis of the percent of the adult, rather than the total, population voting, the difference between Africa and Europe would be even greater, since the difference in age structure of the African and European populations causes an underestimation of the percent of adult population voting in Africa compared to that of Europe.[9]

In addition to the rate of the introduction of elections and mass

9. Estimates of the difference in age structure vary according to the data sources employed and the countries considered. In general, the proportion of the African population that was under nineteen years of age around mid-twentieth century was roughly 5 to 15 percent higher than the proportion in European countries at the time of the introduction of manhood suffrage. This also seems to be the case for those countries which achieved manhood suffrage in the last century. See Van De Walle (1968: tables 2.5 and 2.6); Landry (1945: 126–28); Glass (1950: 369); United Kingdom, Royal Commission on Population (1950: table I); United Nations (1948: table 4): United Nations, Department of Social Affairs, Population Division (1953: 144–45).

participation, the sequence in which they were introduced relative to the timing of other social, economic, and political changes has also received attention. In undertaking an empirical investigation of this comparison, there is a problem in selecting a comparable transition point for the two continents. It was decided to use the date of the introduction of universal manhood suffrage for Europe and the date of independence for Africa. It should be noted that the choice of these dates maximizes the difficulty of reaching the conclusion that elections were introduced at a lower level of development in Africa than in Europe. If alternate dates had been used for Europe, such as the date of universal suffrage or the first date at which 20 percent of the population voted, it would have been easier to show that elections were introduced at a very early level of development in Africa, since these alternate dates are later than the date of manhood suffrage (see Tables 6 and 7). The choice of the year of independence for Africa was made in order to be as consistent as possible in definitions and sources of data. As was indicated above, universal suffrage usually preceded independence by only a couple of years (as did the 20 percent participation date in most, but not all, of Africa). The choice of a later date for Africa, then, also introduces a slight bias against the conclusion that there was an earlier introduction of electoral participation in Africa.

Tables 8 and 9 compare the sequence of the development of electoral participation and education in Africa and Europe. For each country they present the enrollment in primary and secondary schools per 10,000 population in the year of the introduction of manhood suffrage for Europe and in the year of independence for Africa. Whereas in Europe the average primary enrollment per 10,000 was 1,309, for Africa it was only 680. Despite this impressive difference, it is interesting and perhaps somewhat surprising that there is no large gap between the European and African countries. Three African countries fall well within the general European range, and two European countries fall in the middle of the African range.[10] Thus, the difference between Africa and Europe, while substantial, is perhaps somewhat less than might have been expected. Nevertheless, it remains true that with very few excep-

10. For Finland, data were not available until thirteen years after the introduction of universal manhood suffrage; the correct figure would in fact be lower than that presented here.

Table 8. *Primary School Enrollment per 10,000 Population at Introduction of Manhood Suffrage**

Africa[a]		Europe[b]		Breakdown of cases (by quintiles)	Breakdown of value range (by quintiles)
Country	Value	Country	Value		
		Netherlands	1677(+1)		
		Ireland	1608(+4)		
		Belgium	1601	I	I
Gabon	1505				
		Norway	1498		
Congo	1478				
		United Kingdom	1306(+1)		
Rwanda	1253				II
		Sweden	1211	II	
Zaire	1127				
Zambia	1013				
Cameroun	1010				
Kenya	1009				
		France (1851)	994(+12)		III
Malawi	925				
Uganda	759			III	
Ghana	746				
Ivory Coast	728				
Togo	722				
Burundi	637				
Tanzania	597				
CAR	566			IV	
Senegal	510				IV
		Finland	578(+13)		
Sierra Leone	484				
Nigeria	479				
Dahomey	442				
Chad	299				
Mauritania	232				
Guinea	226			V	
Upper Volta	131				V
Mali	78				
Niger	45				
AVERAGE	680		1309		

Source: Banks (1971).

*Missing cases: Gambia, Denmark, Iceland, Luxembourg, Switzerland.

[a]Year of independence. See explanation p. 55.

[b]When data are not available for the year in which manhood suffrage was introduced, the value for the nearest year is given. The number of years between this year and and the year of manhood suffrage is indicated in parentheses.

Table 9. *Secondary School Enrollment per 10,000 Population at Introduction of Manhood Suffrage* *

Africa[a]		Europe[b]		Breakdown of cases (by quintiles)	Breakdown of value range (by quintiles)
Country	Value	Country	Value		
Ghana	223[c]				I, II
		Finland	93(+13)	I	III
		Norway	77		
		Ireland	69		
Gabon	67				
Uganda	65				
Congo	64				IV
		United Kingdom	64		
		Sweden	61	II	
		Belgium	52		
Sierra Leone	47				
		Netherlands	40(+1)		
Zaire	35				
Kenya	35				
Nigeria	34				
Togo	34				
Senegal	33			III	
Cameroun	32				
Ivory Coast	28				
CAR	25				
Malawi	25				
Zambia	25				V
Tanzania	19			IV	
Mauritania	17				
Dahomey	15				
Guinea	11				
		France (1851)	8		
Burundi	5				
Chad	4				
Rwanda	3			V	
Mali	2				
Upper Volta	2				
Niger	0				
AVERAGE	34[d]		58		

Source: Banks (1971).

*Missing cases: Gambia, Denmark, Iceland, Luxembourg, Switzerland.

[a]Year of independence. See explanation p. 55.

[b]When data are not available for the year in which manhood suffrage was introduced, the value for the nearest year is given. The number of years between this year and the year of manhood suffrage is indicated in parentheses.

[c]This value is corroborated in Morrison et al., 1972.

[d]Without Ghana the average is 26.

tions, the introduction of electoral participation in Africa took place at a point of substantially less educational development than in Europe. Furthermore, with either of the alternate dates in the development of European electoral participation (universal suffrage or 20 percent participation), the difference between the two continents would have been greater. Also, had it been possible to correct for differences in the age distribution of European and African populations, that is, had it been possible to look at enrollment as a percent of school-age rather than total population, the contrast would again be greater, since there was a larger proportion of school-age children in the total population in Africa than in Europe at that time.[11]

A similar situation pertains with respect to the sequence of electoral participation and secondary school enrollment (Table 9). Here again, one European country falls below the African average and a few African countries are at the upper end of the distribution. It is interesting to note the extremely high development of Ghana's secondary education relative not only to other African countries but also to all the European countries. On the whole, however, as with primary enrollment, the African average is only half that of the European average.

The same general picture holds for electoral participation and urbanization: compared to Europe, electoral participation was introduced in Africa at a relatively low level of urbanization (Table 10). This is interesting because it is often assumed that, due to various kinds of push-pull factors resulting from "imbalanced" development in the Third World, developing countries are "overurbanized." It may be true that African countries are overurbanized in relation to their level of economic development, but Table 10 shows that they are not overurbanized relative to electoral participation. Quite the contrary: compared to Europe, urbanization in Africa has lagged behind electoral participation.

---

11. It should also be remembered that the levels of enrollment reflected in Tables 8 and 9 had only been achieved very recently in Africa. Hence, when most of the adult population in Africa had been of school age, the level of educational enrollment was lower. In Europe, by contrast, enrollment may have changed more slowly over a generation or two. To the extent that this is the case, the figures in these tables do not reflect consistent differences with respect to the percent of educated adults (or eligible voting population); they overestimate that figure for Africa to a greater extent than for Europe, and therefore underestimate the contrast between the two groups of countries.

Table 10. *Population in Urban Centers of 50,000 or More at Introduction of Manhood Suffrage* (per 1,000 population)*

Africa[a]		Europe[b]		Breakdown of cases (by quintiles)	Breakdown of value range (by quintiles)
Country	Value	Country	Value		
		United Kingdom	365(+1)		I
		Netherlands	333(+1)		
Congo	221				II
		Belgium	205	I	III
		Sweden	130		
		Norway	127		
Senegal	121				
		Ireland	110(+4)		IV
Ghana	101				
		Denmark	97	II	
		Finland	95(+13)		
CAR	90				
Ivory Coast	80				
Sierra Leone	65	France (1851)	65		
Kenya	53				
Togo	46			III	
Nigeria	42				
Cameroun	37				
Chad	33				
Mali	30				
Burundi	28				
Upper Volta	23				
Guinea	22				V
Uganda	9				
Dahomey	0	Luxembourg	0		
Gabon	0	Switzerland	0	IV, V	
Gambia	0				
Malawi	0				
Mauritania	0				
Niger	0				
Rwanda	0				
AVERAGE	44		139		

Source: Banks (1971).

*Missing cases: Zaire, Tanzania, Zambia, Iceland.

[a]Year of independence. See explanation p. 55.

[b]When data are not available for the year when manhood suffrage was introduced, the value for the nearest year is given. The number of years between this year and the year of manhood suffrage is indicated in parentheses.

The relationship between growth of mass media and political participation has also received considerable attention. With reference to radios, there is of course the opposite relationship from those found above: electoral participation in Africa was introduced at a stage of much greater proliferation of radios than was the case in Europe. This is due to the simple fact that commercial radio broadcasting did not begin in Europe until 1927, *after* the introduction of manhood suffrage in all the European countries considered. Even if we look at the date of universal suffrage for Europe, only three European countries fall after 1927, including England in 1929, only two years after the BBC began commercial broadcasting. The other two are Belgium and France, which did have a large number of radios at the time of the introduction of universal suffrage compared to the number in most of Africa (Table 11).

Because of the lack of comparable data, it is impossible to construct a similar table comparing the sequence of electoral participation and economic—as distinct from social—development.

Table 11. *Radios per 10,000 Population at Introduction of Universal Suffrage**

Africa[a]		Europe	
Country	Value	Country	Value
Gambia	1358	France	1320
Gabon	494	Belgium	458
Kenya	272		
Senegal	265		
Mauritania	214		
Ivory Coast	171		
Congo	141		
Ghana	140		
Zaire	121		
CAR	100		
Upper Volta	92		
Niger	69		
Sierra Leone	52		
Tanzania	37		
Togo	34		
Nigeria	26		
Dahomey	25		
Cameroun	21		
Malawi	0		
Uganda	0		

Source: Banks (1971).

*Missing cases: Burundi, Guinea, Rwanda, Zambia.

[a]Year of independence. See explanation p. 55. Other sources report different values for a number of countries, particularly Malawi and Uganda. However, this alternative data leads to essentially the same conclusion in comparison with Europe.

Nevertheless, it seems clear that European countries had reached a level of much greater economic development by the time manhood suffrage was established than had African countries. Comparing nineteenth-century Europe to the present-day developing countries, Hoselitz (1964) states that the late-developers are embarking on industrialization with lower per-capita income, less agricultural land per capita, lower productivity of agriculture, and a lower rate of capital formation. Since the date of manhood suffrage fell in the twentieth century for most European countries, it is clear that Europe was even more economically developed relative to Africa at similar points in the expansion of electoral participation than is suggested in Hoselitz's analysis.

Quite aside from differences in these economic-development indicators, there are contrasts in economic structure that follow from differences in the timing of economic development in the eighteenth and nineteenth centuries rather than the twentieth century. Very briefly, one finds in the history of the late-developers such factors as new forms of capital accumulation, an industrialization model of import substitution, availability of capital-intensive technology, and the role played by multinational corporations. In general, twentieth-century developers, both as colonies and independent states, experience a totally different relationship to the world economy comprising a set of new international economic incentives and constraints as crucial parameters of their economic activity. In this sense too, the context of the introduction of elections in the two continents was entirely dissimilar.

This brief comparison with Europe supports the conventional wisdom that elections and electoral participation were introduced in Africa at a far faster rate and at a much lower level of socioeconomic development than in Western Europe. At the same time, as is suggested by arguments about certain aspects of the "revolution of rising expectations," this occurred in Africa in a context in which certain aspects of communications development, such as the introduction of radios, was far more advanced. Nevertheless, the data also indicate that the African countries varied substantially in rate and sequence, and the experience of a few African colonies is in some aspects closer to the experience of Europe than is sometimes assumed. Similarly, a few European democracies are, perhaps surprisingly, similar to typical African countries in some aspects of rate and sequence. It is not the goal of this discussion to make direct causal inferences from these Africa–Europe comparisons. They do suggest the value of introducing rate and socioeconomic variables into any analysis of the impact of the introduction of elections in Africa, and they point to an important aspect of the broad context in which electoral institutions were dismantled and new types of regimes set up.

3. Pre-Independence Electoral Politics: Mass Participation and Party Dominance

In the approximately fifteen years of decolonization, the suffrage was expanded and electoral participation increased dramatically and quickly along the lines spelled out in Chapter 2. The African masses, who prior to World War II had had no legitimate, institutionalized role in the political system at the territorial level, were now given a role and incorporated into the political system. What were the terms of this incorporation? It is clear that the entry of the masses onto the political stage in Africa had many components of "mobilized" rather than "autonomous" participation. Nevertheless, this mobilization opened the possibility of generating popular demands that the elites could not or preferred not to fulfill, and popular electoral support represented a political resource which could be mobilized by counter-elites. What, then, was the effect of this rapid introduction of elections and electoral participation? In which countries were the nationalist movements able to move into the new institutional context and harness the new resource most successfully? What was the relationship between electoral participation and factionalism among the political elite as reflected in the party system?

Across Africa, there were substantial differences in the degree to which people began to participate in elections and in the degree of fractionalization of the party system that emerged out of this period of electoral politics. How can these differences be accounted for? Three explanations will be considered. First, differences in the rate of introduction of universal suffrage and the number of elections held during the period of decolonization may have had some impact. Second, there is a substantial body of literature which suggests that the level of social mobilization may have been important. Finally, the level of electoral participation may have affected the level of party dominance or, conversely, the level of electoral participation may at least in part be understood in terms of intra-elite political relationships, such as the fractionalization of the party system or the emergence of a relatively cohesive political elite, which affected the effort expended on electoral mobilization. These possibilities will be considered in turn.

Rate of Introduction

The first possibility to be explored is that colonial policy regarding the rate at which elections and universal suffrage were introduced had an impact on the level of electoral participation and on the party system, particularly on the level of dominance the leading party managed to achieve. This analysis will provide an opportunity to explore whether the more rapid introduction of the suffrage enhances or inhibits the capacity of the newly emerging elite to consolidate its position.

Three measures of the rate at which elections were introduced may be considered. The first is the number of years from the first territory-wide election to the introduction of universal suffrage, reflecting the rate of evolution of the franchise. The second is the number of territorial elections held during the pre-independence period, reflecting the amount of experience a colony had with elections prior to independence. The last is the number of elections held with universal suffrage in the decolonization period, reflecting the amount of experience with a fully enfranchised electorate prior to independence. The polarity of these variables should be noted: a higher score indicates a slower rate of introduction or greater pre-independence electoral experience.

Because these rate variables reflect colonial policy, certain problems arise in the analysis. As we saw in Chapter 2, the French colonies held more elections than the others; furthermore, since a single French policy on these matters was applied to all French colonies, there is no variance on these indicators over a substantial number of cases. In addition, even on some variables that do not directly reflect colonial policy, such as level of electoral participation and party dominance, the colonies of the different metropoles tend to cluster together. Therefore it is useful to consider the colonial subgroups separately. Since the three cases in Belgian Africa are an insufficient number for statistical analysis, only British and French Africa will be considered.

Among the British colonies, the evidence suggests that more gradual introduction of electoral politics led to higher levels of electoral participation by the time of independence. Those colonies that had more experience with elections had some tendency toward higher rates of voting in the independence election. (The correlation between voting and number of elections is $r = .31$. If only direct elections are considered the correlation is .57, and it is probably no accident that The Gambia, the only British colony with two elections based on universal suffrage, had the highest rate of electoral participation.) Also, there is some tendency for the levels of voting by the independence election to have been lower in those colonies in which the introduction of the suffrage was telescoped and universal suffrage was introduced shortly after the first territorial election $(r = .42)$.

Because French colonial policy concerning the introduction of elections was identical for all colonies, it is not possible to analyze the correlations involving the rate variables concerned with number of years or number of elections for this colonial subgroup, since there is no variance on these indicators. An analysis of the experience *within* each of the French colonies, however, provides a limited basis for exploring these relationships. Not surprisingly, the trend within each colony shows higher levels of electoral participation with subsequent elections. It is impossible, however, to sort out any possible effect due to the greater degree of political penetration and activation that may come with time or with greater experience with elections from the more obvious effect of the dramatically broadening franchise during that period. It can only be noted that once universal suffrage was introduced, electoral participation did not in all cases increase with additional elections. In most of French Africa, voters went to the polls three times on a territorial basis under the condition of universal suffrage: for elections in 1957 and 1959 and for a referendum in 1958. In virtually every case for which data is available on all three, the 1958 referendum resulted in the highest rate of voting (the sole exception being Mauritania), indicating that the level of participation attained in 1958 was not even sustained, much less increased, in 1959. Because of the importance to the French of the 1958 referendum, which everywhere but Guinea produced overwhelming majorities for the continuation of colonial status in the form of association in the French Community, these results, which may have reflected French intervention either in the conduct of the election or the reporting of the official returns, may not be appropriate bases for comparison (Zolberg, 1964: 240, 1966a: 79). If the trend from the election of 1957 to that of 1959 is considered, there was an increase in rate of participation in only four of the seven colonies on which there is data. On the other hand, those increases were greater than the decline in the rate of participation in the other countries, resulting in an overall average effect of greater participation with additional elections. Thus, the introduction of universal suffrage was an obvious prerequisite for high levels of electoral participation, and although additional elections under the full franchise did not consistently produce higher levels of participation there may be some limited grounds for arguing that among the French colonies, additional elections provided opportunites for further development of party organization, political penetration and activism, and greater mobilization of the vote.

With regard to the impact of the rate of introduction of elections on party dominance, once again the best that can be done among the French colonies is to try to assess what happened with subsequent elections within each colony. Morgenthau has concluded that at least for the earlier part of the period successive elections were accompanied by a process of consolidation. Her argument may be summarized as follows. She suggests that in French Africa, the early elections after 1946 were more like primaries, eliminating and selecting candidates from among a large number of contenders. At this stage there were numerous candidates and parties, as it was relatively easy to run for office when the electorate was so restricted and party organization was still not developed. Most of these "parties" were in fact "one-man shows." In the early years of elections, a number of ethnic parties also emerged, especially after the rural franchise was extended in 1951. In subsequent elections, the trend was toward reducing the number of parties. As party organization developed, the "one-man shows" could no longer hold their own and they disappeared, usually by merging into one of the larger parties. There was a similar trend among the ethnic parties, which merged to form multi-ethnic regional parties. This trend toward reducing the number of parties was clearly accompanied by a trend toward increasing the scope or scale of the parties to include the entire territory. A major reason for these two complementary trends was the evolution of the franchise; as the franchise was enlarged, it became increasingly difficult for the organizationally and politically weaker parties and those that were more limited in their appeal to compete successfully. An extended suffrage meant an expanding political arena and necessitated joining the political battle, making appeals, and mobilizing the electorate on a broadening scale (Morgenthau, 1964: 348–50).

During the period in which the suffrage was being expanded, then, a more nationally oriented and mobilizing party could use successive elections as opportunities to enhance its relative position, while more local parties were eliminated from the competition. Once universal suffrage had been introduced, subsequent elections still provided opportunities for political penetration and electoral mobilization, as Morgenthau suggested for the earlier period, but this opportunity did not so consistently accrue to the advantage of the leading party. Where only one party was able to compete successfully under conditions of universal suffrage, that is, where one party emerged as the overwhelming victor in the first election held under universal suffrage (in 1957), that party was able to use the next election—in some cases with the help of a favorable electoral law—to mobilize the electorate in order virtually to eliminate the remnants of political opposition parties, to the extent that they still existed (e.g., in the Ivory Coast, Senegal, Mauritania, and Mali). Where two parties were more equally adept (or inept) at competing under the conditions of universal suffrage, and the outcome of the first election held under universal suffrage resulted in the continuation of a viable opposition party, the subsequent election did not necessarily benefit the leading party. In a few cases (e.g., Cameroun, Chad, and Upper Volta) the outcome was to the advantage of that party, though in three other cases (Congo-Brazzaville, Dahomey, and Niger) the party that won control of the government in 1957 subsequently fell from power. In many of the cases in which the 1957 election did not result in an overwhelming majority for a single party, the outcome of the 1959 election was influenced by a variety of tactics including gerrymandering, a change of electoral law to increase the distortion of percentage of seats relative to percentage of votes, and sometimes even the arrest of opposition leaders. It may be noted that the failure of an overwhelmingly dominant party to emerge in the 1957 election may have been due at least in part to the inability of any party to mobilize the vote extensively and thereby decisively increase a crucial political resource. The level of electoral participation in these cases is generally substantially lower than in the cases of overwhelming victory in 1957. (This relationship between voter mobilization and party dominance will be further discussed below.) Among the French colonies, then, there was on balance some tendency for greater experience with elections, particularly under conditions of universal suffrage, to lead to greater party dominance.

This picture is not replicated among the British colonies. Rather, party dominance[1] is negatively correlated with all the rate variables ($r = -.60$ with number of elections, $r = -.44$ with number of elections with universal suffrage, and $r = -.60$ with number of years between first election and introduction of universal suffrage).

In part, these negative correlations reflect the impact of the presence (or absence) of substantial settler communities, which affected both British colonial policy and party dominance or fractionalization. In West Africa, where there were relatively few British settlers, elections were introduced earlier. In East Africa, the British were much more hesitant about the extension of electoral politics to the African community, since they were concerned with safeguarding the relative power of the European settler community. Furthermore, in Kenya, Tanzania, Zambia, and Malawi, a pattern of multi-racial politics was introduced in which seats were reserved for the European community and/or separate electoral rolls were provided for the various racial communities.[2] Under these circumstances, politics developed along racial lines, and African political organization did not tend to be as fragmented as it did where there were no opposition parties based on race. Once multi-racialism was abandoned as a constitutional arrangement guaranteeing the (over)representation of minority races in the government, a dominant or single African party emerged more easily than in the colonies that had not had multi-racial politics. In the West, by contrast, electoral politics was introduced earlier, and in the absence of multi-racialism as a unifying issue, African parties proliferated.

1. A description of this variable is presented in Appendix I.
2. Uganda did not have a substantial settler community and multi-racial politics was not introduced; yet the timing of the introduction of electoral politics in Uganda was similar to that of her neighbors, rather than to the nonsettler colonies in the West. See Chapter 2.

The number of elections held in the pre-independence period does not seem to have had any consistent effect on party dominance in an analysis of change over time among the British colonies. There is no evidence that the dominant parties in the East would have lost their position of dominance with subsequent elections, nor are there examples in the West of a dramatic loss of relative dominance with subsequent elections. At the same time, there is little evidence for a strong positive relationship. There seems to be little tendency for subsequent elections in British Africa to have been a mechanism by which a leading party further consolidated its power, as occurred in many French African colonies. In Ghana, Uganda, and Nigeria, the largest party was not able to use subsequent elections to consolidate its power and increase its dominance, though in Zambia and Kenya the leading parties were able to improve their positions. Finally, in The Gambia each subsequent election produced a larger majority for the leading party, although in general the higher levels of dominance were initially achieved through aisle-crossing before the elections, and in Sierra Leone, although the party improved its position relative to the outcome of the previous election, that position was in fact weaker than its position had been prior to the election, an outcome which again reflected aisle-crossing within the legislature.

Though the relationship between number of pre-independence elections and party dominance is inconclusive, other evidence suggests that more gradual introduction of electoral politics in British Africa was associated with less party dominance. The correlation between rate (as measured by the number of years from the first territory-wide election to the introduction of universal suffrage) and party dominance (as measured by the party-dominance-factor score)[3] is negative, as noted above ($r = -.60$). It was noted that this relationship may have been due to multi-racialism. Yet controlling this relationship for multi-racialism only slightly reduces the correlation; that is to say, there seems to be some evidence for the independent effect of rate on party dominance, with more gradual evolution or introduction of electoral politics in British Africa decreasing the ability of a leading party to emerge as dominant and instead leading to party fragmentation. The slower introduction of universal suffrage did not have the effect of institutionalizing the older parties and producing voters who were socialized in their

3. See Appendix I.

favor. Instead, within the parameters of the range of variance found across the British African cases, more gradual introduction of electoral politics and a longer period of decolonization favored the emergence of a greater diversity of political groups and a more fractionalized multi-party system, whereas a more rapid and more telescoped path to independence tended to favor the emergence of a one-party dominant system.

Social Factors

The second set of variables to be considered in explaining levels of electoral participation and party dominance consists of a variety of social factors. Most prominent among these, perhaps, is social mobilization. In addition, communications development, total population, level of economic growth (per-capita GDP in 1958), and ethnic composition will be considered. Following Barrows's (1976) nuanced discussion of the issues of ethnic distribution, three separate measures will be used: the number of ethnic groups, the relative size of the largest group, and the degree to which there are two relatively equal groups.[4]

Deutsch has defined *social mobilization* as an overall process of change in which individuals assume new social roles and new social groups emerge. It is a "concept which brackets together a number of more specific processes of change" (Deutsch, 1961: 493), and the separate indices most often used in measuring social mobilization include economic development, literacy and education, urbanization, size of the nonagricultural work force, percent of work force in wage labor, and media development. In the analysis which follows, per-capita GDP, which is a strictly economic factor, has been kept separate, both because it is a less direct measure and because it is often hypothesized to be a cause, rather than a component, of social mobilization. Indicators of media development have likewise been included in a separate communications variable. The remaining social mobilization indices were entered into a factor analysis for purposes of data reduction.[5] Two factors emerged, which may be labeled *mass* and *elite social mobilization*. The first is most highly correlated with level of literacy and primary education, while the second is most highly correlated with higher education.

---

4. These variables are discussed in Appendix I.
5. See Appendix I.

The well-known and widely tested hypothesis about the relationship between social mobilization and political participation was originally put forward by Deutsch (1961: 499–500): "The increasing numbers of the mobilized population, and the greater scope and urgency of their needs for political decisions and governmental services, tend to translate themselves . . . into increased political participation. . . . When people have the right to vote, the effects of social mobilization are likely to be reflected in the electoral statistics."

While the hypothesized relationship between social mobilization and electoral participation is positive, in the African context that between social mobilization and party dominance is often negative. In explaining the lack of opposition groups to TANU in Tanzania, Bienen (1967: 13) has suggested that the lack of economic development in that country discouraged the formation of economic interest-groups potentially hostile to the regime. Looking at the West African party states, Zolberg (1966a: 71) has observed that "certain categoric groups stand out as sources of political opposition based on education, occupation, and source or amount of income. They include especially civil servants; railroad, harbor, and construction workers; cash-crop farmers." Here too, the idea is that economic development brings with it the emergence of new social groups and interests and a more differentiated class structure, and that this multiplicity of groups, interests, and classes is more conducive to a proliferation of parties and a dispersal of power than to the greater dominance of one party.

Just as colonial policy differed among the metropoles with respect to decolonization and the introduction of electoral politics, so it differed also with respect to a whole range of other matters, including economic and social policy. As a result, there is some tendency for the two colonial subgroups to differ on some of these economic and social indicators. These differences are presented in Table 12.

Perhaps the most striking differences involve total population and education. The average population for the British colonies was nearly four times as large as that for the French colonies. This difference, of course, is somewhat exaggerated by the single case of Nigeria, which alone is several times the size of the Belgian Congo, the next largest colony; omitting Nigeria from this comparison, however, but including The Gambia, with only one-third of a million people by 1967, the average population among the British colonies is still twice as great as that among the French colonies.

Table 12. *Differences between French and British Colonies*

	French Africa (mean)	British Africa (mean)
Variables on Which British Colonies Are Higher		
Population (millions)	3.00	11.40
Mass social mobilization[a]	−0.48	0.52
Percent literate	3.50	15.00
Primary school enrollment (per capita)	27.00	45.00
Secondary school enrollment (per capita)	4.80	11.30
Number of linguistic groups	25.00	39.00
Variables on Which French Colonies Are Higher		
GDP per capita, 1958 (U.S. $)	99.00	78.00
Elite social mobilization[a]	0.22	−0.13
Enrollment in higher education, 1961 (percent age group)	23.60	16.40
Newspaper circulation per 10,000, 1964	69.00	20.00
Electoral participation	24.00	18.00
Party dominance[a]	2.60	−2.60

[a]These are standardized variables derived from a factor analysis, as explained in Appendix I. For these twenty-three cases (that is, the French and British colonies only), mass social mobilization has a mean of −0.09 and a standard deviation of 0.83; elite social mobilization has a mean of 0.08 and a standard deviation of 1.03; party dominance has a mean of 0.05 and a standard deviation of 0.96.

Despite the larger average size of the British colonies, the British tended to provide more education per capita than did the French. This difference in education is particularly great with respect to literacy and to primary and secondary school enrollment. The British colonies also tend to be higher on the mass-social-mobilization factor, which reflects these differences in education. The French colonies, however, have a higher average level of enrollment at the post-secondary level and score higher on the elite-social-mobilization factor. There is no significant difference among the colonies with respect to the relative size of the wage-earning population or the number in agricultural labor, though the French colonies tend somewhat to have higher levels of per-capita GDP.

There is also a tendency for the British to have erected colonial boundaries that include more linguistic groups. This is primarily a result of the larger population contained within the British colonies, and the French colonies tend to have more languages per million population. There is no difference between the two colonial sub-groups in the relative size of the largest linguistic group or in its primacy relative to the second largest.

As noted above, the two sets of colonies tend to differ as well on the political variables which are the object of the present inquiry. The French colonies tend to have higher levels of both electoral participation, as measured by the percent of the population voting in the independence election (an average of 24 percent for French Africa compared to 18 percent for British Africa) and of party dominance (as measured by the party-dominance-factor score). The difference with respect to the latter is apparent in all the component variables except percent voting for the leading party in the independence election and the number of parties in the ruling coalition at independence. In one sense, the extent of the contrast in party dominance is masked by the special cases of settler politics in some British colonies. Only among these cases were high levels of party dominance achieved in British Africa. Thus, if those cases were omitted (leaving those more contextually similar to the French African cases in their absence of multi-racial politics), the contrast between the two groupings in terms of party dominance would be even more striking.

Major differences thus emerge between the two colonial sub-groups among the variables of greatest concern to this study; hence, it is appropriate to continue to look at the two colonial groupings separately. The analysis will begin by comparing the relationship between electoral participation and the social and economic variables for French and British Africa. Table 13 presents all the correlations with participation that are equal to at least $r = \pm .3$. The most striking things about this comparison are, first, how different the correlates are for the two groups of colonies and, second, how few strong social predictors there are for British Africa. (More important than the social factors in explaining level of electoral participation in British Africa are timing and rate of introduction of elections, already discussed; another important factor will be considered below.)

The one socioeconomic variable that is correlated with participation among the British colonies is a measure of communications infrastructure.[6] This relationship, which is even stronger

6. See Appendix I.

Table 13. *Social and Economic Correlates of Voting**

	French Africa	British Africa
GDP per capita, 1958	.48	
Elite social mobilization	.51	
Communications	.69	.38
Population	−.30	
Ethnic composition		
Primacy of first to second largest		
linguistic group	.31	−.44
Number of linguistic groups		(−.28)
Largest linguistic group as percent		
of total population		(−.28)

*Pearson product-moment correlations. Only those correlations greater than or equal to ± .3 are presented.

among the French colonies (the correlation for all colonies is $r =$ .40), is not surprising, since both the decision to vote and the very act of voting are dependent on communications development.

Among the French colonies there seems to be some support for the social-mobilization hypothesis. In addition to communications, participation is correlated with per-capita GDP and one of the social-mobilization factors—elite mobilization. These, furthermore, are themselves highly correlated, thus comprising the kind of social-development syndrome we might expect. The fact that the second social-mobilization factor, mass mobilization, is not correlated with participation $(r = -.04)$, however, may be suggestive. This contrast may indicate that even more important than the hypothesized social-mobilization effect, which explains higher levels of participation in terms of the movement of the participant into more "modern" situations of urban residence, literacy, and non-traditional occupations, is a process of voter mobilization by elite groups; that is to say, the pattern in French Africa may be one not so much of mass social mobilization leading to participation but of a high level of elite social mobilization producing an available pool from which political leaders and local political cadres were drawn, who in turn mobilized the vote among the populace at large.

Only one ethnic-composition variable is correlated with voting, and its effects are different for the two colonial subgroups. Among the French colonies, greater electoral participation is correlated with a greater degree of primacy of the largest ethnic (linguistic) group relative to the second, while among the British colonies it is correlated with greater parity (and presumably competition) of the two largest groups. In addition, the two other indicators of ethnic diversity are negatively, but weakly, correlated with voting among the British colonies.

Finally, it may be noted that total population is negatively correlated with voting among the French colonies, suggesting the more difficult organizational tasks of political penetration for a larger population. Why this may have been less of a factor in British Africa, as well as some of the other contrasts noted in this section, will be discussed below.

Table 14 presents the social and economic correlates of party dominance among the French and British colonies. It can be seen that the correlates of party dominance are quite different from those of electoral participation, and in this case there are very few correlates for the French colonies. Economic variables are not correlated with party dominance, though the social-mobilization variables which are said to be their concomitant are. For both colonial groupings, party dominance is negatively correlated with social mobilization. For the British colonies, however, this effect refers to elite mobilization: the greater the elite mobilization, the greater, presumably, the emergence of more diverse elite groups and interests and hence the greater the multiplicity of political organizations they formed. Under these circumstances party dominance was lower. Among the French colonies, the correlation is with mass mobili-

Table 14. *Social and Economic Correlates of Party Dominance* *

	French Africa	British Africa
Social mobilization		
Mass	−.41	
Elite		−.41
Newspaper circulation		−.43
Population size		−.34
Ethnic composition		
Percent largest linguist group		.33
Primacy of first to second		
largest linguistic group		.53

*Pearson product-moment correlations. Only those correlations greater than or equal to ± .3 are presented.

zation. Perhaps the more socially mobilized, the more literate and educated the electorate, the less likely it was to fall in line behind a dominant party. Finally, it may be noted that for British Africa population and newspaper circulation are negatively correlated with party dominance, while the primacy and size of the largest ethnic group are positively correlated with it.

To conclude, although some correlations were found between these socioeconomic variables and levels of participation and party dominance, hypotheses related to social mobilization do not appear to be a principal explanation of these political outcomes—at least at this macro-level of comparison. We will therefore turn to the possibility that *political* explanations may take us further in accounting for these outcomes.

Electoral Participation and Party Dominance

If one considers all twenty-six colonies, no relationship is found between electoral participation and the ability of a single party to achieve dominance over its competitors ($r = -.05$). Within colonial subgroups, however, a different picture emerges. Among the British colonies, the relationship is negative ($r = -.74$). The introduction of social control variables does not substantially affect this relationship.[7] Among the French colonies, by contrast, the relationship is positive. Although the bivariate correlation is modest ($r = .25$), the introduction of elite social mobilization as a control increases

7. Unfortunately, because of the small case-base involved, especially within colonial subgroups, the use of multivariate analysis to introduce control variables is hazardous at best. The procedure adopted in this chapter and the next is to introduce one control variable at a time and to see whether or not the zero-order relationship was substantially changed, and in what direction. To simplify the presentation, these partial correlations are generally not presented unless they suggest that the zero-order correlation is misleading.

In connection with this problem of a small case-base, it should be noted that one important means of preserving the whole case-base would be to insert into a multiple-regression analysis a dummy variable representing metropole. However, this would in effect assess the relationship between participation and dominance "controlling" for colonial grouping. What we are instead interested in is the hypothesis that this relationship is different within the two colonial subgroups; hence this disaggregated approach is more appropriate. It will be shown that there are, in fact, substantial differences in the relationships in the colonial subgroups. The analysis will thus follow the procedure that Przeworski and Teune (1970: 43ff.) have described as "comparing relationships," in which attributes that distinguish the subgroups—experience with colonial rule—are used to explain the contrasting relationships that emerge within subgroups.

the correlation to $r = .45$. A further point might be made about the colony for which there was the largest error of prediction in this correlation, the CAR. The leading party in the CAR had achieved a very high level of dominance and the country had previously attained a very high rate of electoral participation, yet the rate of participation in the 1959 election on which the scoring of the participation variable is based was very low. That election took place shortly after the death of Boganda, the leader of the party and of the nationalist movement. At that time, the party was deeply engaged in a factional struggle (indeed, shortly after the election the party split into two separate parties) based on the competition of two potential heirs to Boganda's leadership. Under these conditions of leadership crisis (which is not reflected in the party-dominance score), there was little mobilization and very widespread abstention, resulting in the lowest rate of participation in French Africa and one of the lowest rates for any of the African colonies.[8] If the CAR is omitted from the correlations, the bivariate relationship increases to $r = .37$, and controlling for the two social-mobilization factors (one at a time) increases the correlation to .50 and .55.

Three hypotheses concerning the linkages between voting and party dominance may help to interpret these opposite relationships in the British and French colonies. The first hypothesis posits a negative relationship in which voting affects dominance: higher levels of voting have a fragmenting influence which makes party dominance more difficult to achieve. According to the other hypotheses, the causation goes in the other direction, from dominance to voting. The second hypothesis posits a positive relationship in which the presence of a dominant party may stimulate a bandwagon effect and/or a certain kind of dominant party may actively mobilize the vote in a plebiscitary effort to broaden its support. In the pre-independence context, dominant parties may have found it advantageous to mobilize the vote in order to press for nationalist demands and to consolidate their power, even at the risk of increasing demand-making in other areas. The third hypothesis posits a negative relationship in which a lower level of dominance, i.e.,

8. As an indication of the extent to which the low level of participation in the CAR was the result of this leadership crisis, it may be noted that the average drop in rate of participation between the 1958 referendum and the 1959 election for the other French colonies that participated in both was 20 percent, while that for the CAR was 82 percent.

a higher level of party competition, results in greater voting. This corresponds to the pattern reported in the United States, where it has been suggested that turnout is greater in close elections and was therefore relatively low in the traditionally one-party-dominant South. This negative relationship between party dominance and voting may be due both to the perception of voters that their vote is potentially more important in a close contest and to the competitive tactics of party leaders who, facing a close election, make a greater effort to mobilize the vote.

Among the French colonies, then, the relationship between electoral participation and party dominance is positive, and only the second hypothesis posits a positive relationship: voting was greater where there was a more dominant party that attracted or mobilized the vote. This relationship is consistent with the finding (discussed above) that those parties that did very well and emerged as most dominant in 1957 were able to use the 1959 election as an opportunity for the plebiscitary mobilization of support.

Among the British colonies, the relationship between voting and party dominance is negative, corresponding to either of two of the above hypotheses: either party competition led to greater mobilization of the vote and/or the incentive to vote was lower where one party was more dominant; or the participation of more people, representing more diverse groups and interests, had a fragmenting effect, making dominance more difficult to attain. It is the first of these two explanations which seems to apply to British Africa. This interpretation, which is more consistent with the absence of a positive correlation between mass social mobilization and voting (a correlation which would be more strongly implied in the second hypothesis), is based on an examination of variations across constituencies within colonies. The two colonies that were lowest on voting turnout were as low as they were because one party was so dominant that there were many uncontested constituencies, in which no voting took place. In Tanzania, only thirteen of the seventy-one constituencies were contested in the independence election. In Zambia, total voting turnout was similarly low because nearly a third of the constituencies were uncontested. The most extreme case was Malawi, where none of the constituencies was contested and no voting took place at all.

This relationship between party dominance and participation is not limited to the effect of voting in the extreme case of uncontested constituencies; it is a continuous relationship. Although there were few uncontested constituencies in Ghana in 1956, Austin has made the same argument about the inverse relation between party dominance and voting. He suggests that in the south, "[t]he low registration figure was . . . the result . . . of an indifference towards the election in areas where the CPP was dominant, and the contest a foregone conclusion" (1966: 340). Post argues that a similar process occurred in Nigeria and shows that in the 1959 election turnout was higher in non-Ibo constituencies in the East and in non-Yoruba constituencies in the West, because of the greater competition in those areas (1964: 351–54). Thus in British Africa, as in French Africa, party dominance appears to be a cause, rather than a consequence, of electoral participation; unlike French Africa, however, party fragmentation rather than dominance produced higher levels of electoral participation.

The relationship between participation and party dominance for British Africa is summarized in Figure 1. The rate of introduction of electoral politics among Africans, which was the immediate result of colonial policy, depended in part on the presence or absence of a substantial British settler community.[9] Where there were relatively few settlers, the colonies moved earlier to a stage of African political participation in territory-wide elections, and universal suffrage was introduced gradually; where it happened later, the trend of events elsewhere on the continent led to the telescoping of the traditional stages of the British system of evolution toward self-government and independence. This telescoping of events meant fewer elections, provided that the early multi-tiered, indirect elections in West Africa are included in the comparison. It was this stage in particular that was skipped in East Africa, and if only direct elections are considered, there is no real difference in number of elections. Both the factors of rate and of multi-racial or settler politics (involving special provisions for disproportionate settler representation) affected party dominance. The rate variables remain highly correlated with party dominance when the relationship is controlled for multi-racial politics. Party dominance in turn affected the level of electoral participation. The rate variables also affected participation; greater elapsed time and a greater number of elections provided more op-

9. Uganda has already been discussed as an exception. That other factors were involved is evident also in the timing of introduction of electoral politics in Sierra Leone and Gambia.

Figure 1. Party dominance and electoral participation in British Africa.

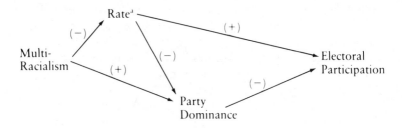

ᵃSince the rate variables are measured in terms of number of years or number of elections, higher values reflect a slower rate and lower values reflect a greater telescoping of stages.

portunities for political penetration and mobilization. Once again, however, the relationship between party dominance and participation remains very strong when the rate variables are introduced as controls, and this relationship is further supported by a comparison of constituencies within colonies.

Impact of Patterns of Colonial Rule

In the above analysis, several contrasts between French and British colonial experiences with the introduction of electoral politics were noted. How can those differences be accounted for? Part of the explanation may be found in differences between French and British colonial rule.

Party Dominance

First we may consider the question of why there tended in general to be higher levels of party dominance in French Africa than in British Africa. Part of the explanation lies in the electoral systems introduced by the two metropoles. British Africa had single-member constituencies, and often only the name of the candidate, with no party identification, appeared on the ballot. French Africa, on the other hand, had multi-member list systems in which lists were identified by party name, and voters chose a party rather than an individual candidate (Mackenzie and Robinson, 1960: 466). The French system thus tended to favor emergence of a dominant party, both because it was easier to make an appeal on the basis of party and because the electoral system in French Africa produced greater distortion in favor of the strongest party and tended to result in the elimination of weak ones. Under the winner-take-all list system, a party had to put up an entire list in a given constituency; it had to enter and win what is equivalent to several single-member constituencies in the British system, in terms of size and diversity of population, and compete for several seats at a time. In the British system, on the other hand, a weak or local party had the possibility of winning a single seat at a time; hence, in the British system, smaller opposition parties had a better chance.

The difference in level of party dominance between French and British Africa is also related to the nature of the two types of colonial rule and the degree to which colonial rule helped either to foster elite cohesion or to perpetuate and perhaps even heighten elite fractionalization. In this regard, one important difference in colonial policy is the difference in general approach, goals, and ideals that is sometimes referred to as British "empiricism" as opposed to French "Cartesianism" (Hodgkin, 1957: 33). In the present context the relevant aspect of this difference is that the French tended to adopt a single policy for all her African colonies, while the British tended to adopt a separate policy for each African colony, and even for different regions within a colony, albeit within a common framework. The "assimilationist" approach of the French, as opposed to the "indigenous" or "accommodationist" approach of the British, is also involved here. The French introduced common legal, political, and administrative institutions throughout French Africa, while the British were more institutionally flexible, seeking to preserve and accommodate diverse ethnic traditions, identities, and institutions.

In accordance with this orientation, France introduced more uniform institutions throughout her colonies and reduced the influence of ethnic differentiation by limiting, much more than the British did, the power of the chiefs and their traditional institutions. As Crowder has stressed:

The French-speaking states inherited a uniform pattern of administration, with emphasis on the powers of the central government, whilst the former British states inherited patterns of administration whose original emphasis was primarily on local government institutions, sharply differentiated according to ethnic origin, and resulting in many cases in strong centrifugal tendencies. . . . Traditional political institutions and ethnic differences are not nearly such great barriers to national unity in the French-speaking African states as in the former British colonies. (1970: 301)

This greater preservation of traditional institutions by the British not only had the effect of politicizing ethnic diversity to a greater extent but also led to a conflict between the traditional elite and a new elite. At the same time that the British sought to preserve traditional rule, they set up an elected legislative assembly which was dominated not by chiefs but by the new elite, an elite whose status was based on achieved rather than ascribed position (see Coleman, 1965: 160–61; Post, 1970: 41ff.). In this way, the British sponsored two systems of authority and legitimacy which would ultimately come into conflict. This contrasts with the French experience, under which only one system of authority was sponsored and the traditional system had been greatly weakened by colonial rule.

This assimilationist-accommodationist difference is also reflected in the constitutional arrangements in the African colonies. In these constitutional arrangements, the British often attempted to accommodate ethnic diversity and, at various stages, to preserve the authority of traditional rulers. Thus, various schemes of federalism were considered, and two countries became independent as federal systems. There were also various constitutional schemes in which legislative seats were reserved for chiefs. This orientation of British policy was responsible for the unworkable constitution under which Uganda became independent.

The pattern of "constitution-mongering" to safeguard the position of minorities (Crowder, 1970: 302) contrasts sharply with the situation in French Africa, where all colonies were given identical, and unitary, constitutions. The French policy diminished ethnic identities, while the British policy preserved and even heightened them. "The whole question of federalism, its actual achievement, as in Nigeria or Uganda, or even its possibility, as in Gold Coast, also meant greater regional identity and consciousness" (Coleman, 1965: 322). Coleman suggests that this policy was rooted in a

Burkean concept of nationalism, which admits of a multiplicity of loyalties, and contrasts it to the French Jacobin nationalism, which eliminates all intermediate groups (Coleman, 1965: 321–22).

The assimilationist-accommodationist distinction was also seen in language policy. All French education was in French, whereas in British Africa, primary education was conducted in the indigenous languages. As a result, the French language became more of a lingua franca and a force for cohesion in the French colonies than English did in the British colonies.[10] Thus, in a number of policy areas, Britain accommodated or encouraged social diversity among groups within her colonies, whereas France adopted a uniform policy throughout the colonies and attempted to minimize social diversity.

A closely related difference in colonial rule that had implications for elite cohesion and party dominance was that between direct and indirect rule. Many early analyses of African political history exaggerated the differences between direct rule and indirect rule, and as a result, type of colonial rule has generally been dropped from recent analyses. Nevertheless, there were important differences between French direct and British indirect rule: (1) the British relied more heavily upon and were more predisposed to rule through traditional authorities—though this was a matter of degree; (2) the role and prestige of the chief, whether traditional or appointed, was different; and (3) the most basic difference between indirect and direct rule was that between local self-government and central administration.[11]

The first point of difference, then, is that the British tended more often to preserve and even to enhance the role of the traditional chief, while the French more often bypassed the traditional chief and diminished his power and legitimacy. Britain was concerned with appointing traditional chiefs to be responsible for a territory defined by traditional boundaries. French policy was the opposite: the French were often hostile to traditional chiefs, whom they were anxious to replace. Even when they recognized the advantages of traditional chiefs, they often took literacy rather than traditional

10. It must be remembered, however, that this difference between the two regions was made somewhat less important by the fact that the rate of school enrollment was lower in French Africa than in British Africa.

11. The discussion which follows is taken largely from the Crowder (1964) and Crowder and Ikime (1970) discussions of the differences between direct and indirect rule.

standing as a prime qualification for appointment. Furthermore, they were more interested in carving out administrative units of equal size than in preserving traditional units, and they deliberately reduced the size of the great chiefdoms. All of these differences, however, were largely differences of degree.

The most striking aspect of the difference between direct and indirect rule is that British indirect rule meant local self-government and French direct rule meant central administration. The role of the chief was very different under these two systems. As head of a local self-government unit, or "Native Authority," the chief in British Africa had the power to collect taxes and control a budget, administer customary law, and control the appointment and dismissal of officials. The Native Authorities were considered legislative bodies, and the political officer, representing the colonial administration, acted only as an adviser to the Native Authority insofar as local government affairs were concerned. The role of the French chiefs was closer to that of an administrative agent. Crowder and Ikime have summed up this contrast:

> The French chiefs had no criminal jurisdiction over their subjects, no police force, no prisons. Their jurisdiction in civil cases was severely limited. . . . [T]heir judicial role was reduced to a shadow of what it was in pre-colonial times. . . . Furthermore, the French chiefs had no "native authority" of their own with a budget and control of appointments as the British chief did. He collected taxes as his British counterpart did, but retained no percentage to run "local government." He thus had no patronage to offer. . . . While the British chief retained most of his traditional powers, the French chief did not. By and large the latter was required to do the dirty work of the French administration: collect taxes, recruit and supervise forced labor, round up soldiers for the army. His traditional functions of justice, policing the state, and of administering the government of his people were removed from him. . . . We can distinguish between the French and British chief under colonial rule: the French chief was an official or "fonctionnaire" of the French bureaucratic hierarchy and like all subordinate bureaucrats had a set of tasks, with no initiative of his own. On the other hand the British chief had a dual role: in local government he was an authority in his own right, though this authority was carefully circumscribed, even if it was considerable. . . . However, insofar as he was an agent of the central government required to execute decisions . . . made by the central government, he was just as much a bureaucrat as the French chief. (1970: xv–xviii)

This difference in the chief's role was obviously accompanied by differences in his power and prestige. Crowder and Ikime report that under indirect rule chiefs tended to increase their power, as the colonial regime had the effect of eliminating the traditional checks and balances to the chief's power, but left him largely free to govern as he had in pre-colonial times (Crowder and Ikime, 1970: xiv, xxiv). The French chiefs, on the other hand, lost both their power and the respect of their people. They became mere "agents of the law, in this case the unpopular system of summary administrative justice known as the *indigénat*" (Crowder, 1964: 200).

In his role as administrative agent the French chief tended to become allied with "French-backed conservative politicians to whom the French 'guaranteed' the support of the chiefs against the radical politicians" (Crowder and Ikime, 1970: xxiii). Because of this and his unpopular tasks,

> the chief in French West Africa became a more obvious target for the anti-colonial radical than the chief in British West Africa, who at least by the Second World War was no longer concerned with forced labour and had never been concerned with compulsory recruitment (officially) or with compulsory crop cultivation. Furthermore, divested of his judicial and police functions, the French chief had no formal power of his own and was in appearance and fact a mere administrative agent or "lackey" of the French. (Crowder and Ikime, 1970: xxiii)

Thus, the French chief had little say in nationalist movements, and was considered an unimportant cog in the colonial administrative machinery who, like the rest of the administration, was to be replaced. Consequently, chieftaincy became relatively unimportant politically in most of French Africa.

The situation in British Africa was quite different. There, as noted above, two parallel systems of status, two sources of class formation and consolidation, were established and maintained, one based on traditional standing and reinforced by indirect rule and the other based on the "reform" of the colonial state during the period of decolonization and on the expansion of capitalism. The greater tendency to encourage the emergence or preservation of a "neo-traditional" (Kilson, 1970) elite in British Africa meant that the elite tended to be fragmented. Retaining real authority, legitimacy, respect, and the possibility of dispensing patronage, chiefs under the

British had their own power base. In this context, the elite was more differentiated, and as a result the party system that reflected this was more fragmented.

Not only was there greater differentiation within the elite along the neotraditional/modern lines, but in addition there may have been in British Africa greater differentation within this latter category as well. An important source of differentiation within the modern elite was that between an "old" and a "new," urban, educated elite. From these two groups emerged two conflicting types of nationalist movement. From the first arose what Markovitz (1977: 178) has called "the genteel nationalism carried on as a leisure activity by the small class of petty bourgeois Africans aspiring to the upper status of the colonial establishment." This class, comprised especially of higher civil servants, merchants, and members of the liberal professions, was frustrated by its lack of access to positions and status reserved for the metropolitan elite within the colony, but its strategy of pressure for change, usually limited to equal access and the extension of their privileges, did not include mobilization of mass support. The second form of nationalism, more militant in its anticolonialist demands and more oriented toward mobilizing mass support, was based in a newer, lower-middle class that emerged from the economic expansion of wartime activity (Wallerstein, 1967: 499). Although the split and conflict between these two elements of the emerging elite has been given substantial attention in histories and analyses of African nationalism and although it is asserted that "the types of nationalism and the classes upon which they were based determined the outcome of the move from colony to nation" (Markovitz, 1977: 179), few studies have systematically compared colonies in this regard.

In spite of this lack of comparative data, some preliminary evidence can be gathered that suggests that this conflict may have been greater in the nonmulti-racial British colonies because of the greater degree to which an "old" elite emerged there. One source of evidence is the extent of education provided or permitted (through missionary schools) by the colonial powers at an early period (Morrison et al., 1972: 62; Kilson, 1970: 352–54). Because education was introduced in British Africa both earlier and on a larger scale, those colonies tended toward greater differentiation of the elite along these lines. Various accounts support this interpretation of the difference between French and British Africa. Wallerstein's analysis of West Africa (1967: 502–6) suggests that there was no politically significant old urban elite in the Ivory Coast, Guinea, Mali, Niger, Upper Volta, or Mauritania. It is true that there was an old elite in the French colonies of Senegal, Togo, and Dahomey; nevertheless, there does in general seem to be a contrast between French and British Africa which helps to explain the differences found in the analysis of the two groups of countries.

This point perhaps merits further elaboration. The theoretically interesting variables are those that reflect the nature of the elite being formed in the colonial period. If systematic data were available for a number of cases, it would of course be preferable to enter such factors directly into the comparative analysis supplanting the crude British-French dichotomy in favor of a more sensitive distinction that would also take into account differences within the colonial groupings. Unfortunately, such data, not now available, are beyond the scope of the present research to generate. In the absence of systematic data, the next best approximation has been to observe a tendency toward a general difference in party dominance, for example, between the two colonial groupings and then to explore the general, more or less consistent differences between them that might help to explain the observed tendency.

Electoral Participation and the
Participation-Dominance Relationship

Another set of questions concerning the contrasts between French and British Africa is why in general levels of electoral participation were higher in French Africa and why the relationship between party dominance and electoral participation was quite different for the two groups, that is, why the most dominant parties in French Africa tended to mobilize high levels of voting whereas those in British colonies did not, higher levels of voting in the British colonies being instead associated with greater party competition.

There are perhaps two reasons why French Africa had higher levels of electoral participation than British Africa. First, the French colonies held more elections than the British. Each subsequent election provided an additional opportunity to extend party organization and to mobilize the electorate. This effect was seen in the correlations among the British colonies. Although the French colonies did not consistently use the second election under universal suffrage to mobilize the vote further, the greater number of elections which preceded the introduction of universal suffrage among the French colonies may explain the fact that the rate of participation in the first election with universal suffrage tended to be higher among the French colonies than among the British colonies.

The second explanation concerns the nature of the electoral systems introduced by the two metropoles. As noted, in British Africa no voting took place in uncontested constituencies; whereas in French Africa, voting did take place in such constituencies and, furthermore, substantial turnout was mobilized in these constituencies. In the 1957 election in the Ivory Coast, for instance, it was *not* the unopposed constituencies that had the lowest rates of turnout (Zolberg, 1964: 214). This more mobilizational electoral system was perhaps reinforced by different norms regarding elections. The French African parties were directly linked to the French Communist and Socialist parties and may thus have been more directly aware of mobilizational ideologies and of the methods used by Communist parties in the Soviet Union and elsewhere for mobilizing participation and support. There were no such links in British Africa. The British experience provided an example that was more oriented toward competitive democracy and the use of elections for choosing among alternate candidates. In the post-independence period, even the one-party regimes in ex-British Africa have not mobilized the vote for support in the same way as their counterparts in ex-French Africa. Malawi continued until 1978 the pattern of holding one-party elections in which no voting took place at all because all the constituencies were uncontested. Perhaps most interestingly, Nkrumah, despite his similarity to French African leaders in many respects, particularly in his ideology and his move to form a one-party regime, also failed to use elections for support mobilization; instead, the winners in the non-competitive one-party elections of 1965 were simply declared, as in Malawi. Finally, as will be discussed below, the competitive form of one-party elections has been introduced in the former British colonies (and recently in Zaire).

These two factors that help to explain why voting participation was greater in French Africa also help to account in part for the negative relationship between party dominance and voting in the British colonies. It has been seen that the most dominant parties in British Africa emerged in those colonies that were involved in multiracial politics and in which electoral politics started relatively late and lasted for a relatively short period before independence. This shorter time (along with some tendency to have held fewer elections in these colonies, thus affording fewer opportunities for political penetration, mobilization, and organizational development) meant less electoral participation, and this is part of the explanation for the low levels of electoral participation in those British colonies with the most dominant parties. Further, it was in those British colonies with dominant parties that the level of voting was most adversely affected by the practice of nonvoting in uncontested constituencies. The extent to which this practice can affect the level of voting was seen in the case of the 1960–61 election in Tanzania, where only one-seventh of the constituencies were contested, and in Malawi, where none was contested in 1964. Yet, as we have seen, the negative relationship between electoral participation and party dominance in British Africa is not completely explained by rate factors, nor is it limited to the extreme case of uncontested constituencies. The contrast between the two colonial groupings—the negative correlation among the British colonies and the positive correlation among the French colonies—remains. How is it to be explained?

The broad differences in the two patterns can perhaps be explained in terms of the potential for a bandwagon effect or for a process of fragmentation, as described by Zolberg (1966a: 19–22) in his analysis of electoral politics during the decolonization period, and the way in which these two tendencies were mediated by the differing roles and positions of local or regional leaders that resulted from differences between French and British colonial rule. The bandwagon effect refers to the propensity, especially for new participants, to respond to the appeals of and to identify with the most dominant party. Zolberg argues that in the African context this process is likely to occur unless it is inhibited by factors such as the politicization of primary-group ties. The fragmentation process refers to the potential for the splintering of the mass movement (or, it may be added, the prevention of its emergence in relatively cohesive form) due to the entry into the political arena of new political entrepreneurs. Once again, Zolberg observes that these competing elite groups tend to make their appeal for popular support on the basis of primary-group ties.

The opposite correlations between party dominance and electoral participation found for the two colonial subgroupings indicate that the bandwagon effect was stronger among the French colonies, whereas the fragmentation effect, especially in terms of the prevention of the emergence of a dominant, cohesive party, was stronger among the British colonies. The bandwagon effect is a description of a process in which a dominant party is successful in mobilizing and attracting supporters (hence the positive correlation between party dominance and electoral participation among the French colonies); and the fragmentation effect describes a process in which political competition provides the context in which higher levels of electoral participation are mobilized (hence the negative correlation between party dominance and electoral participation among the British colonies).

It will be remembered that French direct rule tended to centralize power and eliminate or at least reduce the political importance of local, traditional leaders while British indirect rule left power more decentralized and tended to sustain the political importance of chiefs as leaders of groups based on primary ties. This contrast may help to explain the difference in potential for fragmentation or bandwagon processes between the two colonial subgroupings. In French Africa, where the impact of local and traditional leaders as power brokers was relatively limited and power was comparatively centralized, political aspirants and leaders had no choice but to operate on a territorial level. There was less opportunity to politicize ethnic groups. This is not to say that ethnic groups were not politicized in French Africa but, rather, that in general they were less politicized than they were in British Africa. This is a point made by Zolberg (1966a: 26) as well, in his comparison of the Ivory Coast and Ghana: "The generally weaker position of traditional authorities in French-speaking Africa deprived the Ivory Coast ethnic parties of the sort of ready-made organ through chiefs and their councils available to [their] counterparts in Ghana." In this situation, as the franchise was extended and new participants entered, the result was likely to be a bandwagon effect. Under British rule, on the other hand, power resided locally to a greater degree as local chiefs were allowed to maintain their power bases and their position was in some ways even enhanced. In this situation, voter participation was stimulated by and mediated through local leaders of ethnic groups. The voters were thus less directly available for mobilization by a national party and the bandwagon effect was less likely to occur.

Drawing on the survey of Birmingham and Jahoda (1955) of the 1954 election in Ghana, Zolberg (1966a: 20) makes a similar point: "[A]ffiliation of individuals to parties and candidates *opposed* to the CPP tended to be mediated by personal links. But in the *absence* of such links, 'voters seemed to fall in with the powerful propaganda of the CPP.'" This example also draws attention to important differences *within* a given colony and, of course, across colonies within the metropolitan grouping. However, the existence of such differences does not invalidate the proposition that the treatment of local chiefs under colonial rule in British Africa tended to increase the number of these "personal links," or the proposition that a bandwagon effect was therefore less likely to occur, or at least to be as widespread, as it would have been in otherwise similar circumstances in French Africa.

For the same reasons that the bandwagon effect was more limited in British Africa, the fragmentation tendency was stronger. The presence of local leaders with significant political power provided an additional basis for the emergence of rival political elites and therefore of opposition and fragmentation. The process of fragmentation was thus more likely to go further in splintering the mass movement or in preventing its emergence and/or final consolidation of power in British Africa than in French Africa. Indeed, it is not simply a coincidence that of the five West African countries analyzed by Zolberg, only Ghana, the only one of the five under British rule, failed to become independent with a party that had consolidated its control of the government. The leading parties in the other countries, despite the fact that they too experienced some of the same fragmenting pressures, all managed to control *all* of the legislative seats at the time of independence. In Ghana, the CPP controlled only 68 percent of the seats—by African standards, a relatively low percentage.

In addition, it may be noted that the greater pressures for fragmentation in British Africa may help to explain why the leading parties in these colonies, especially in the nonmulti-racial colonies, were rarely able to use successive elections to improve their positions in the way that many of the leading parties in the French colonies did.

To summarize, the greater possibility of a bandwagon effect in a situation of relatively weak intermediate groups in French Africa is a possible explanation of why the strongest parties in French Africa mobilized the vote. The presence of stronger intermediate groups in the form of a neotraditional elite in British Africa is an additional possible explanation of the tendency for greater voter turnout to be due not to mobilization by dominant parties but, rather, at least in part, to competition among parties. In a situation of greater decentralization of power, the neotraditional elite comprised a conservative class that retained its own locally and ethnically delimited power base and was interested in using that power base to defend its interests and preserve its privileges. Where the locally based neotraditional elites were relatively strong, they were often able to mobilize the vote in support of ethnic or regional parties that competed with those of the modern elite. Where regional parties based on neotraditional elites were not important, those elites were able to use their role as powerbrokers to greater advantage in situations of party competition in which they could bargain for concessions to enhance their positions by delivering the vote in a more strategic context. Under these circumstances, then, electoral participation was mobilized by these intermediate powerbrokers and was a concomitant of political fragmentation rather than of political cohesion and party dominance.

Conclusion

Several findings related to the introduction of electoral politics have emerged in this analysis. The level of electoral participation attained by independence was not stimulated primarily by the level of mass social mobilization, as is often asserted, nor was the impact of relatively high levels of participation so "disruptive" of political cohesion and elite interests as is often hypothesized to be the case under conditions such as those found in Africa. Rather, level of participation tended to be an outcome rather than a cause of elite political cohesion, although this relationship took a different form in the two groups of colonies.

Among the French colonies, higher levels of voting were due to the plebiscitary mobilization of electoral support and the bandwagon effect which accompanied very high levels of party dominance. High levels of electoral participation thus represented support mobilized by a highly dominant party. Among the British colonies, higher levels of electoral participation were due to the mobilization of the vote by a fragmented, often locally based elite in a situation of greater party competition. Higher levels of participation were thus not the result of the strategy of a dominant party for increasing its support and relative strength, as they were generally in French Africa; they were instead likely to be part of an outcome of elite fractionalization and party competition.

This contrast was seen in the opposite correlations between electoral participation and party dominance and in the pattern observed in French Africa, but not in British Africa, in which the highly dominant parties were able to use subsequent elections to mobilize very high turnout. The contrast between the plebiscitary mobilization from a relatively cohesive center and mobilization by competing, often dispersed and local elites is also consistent with the stronger correlation between communications development and participation for French Africa than for British Africa and with the positive correlation for French Africa compared to the negative correlation for British Africa between voting and primacy of the largest ethnic group. It is also consistent with the correlation between elite social mobilization and voting for French Africa and the absence of any correlation for British Africa, where local and traditional leaders were presumably more likely to mobilize the vote.

The two patterns can be explained in part by differences in the nature of colonial rule and in the pattern of decolonization, particularly the electoral system and the rate at which electoral politics were introduced. Direct rule and list voting meant that in French Africa a dominant party was more likely to emerge and to mobilize the vote as a political resource. In British Africa, indirect rule encouraged the diffusion of power and the fragmentation of the political elite. Under these circumstances a dominant party was less likely to emerge except in the context of a large settler community where multi-racial politics and a telescoped or foreshortened experience with electoral politics favored the emergence of a cohesive African political elite. In addition, the characteristics of the electoral system introduced by the British on the one hand reinforced political fragmentation and on the other did not admit of the possibility of plebiscitary mobilization of the electorate by a dominant party. As a result, in British Africa an expanded franchise did not provide a political resource for the dominant party to the extent that it did in French Africa; it was a resource which various factions of the political elite could mobilize. Thus among the French colonies, the introduction of universal suffrage and the possibility of electoral mobilization tended to facilitate formation of a relatively cohesive ruling elite and increased the resources of that elite to govern, while among the British colonies it tended to inhibit the formation of a relatively united or dominant ruling elite. These were the different heritages of the period of decolonization and the introduction of electoral politics in Africa.

4. Post-Independence Political Change: One-Party and Military Rule

Soon after independence it became clear that the Western democratic model, based on multi-party competitive elections, would not be followed in Africa. Leaders of the newly independent nations moved rapidly and deliberately to eliminate competitive party politics. This process occurred in two interrelated phases.

The first phase involved the attempt to form one-party regimes. The effective monopoly of power by a single party was achieved in some countries even before independence, during the period of decolonization. In most of these cases, the overwhelming electoral victory of a single party or the merger of two parties into one made it possible for that party effectively to eliminate all competition. By 1960, the year in which most of colonial tropical Africa became independent, nine countries had one-party regimes. Amid statements by both political leaders and social scientists justifying or rationalizing the one-party development as a potentially "democratic" form of government suitable to the multi-ethnic societies of Africa,[1] there followed in the next half-decade the formation of seven additional one-party regimes. In most of these later cases, however, the one-party status did not result from electoral victory or merger but from the banning of all opposition parties or from the outright rigging of elections. Even in those one-party regimes which achieved that status by more legitimate means, the supremacy of the single party was maintained by repressing the opposition and was sometimes ratified in law or in new constitutions proclaiming that only one party could legally exist.

1. See, for instance, Wallerstein (1961) and excerpts from Sékou Touré, Madeira Keita, Kofi Baako, and Julius Nyerere in Sigmund (1964).

The second phase of the attempt to eliminate competitive party politics took the form of the military coup, through which civilian governments in some of the new independent states were overthrown by the armed forces. This phase became dominant in 1966. The first military coup in tropical Africa occurred in 1960 in the Congo (Zaire), following closely on the heels of independence. In 1963 three more coups occurred, in the Congo (Brazzaville), Dahomey, and Togo. In all four cases, the military did not stay in power but instead intervened to bring about a change in the civilian government. The next two years brought four more coups, but three of these were in countries where coups had already occurred and the other, in Gabon, was reversed by the intervention of French troops, which restored the former civilian government. The military coup was definitely a fact of political life on the African continent, but it did not yet appear to be a pervasive phenomenon.

The events of 1966 changed this assessment. Coups took place in five additional countries (indeed, two of these countries had two coups each) and for the first time the list included ex-British as well as ex-French and ex-Belgian colonies. By the end of the decade there had been eight additional coups, bringing the total up to twenty-two in twelve countries. In the 1970s this trend continued. Between 1970 and 1975 eight more coups occurred, four of which took place in countries that had not previously had a coup. This brought the total up to thirty in sixteen countries.

The year 1966 also signaled a change in the role of the military after coups. A coup no longer signified a short-term intervention for the purpose of installing a new civilian government. The military expanded their role, not only seizing power to oust the civilian regime but retaining it and setting up a military regime.[2] In 1975 fourteen tropical African countries were ruled by governments which had come to power in military coups. The military regime had become a dominant feature of African political life.

---

2. Though I refer in this analysis to "military" and "civilian" regimes, I do not mean by these descriptive terms to imply that the fact of military or civilian incumbency is the basic feature that differentiates these regimes. For present purposes, the important features of civilian regimes is that they are multi-party competitive, one-party plebiscitary, or one-party competitive, while for military regimes the important point is that they are nonelectoral, though there is some tendency to transform these nonelectoral regimes into one-party regimes (and to turn them into civilian regimes in the process). See Chapter 5.

Throughout tropical Africa, there is hardly a country which did not establish either a one-party or a military regime. Of the twenty-six countries presently under consideration, only The Gambia has retained a multi-party regime based on competitive elections. How can the appearance of one or the other of these regime changes be explained? Did they occur randomly across the continent or can they be attributed to factors such as differences in colonial background, level of economic and social modernization, or characteristics of the pre-independence experience with electoral politics? Because military coups seemed to occur in countries that differed in terms of these traits, many observers have concluded that coups were randomly distributed throughout Africa—and, more specifically for present purposes, that the formation of a one-party regime was irrelevant in explaining the occurrence of a coup.[3] This assessment needs further evaluation. What is the relationship between the two types of regime change: the emergence of a one-party and of a military regime? Is there some sense in which one-party regimes and military regimes can be considered as alternative responses to the problems of the post-independence period? It will be argued that these two types of regime change are not random and that they are related. Leaders in different countries adopted distinct approaches in their attempt (or lack of attempt) to form one-party regimes. Certain approaches tended to result in fairly long-lived civilian one-party rule, whereas others contributed to military inter-

3. See especially Zolberg (1968a). Though many analysts still assert that coups occur randomly and Zolberg continues to be widely quoted on this point, there have since been many attempts to explain the incidence of coups in terms of a variety of factors. See, for instance, Morrison and Stevenson (1972); Welfling (1973); Hakes (1973); McKown (1975); Barrows (1976); and Jackman (1978). Particularly relevant from the point of view of the present discussion are the analyses of Welfling and Jackman, which relate coups to characteristics of the party system, and in the case of Jackman, also to level of pre-independence electoral participation. Welfling's study focuses on party institutionalization. Though this variable is conceptually different from the party variables employed here, it does rank African countries in roughly similar ways. Hence, though the two studies employ different analytic frameworks and seek to explain different things, they do tap the same underlying relationship between characteristics of the party system and military coups. Jackman's independent variables—pre-independence levels of party dominance and electoral participation—are close to those used here, although they are not measured identically. He uncovered a similar relationship between party dominance and coups. However, since he did not deal with the distinctions among colonial groupings, the substantive thrust of other parts of his analysis is different from that presented here. Neither Welfling nor Jackman considered the relationship between coups and types of one-party regime.

vention. Specifically, if one considers not simply whether or not a one-party regime was formed but also the means by which a one-party regime was formed, it becomes apparent that type of one-party regime formation and the incidence of military coups and military regimes are closely related phenomena. The pattern of one-party regime formation in turn depended in large measure on the degree of cohesion among the political elite, as seen in the level of dominance the leading party had managed to achieve in the multi-party competitive elections held during the pre-independence period, and on colonial ruler.

Patterns of One-Party Regime Formation

The first important consequence of the patterns of pre-independence electoral politics discussed in the previous chapter was for the party system—specifically, for whether or not a one-party regime was formed and how it was formed. For present purposes, a one-party regime will be defined as involving cases in which only one party holds seats in the national legislature. Most analyses of African politics have simply considered whether or not a one-party regime was formed. It is important, however, to consider the various ways in which one-party regimes have been instituted.[4] In some cases, they have been established in the context of a broadly popular party with little opposition; in others, they have been formed in a situation of substantially less party strength and popular support. Within the African context, we may consider three patterns of one-party regime formation. One-party regimes have been formed by the total electoral success of a leading party, by the merger of parties, and by coercion, i.e., by the banning or repression of opposition parties. In addition, in some cases one-party regimes

4. Bienen (1970) and Finer (1967) have both suggested that the concept of one-party regime should be broken down and that distinctions should be made among different kinds of one-party regimes. However, to my knowledge, no systematic analysis of different types of one-party regimes has been undertaken, except for the distinctions made by Huntington (1970), which continue to group virtually all the African single-party regimes within the same category. Even Finer, in the analysis that follows his criticism of a blanket single-party concept, analyzed all one-party regimes on the African continent as a single group, without making distinctions among them. His analysis is particularly interesting for present purposes because, without making distinctions within the one-party category, he found that one-party and multi-party regimes are equally likely to experience military intervention, an assertion about which more will be said below.

were never formed. These four categories may be seen as reflecting the degree to which a one-party regime was formed as a "legitimate" consequence of the results of elections, with the final category reflecting the absence of one-party regime formation.[5]

The type of one-party regime formation that occurred in each country depended in part on the degree of party dominance in the pre-independence period, with the more dominant parties being more likely to establish a one-party regime and to do so by more "legitimate" means, according to the norms of the electoral system introduced during the period of decolonization (rho = .65). This relationship is found within the colonial subgroups as well. This connection between party dominance and one-party regime formation is hardly surprising, yet it has not received explicit attention in analyses of African politics. The introduction of social, economic, and ethnic-composition factors as control variables does not significantly alter this relationship.[6]

The pattern of one-party regime formation, then, depended in part on the degree of dominance of the leading party in each country. Where a one-party regime was formed by election, political cohesion was greatest and the dominant party had least opposition and was able to fill all the elected legislative seats on its own. The cases of one-party regime formation by merger represent a situation of somewhat lower elite cohesion. In these cases one party became clearly dominant but faced some opposition from a much weaker party which it could not eliminate electorally. It was nonetheless sufficiently dominant that the opposition party finally decided it would fare better inside the dominant party than in opposition to it. One-party regimes formed by electoral victory or by merger, then, were based on clearly dominant parties. They had been able decisively to eliminate the opposition parties, and, furthermore, had done so in a manner that was defined as legitimate—according to

5. While it is not strictly speaking an ordinal scale, for the purpose of the present analysis there is a clear ordering among the categories that makes it appropriate to treat these categories as if they were ordinal.

6. The statistic rho, rather than a Pearson product-moment correlation, was used because of the noninterval nature of the dependent variable. A computer program that permitted calculating partial coefficients for rho was unfortunately not conveniently available. In order to introduce control variables, therefore, the analysis was redone with a product-moment correlation (values for the zero-order correlations differed little for the two statistics). These partial correlations, which are presented in Appendix II, are very similar to the original bivariate correlation.

the rules of the political game introduced during the period of decolonization. Thus, in the immediate post-independence period, these parties were in a relatively favorable position in terms of legitimacy as well as political dominance.

Where a one-party regime was not established by election or merger, the dominant parties had been relatively weak in the pre-independence period and had never been able to establish as broad an electoral base. These parties were thus unable either to eliminate the opposition in an election or to absorb it through merger. In these cases the most dominant party, with few exceptions, did not have the same capacity to institute a durable one-party regime. The political leaders in many of these countries attempted to set up a one-party regime through coercive means by simply outlawing opposition parties or by effectively prohibiting the opposition from contesting elections. In other countries, leaders did not attempt to institute a one-party regime by such measures but tried to work within the framework of a multi-party system.

The countries that formed one-party regimes by coercion cannot be distinguished in terms of degree of party dominance from those that never formed one-party regimes. Rather, the choice between these two alternatives appears to be related primarily to a difference in former colonial ruler, political elites in ex-French colonies tending to choose differently from those in ex-British colonies. In former French colonies, the political leaders tended to proceed relatively quickly to establish their dominance, either by overtly banning opposition parties or by effectively prohibiting them from contesting elections. Multi-party regimes were not retained in any of the ex-French African countries (see Table 15).

Table 15. *Type of One-Party Regime Formation by Colonial Grouping* (to 1975)

	Election	Merger	Coercion	One-party regime not formed
French	3	3	8	0
British	2	0	4	3[a]
Belgian	1	0	0	2
TOTAL	6	3	12	5

[a]This includes Sierra Leone, which formed a one-party regime in 1978.

The seven ex-British African countries that had not established a one-party regime by election or merger exhibited much greater hesitancy to ban the opposition and a greater tendency to retain a multi-party regime for a longer period. In five of these countries, multi-party elections continued to be held after independence, though in two of them, Kenya and Zambia, one-party regimes were eventually formed, six and eight years later, respectively, by banning the opposition. (In Kenya, a short-lived one-party regime had been formed by merger five years earlier.) This greater hesitancy can also be seen in Ghana and Uganda, the two remaining ex-British colonies that formed a one-party regime by coercion. Though they did not continue to hold multi-party elections, they waited a substantial interval after independence—seven years—before moving to establish one-party regimes. This pattern contrasts markedly with the ex-French colonies that did not form a one-party regime by election or merger. Nearly all of these countries had moved to form a one-party regime by coercion within a year or two of independence. It may be noted that the ex-Belgian African countries likewise showed greater hesitancy in banning the opposition and immediately establishing a one-party regime.

This finding gives new credence to the earlier argument about the difference in political norms that took root in British and in French Africa.[7] Post has suggested that in contrast to the British,

> the French left behind them an institutional pattern which put far less emphasis on the formal balancing of interests through such devices as bicameral legislatures, entrenched positions for chiefs, and official oppositions. Their legacy was rather one of greatly centralized decision-making and administration, and of the supremacy of the executive over all other branches of government. (1968b: 193)

Furthermore, the ex-British colonies had in their former colonial ruler a model of greater continuity in competitive electoral politics. For the ex-French colonies the model provided by the metropole involved a far more uneven history of competitive elections (Zolberg, 1964: 104–5). Finally, the French Communist Party had been linked to the dominant parties in most of the French colonies, so that one-party ideologies may have been more readily diffused to French Africa.

7. See Zolberg (1966a: 78–79) for a similar argument concerning the party-states of West Africa.

In addition to the effects of pre-independence party dominance and colonial ruler, there was an independent effect of electoral participation on type of one-party regime formation. The impact of voting turnout was quite different for the British and French colonies, being negative (rho = −.75) for the former and positive (rho = .30) for the latter. It thus seems that higher levels of voting aided one-party regime formation by legitimate means among the French colonies and hindered it among the British colonies.[8]

This contrast reflects the different causes of turnout in the two colonial groupings. Among the French colonies, greater participation occurred where there was greater party dominance, and it seemed to be the result of the mobilization of the electorate by these parties. It served as a source of support for those parties that had already achieved a high level of dominance, enabling them to form a one-party regime by election or merger. Among the British colonies, greater voter turnout was not the result of the strategy of a dominant party to demonstrate more support and thereby unequivocally eliminate its opponents; rather, it was the result of colonial policy concerning the evolution and transfer of electoral arrangements to the colonies and was also a result of party competition. As such, it was not within the control of the dominant party. Thus, while greater turnout aided the formation of one-party regimes by election or merger among the French colonies, this was far from being the case among the British colonies.

One-Party Regime Formation and Military Intervention

During the first years following independence in Africa, then, there were one-party regimes that had emerged as a result of the electoral process introduced during the period of decolonization, one-party regimes that were imposed by coercion around the time of independence or immediately thereafter, and multi-party regimes. How did these various regimes fare in the decade and a half

8. Once again, in calculating the partial correlations, product-moment correlations were substituted for the nonparametric Spearman correlation. Among the French colonies the relationship was depressed by only .07 when party dominance was introduced as a control variable, and remained unchanged or increased with social and economic control variables. Among the ex-British colonies, the partial correlations also tended to be the same or higher than the original bivariate correlation, except when party dominance was introduced, in which case it was still a strong −.60.

that followed? To what extent did each type serve the inheritance elite as a vehicle for rule? Alternatively, to what extent was each the prelude to military intervention and the establishment of military rule?

Of these three categories of regime, only the first, as a group, managed to survive throughout the first fifteen years of the post-independence period; most of the others were overthrown in military coups. This relationship between type of one-party regime formation and survival of the independence regime is presented in Table 16.

It is apparent that multi-party regimes were least equipped to provide a basis for extended rule and were almost universally unable to survive in the post-independence period. All experienced military take-overs, with the sole exception of The Gambia, the smallest of the countries considered here and the only one that does not have an army. One-party regimes had a significantly higher survival rate, with nearly half of them still in place by 1975. Thus, despite more recent contentions that coups do not occur in any regular pattern in Africa, the assertions of Von der Mehden (1964: 65) and Huntington (1969: chapter 7) that one-party regimes are less likely to be ousted by a military coup seem to be upheld in the African context. Nevertheless, by looking closely at the cases within the one-party category, one can gain a more subtle understanding of the relationship between party system and military coups. In fact, one-party regimes formed by coercion were nearly as likely to succumb to a military coup as were the multi-party regimes. Quite a different picture is presented, however, by the one-party regimes

Table 16. *Type of One-Party Regime Formation by Survival of Regime* (to 1975)

	Survival	
	Yes	No
One-party regime not formed	1	4
One-party regime formed	9	12
By election or merger	7	2
By coercion	2	10[a]

[a]This includes Gabon, where French intervention restored the post-independence government to power following its overthrow.

formed by election or merger, most of which stayed in power throughout the first decade and a half of the post-independence period.

In order to gain a better understanding of these regime changes and the relationship between one-party regime formation and military coups, it is useful to explore in greater detail the post-independence electoral policy adopted by the newly independent civilian regimes. While in some cases the holding of elections did not disrupt civilian rule, in other cases post-independence elections triggered crises that highlighted the inability of a factionalized civilian regime to provide a basis for stable rule. Such elections were factors in precipitating the overthrow of the civilian government, usually by military coup. Given the frequency with which this happened, it is interesting that civilian regimes in Africa were consistently reluctant to dispense with elections. Uganda was the only post-independence civilian regime to adopt a policy of suspending elections. Table 17 provides an overview of the relationship between the types of one-party regime formation, post-independence electoral policy, and occurrence of military coups.

Where one-party regimes were established by election or merger, the policy of holding regularly scheduled one-party elections was adopted. As mentioned above, these elections served to ratify the continued dominance of the coalition that had won the pre-independence electoral contests and did not trigger crises in the way they did elsewhere. Quite the contrary, elections in these countries can be seen as attempts by the elite to maintain and institutionalize their dominance and to legitimate and sustain the new political order; and whether or not they are actually successful in this, these elections have not tended to heighten tensions in a way that has led to the overthrow of the government by military intervention. (We will return to a discussion of these elections in the next chapter.)

As we have seen, civilian regimes in the other countries have tended to be overthrown. What was the role of elections in these events? To what extent did elections become a focus of conflict in which existing tensions mounted and intensified, resulting in the incapacity of the government to rule?

Ratification Elections

The first wave of coups in tropical Africa, with the exception of the 1960 coup in the Congo (Zaire), which will be discussed below, occurred in those ex-French African countries where elite cohesion

Table 17. *Initial Electoral Policy of Post-Independence Civilian Regimes*

	Regular one-party elections	One-party election for ratification	Multi-party elections	Suspension of elections	Other[a]
One-party regime by election or merger	Guinea Ivory Coast Mauritania *Mali Malawi[b] Tanzania *Rwanda[c] Senegal				Cameroun
One-party regime by coercion	*CAR *Niger *Upper Volta	*Benin *Chad *Gabon[d] *Togo		*Uganda	Kenya Zambia *Ghana *Congo
One-party regime not formed			Gambia *Burundi *Nigeria *Sierra Leone		*Zaire

*Indicates civilian regime overthrown by military coups in first decade-and-a-half of independence period.

[a]Cameroun, Kenya, Zambia, and Ghana followed "mixed" patterns, each holding competitive elections or by-elections before instituting a one-party regime several years after independence. In Cameroun, one-party regime formation took place in somewhat different steps at both state and federal levels, and involved erosion, outmaneuvering, and finally some elimination of the opposition. In Kenya a one-party regime was formed by merger around the time of independence. A split in the party reinstituted multi-partyism; following a competitive by-election, the opposition party was banned, and the country returned to a one-party regime. In the Congo, the move to establish a one-party regime set off popular demonstrations and calls for the overthrow of the government. Military intervention followed and a one-party regime was instituted under different leadership. That regime too was overthrown. In Zaire, as in the Congo, the military overthrew the government before any electoral policy could emerge.

[b]Following the British practice for uncontested constituencies, no voting took place in the one-party non-competitive elections in Malawi.

[c]The pattern followed by Rwanda is distinct. Like Cameroun, a one-party regime was formed after independence, not before it as in the other countries where one was formed by election or merger; and though there was some erosion and outmaneuvering of the opposition parties, the heavy hand of the government also played a role. In the end one-party status was attained when opposition parties abstained from the first post-independence elections.

[d]The success of the 1965 military coup was reversed by the intervention of French forces. The restored civilian government subsequently formed a one-party regime and has continued in power.

was the lowest and where a one-party regime was not established in the period of decolonization. The electoral policy in these countries was to hold a one-party or one-list election shortly after independence as a means of establishing or ratifying the formation of a one-party regime. Such elections occurred in four former French colonies: Togo, Dahomey (Benin), Gabon and Chad.

In Togo and Dahomey, the technique employed was a change of electoral law to institute list voting in a single, nationwide constituency, thus automatically assuring a one-party outcome. In Togo, this electoral provision was supplemented, for good measure, by the disqualification of the opposition list on technicalities (the government claimed the opposition filed late, while the opposition maintained that it had been prevented from filing on time). In Dahomey, whose tripartite politics based on shifting coalitions and realignments among three major parties was described in terms of the formula of "any-two-against-the-third" (Ronen, 1975: 126), the winning list was produced by a merger of two of the parties. The third party, which was the one that had polled the most votes in the elections of the previous year, was thereby totally excluded from the formal political process. Following the election, that party was banned and its leader jailed.

In the elections in Gabon and Chad, no provision was made for an opposition list; rather, only one list was allowed, and other parties were banned. In both cases, however, the single list represented a coalition or national-union list of the two major parties.

This tactic of using an election to establish or ratify a one-party regime was rarely successful. The one-party regimes established by election or merger before independence were based on relatively dominant parties which had either won all seats in competitive contests or had managed to win so many seats that the effectiveness of an opposition party was called into question and the opposition party decided that it could fare better inside than it could outside the dominant party. The one-party regimes in this second group of countries were based not on dominant parties but on the banning of parties that had previously had substantial strength and/or on the attempted merger of two more nearly equal parties. In these cases the one-party regime was a more artificial device which could not contain the underlying reality of political fractionalization. Unlike the regimes in the first group of countries, among which only Mali and Rwanda had coups in the post-independence period being considered, the resulting regime in each of the countries that had held ratification elections was overthrown. While in some cases the connection between coups and these elections is less direct than in the cases of competitive elections described below, it seems certain that in most of these countries the manipulation of elections was one important source of dissatisfaction and thus one cause for the coup that followed. Clearly, coups are the result of a great variety of causes, a different combination of which probably comes into play in each case.[9] The aim here is not to attempt a causal analysis of coups in Africa but to show how regime manipulation in general, and the manipulation of elections in particular, contributed to the general context of crisis in which civilian sectors intensified their opposition to the government and in which the military ultimately intervened.

The elections held to establish and ratify a one-party regime, then, could not create political unity where none had existed. On the contrary, they tended to focus and heighten political factionalism and rivalry. The 1963 coup in Togo can be linked to dissatisfaction over the suppression of the opposition that followed the rigged 1961 election. In the other three countries the mergers among parties on which the single-party regime was based did not last long. In Dahomey, the two leaders of the "merged" parties, Apithy and Maga, were soon involved in an effort to undercut each other. The 1963 coup was in part a result of this rivalry, of the utter weakness of the government which was based on the "merger," and of the incongruence of the regime with the realities of the process then taking place—a realignment of political forces into a different combination of two against the third. In Gabon and Chad the mergers or coalitions on which the single-party regimes were based also fell apart quickly, and in both cases the president moved to exclude the former coalition partner. Almost immediately in Chad, and more gradually in Gabon, new one-party elections were called to create and ratify a one-party regime based not on a national-union list, but, this time, on the single party. In Gabon, this move heightened tensions and the military coup preceded the election by a few days in order to prevent the formation of a one-party regime based on the BDG. The opposition leader was installed as head of state, but French troops intervened and restored the former president to power. Chad is the only country in this group that did not have a coup at the time of, or shortly

9. For an inventory of arguments about the causes of coups see Welch (1970c: 17–35) and Thompson (1975).

following, the formation of a one-party regime. The underlying political divisions were never resolved, however, and the post-independence period was marked by violence and civil war, a coup at the end of that period, and a subsequent inability to establish stable rule.

One ex-British colony, Ghana, adopted an electoral policy that has certain parallels with those just considered. While these former French colonies had moved quickly to establish a one-party regime and to ratify it electorally, however, Ghana moved slowly. Legislative elections were suspended, although by-elections and presidential elections were held. In 1964, seven years after independence, the final move to a one-party regime was made, and it was ratified not by a one-party election, as in the above countries, but by a referendum on the constitution. In the legislative "elections" that followed, no actual voting took place; the electoral victories of the unopposed candidates were simply declared, following British electoral practice. The leaders of the coup in Ghana, which followed the one-party regime referendum by just one year, explained their intervention as a reaction to the coercive concentration of power in the hands of Nkrumah.[10] In analyzing the causes of the 1966 coup, Austin (1975: 4–5) has emphasized the role of electoral manipulation and the repressive attempt to establish the political monopoly of single-party government in a situation in which no "natural" dominance existed.

Regularly Scheduled One-Party Elections

In a third group of countries, where one-party regimes were also established by coercion, no similar attempt was made to hold an early post-independence election as a mechanism either to establish the one-party status or to ratify it. A one-party regime was established by banning the opposition, and an attempt was made to follow the electoral pattern of the first group of countries discussed, that is, to hold regularly scheduled elections on a one-party basis. The parties in these countries managed to achieve higher levels of dominance in the pre-independence period than those in the second group of countries, though they were not generally as high as the levels achieved in those countries that established a one-party re-

10. See the radio broadcast of February 24, 1966, excerpted in Morrison et al. (1972: 256).

gime by election or merger. A one-party regime was actually instituted in Upper Volta and Niger before independence. In both cases the largest party had won an overwhelming (but not total) victory in the last election before independence.[11] This victory, however, took place in a context of deep political divisions, and the final establishment of a one-party regime took place by banning the opposition just before independence. A variant of this pattern occurred in the CAR, where substantial political cohesion was forged under the leadership of Boganda during the pre-independence period. In the elections of 1957 and 1959 the leading party won all seats in the assembly. However, the unity achieved under Boganda broke down after his death in 1959. Shortly after the election, the party split into two factions, each claiming to be the heir of Boganda. This rivalry broke into the open when one faction split from the party and founded a new party. As a result, independence coincided with a major division in the elite. In the months following independence, the Dacko faction predominated, and the opposition party was suppressed and its leader imprisoned. The remaining small parties were dissolved in 1962. In 1964 and 1965, several years after the elimination of the major opposition groups, one-party elections were held in all three countries. Because these elections were less directly associated with the establishment of a one-party regime and the forced monopolization of power, their connection with the subsequent military intervention is less clear. Nevertheless, it is interesting to observe that in Upper Volta the government was overthrown within two months after the election, in which the single list that was presented had the effect of isolating the president (see Skurnik, 1970: 66; Le Vine, 1970: 1049; and Chapter 5 below). In the CAR and Niger the elections did not seem to heighten divisions and dissatisfaction in the same way. Both countries had coups, but the elections were not part of the immediate political context in which the government was overthrown.

Multi-Party Elections

The most direct link between elections and the collapse of civilian rule is seen in those countries that did not initially attempt to form a one-party regime but instead continued to hold regularly sche-

---

11. The victories were more impressive in terms of number of seats won than they were with respect to percent of the vote for the party. Interestingly, for former French Africa the former is generally more highly correlated with the other political variables discussed in this study than is the latter.

duled competitive elections. Such elections were held in the former British and Belgian colonies—in Nigeria in 1964, Burundi in 1965, Sierra Leone in 1967, and Zaire in 1960 and 1965. Although, again, the elections cannot be singled out as *the* cause of the coups which followed and in fact can be seen as reflecting rather than causing the political fractionalization that made the regime so fragile, in each case the election became a focus for unbridgeable political rivalries, thus contributing to the underlying situation which resulted in the overthrow of the government. In Burundi, the elections resulted in a clear Hutu victory, which was difficult for the Tutsi king to accept. As a consequence, the issue of monarchical rule versus parliamentary government was brought to the fore and came to coincide with ethnic rivalries. One unsuccessful and two successful coups followed within the next year and a half (see Lemarchand, 1970a: 295ff., 411ff.). In Sierra Leone, the army intervened in direct response to an election which was bitterly disputed. As Welch put it, "The first coup in Sierra Leone grew out of the results of 'democracy'" (1970b: 53). Finally, in Nigeria, major causes of the coup of January, 1966 (which, though unsuccessful, brought down the civilian government) were regional tensions and the decline of electoral legitimacy that accompanied the 1964 federal elections and the 1965 elections in the Western Region (see Zolberg, 1969: 189–90; O'Connell, 1970: 1020–23). In Zaire, the army intervened twice following elections. The election of 1960 "formally registered the fragmentation of Congolese political movements. . . . The leading three parties had between them only a bare majority . . . ; nine parties had seven or more seats" (Young, 1965: 302). Under these conditions the fragile regime that emerged soon broke down as Prime Minister Lumumba and President Kasavubu tried to remove each other from office (Morrison et al., 1972: 222). The military then intervened. Civilian rule was soon reestablished and elections were again held in 1965, following a five-year period, after the first coup, in which four people had held the post of prime minister. The results of the 1965 elections were widely disputed, and within a few months the military again intervened (Morrison et al., 1972: 220).

Thus, where elite cohesion and party dominance were low and a one-party regime could not be established by election or merger in the electoral period before independence, post-independence elections often served to heighten tensions among political factions and to bring into dramatic relief the inability of a civilian regime based on these factions to provide a basis for stable rule. This occurred both in those cases in which multi-party elections were held in an unsuccessful attempt to sustain a democratic regime and in those in which manipulated elections were held in an unsuccessful attempt to establish or ratify a one-party regime. Most of these regimes have been overthrown and military regimes have been established.

It should be added that in a few countries, particularly those which experienced the first wave of coups in Africa (discussed above as those having ratification elections), civilian rule was restored immediately following the military intervention that toppled the initial civilian regime. Sometimes those civilian regimes were one-party, in other cases they were multi-party, but in every case, with the exception of Gabon, the new civilian regime in turn was overthrown by the military within a few years. In the post-independence period, the only regimes in Africa that have displayed any substantial degree of longevity are, as a general rule, those one-party regimes which were formed by election or merger, those which allow electoral competition within the one-party structure (see below), and some military regimes. These three types of regime will be discussed in the next chapter.

Regime Instability

Up to this point the analysis has focused on the problem of explaining broad patterns of initial post-independence regime change involving the emergence of one-party or military regimes. In addition, the heritage of pre-independence politics helps to explain the incidence of military coups and elite instability, as measured by the number of successful coups, attempted coups, and plots. That is to say, the pre-independence period affected not only initial post-independence regime survival but also the prospects for establishing any type of stable regime, since post-coup regimes experienced more coup attempts and plots and tended themselves to be overthrown.

Not surprisingly, countries that achieved higher levels of party dominance in the pre-independence period and scored higher in terms of forming one-party regimes by legitimate means experienced less elite instability in the post-independence period. This relationship holds for both colonial subgroups.[12] Given the small

12. The correlation of party dominance with elite instability and number of coups was −.50 and −.54 respectively, for 26 cases; −.41 and −.54 for ex-French Africa; and −.61 and −.68 for ex-British Africa. The correlations with type of one-party regime formation are −.44 and −.45 for 26 cases; −.57 and −.52 for ex-French

case-base and the high correlation between these two explanatory variables, it is not feasible to assess their relative impact on instability. In fact, for the larger concerns of this analysis it is not essential to do so, since dominance and type of one-party regime formation in a sense measure the same underlying phenomenon at two different times. The basic point is that to the extent a leading party achieved dominance in the pre-independence period and established a one-party regime through relatively legitimate means, there was subsequently less instability.

At the level of bivariate correlations, no relationship is found between level of participation in the independence election and elite instability or number of coups, either for the twenty-six cases or for the two colonial subgroups. For the ex-French colonies, this relationship remains unchanged when control variables are introduced. For the ex-British colonies, however, introducing party dominance as a control pushes the correlation between voting and instability in a strong, *negative* direction ($-.65$), suggesting that higher levels of mass electoral participation contributed to regime stability. Again, given the small case-base and the high correlation between these two explanatory variables, this partial correlation hardly provides a firm basis for causal inferences. However, we may note that such a reversal in the role of electoral participation in ex-British Africa would be consistent with the idea that the democratic norms of legitimacy may have been accepted to a somewhat greater extent in British Africa than in French Africa. Removing the effect of party dominance, it may be that the presence of a government based on broad electoral participation was more of a deterrent to military take-over in British Africa.

Summary of the Argument

The effects of the introduction of electoral politics on post-independence regime change can now be summarized (see Figure 2). The achievement of a higher degree of party dominance in the pre-independence period increased the likelihood that a one-party re-

---

Africa; and $-.35$ and $-.57$ for ex-British Africa. The introduction of socioeconomic control variables does not significantly change these relationships, except that for many of these it reduces the correlation between one-party regime formation and elite instability (but not coups) for ex-British Africa.

Figure 2. Factors shaping post-independence regime change.

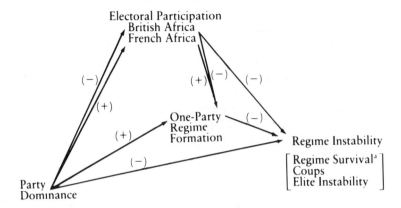

[a]Survival of civilian regime has the opposite polarity from the other two instability variables.

gime would be formed according to the norms of the existing electoral system. This relationship is primarily a direct one, involving the link between party dominance and type of one-party regime formation. However, the relationship is reinforced by the intervening role of electoral participation—though in different ways for different colonial subgroups. Among the British colonies, lower levels of dominance and higher levels of party competition encouraged higher levels of participation, which in turn appeared to have inhibited the ability of the leading party to form a one-party regime by election or merger. Among the French colonies, higher levels of dominance encouraged higher levels of participation, which in turn appeared to facilitate one-party regime formation within the norms of the electoral system. Thus, although electoral participation has opposite causes and effects in the two colonial subgroups, in both cases the net effect of electoral participation as an intervening variable was to reinforce the ability or inability of dominant parties to consolidate one-party regimes. To the extent that a political elite was able to consolidate its position under the electoral system and form a one-party regime according to the norms of that system, that elite was generally able to maintain continuous rule throughout the post-independence period. Furthermore, where the elite was politically more fragmented and party dominance was low, coups and elite instability occurred more often. Finally, although in ex-British Africa greater electoral participation was part of a syndrome of greater competition among a divided political elite resulting in an inability to form a dominant coalition and party on which to base stable rule, the evidence suggests that, controlling for party dominance, greater electoral participation may in fact have contributed to regime survival and stability.

Conclusion

Across tropical Africa, the immediate post-independence period saw a rapid dismantling of the multi-party competitive regimes introduced in the period of decolonization. Such regimes, though appropriate exit devices for the departing colonial powers and for the transfer of power to an indigenous African elite, were inappropriate mechanisms for that emerging elite to consolidate political rule in the new states. As Heeger (1974: 47) has suggested, independence presents a "crisis of management" for the new political leaders who were confronted with the problem of consolidating their position by seeking cohesion among contending elite factions, mass compliance to elite preferences and policy, and at least the appearance of mass support. In this context, the multi-party regimes were replaced either by one-party regimes which were potentially more conducive to the needs of the inheritance elite, or, after a period of regime experimentation, by military regimes which reflected the failure of the new civilian elite to establish a dominant position from which to rule.

Despite the usually immediate abandonment of the multi-party competitive regimes following independence, the relatively brief period of decolonization and the introduction of competitive-party electoral politics during that period should not be seen simply as an aberration without consequence. That experience was the stage on which the drama of Black African politics opened, introducing the players and providing the context out of which the protagonists would emerge. I have tried to show how patterns of post-independence regime change were directly connected with experiences during this initial period.

The extension of mass suffrage involved the creation of a political resource that figured prominently in intra-elite politics. In the pre-independence period it was a decisive resource in that the party better able to attract mass support became the heir to the colonial state.

The regime changes that occurred in the immediate post-independence period signalled the unworkability or abandonment of the multi-party competitive election or of the vote as a means for adjusting the claims of contending elites. Interestingly, in the search for a new form of regime through which to rule, a solution was found (somewhat ironically) only among those countries where the introduction of multi-party competitive elections resulted in the monopoly of power by the dominant party in the context of free competition; that is, where all major political factions either joined the coalition or were defeated in a political game they had accepted. In most of these cases there has been *relatively* less opposition to the maintenance of one-party regimes (usually perpetuated by repressive means), since the one-party regime represented the same coalition. There is, of course, no reason to think that this situation will continue indefinitely. Members of the coalition may leave or may be expelled. Internal splintering may occur and new coalitions may develop. Increasingly, the contest during which the coalition was formed and the opposition defeated will seem more distant and less relevant. In some instances, it may be possible to accommodate these changes and even bring to power an altered coalition within the structure of the one-party regime; however, it seems probable that the stability of many of these regimes will decline. Nevertheless, in the initial post-independence period these regimes as a group have unquestionably been more stable.

Where a one-party regime did not emerge out of the pre-independence electoral game, the new civilian political elite was generally unsuccessful in establishing a post-independence regime on which it could base extended rule. When a one-party regime was imposed, it met with greater opposition, since it was not the product of the formation of a coalition of the whole but was a means of depriving opposing elite factions of a valuable political resource, popular support. In these cases, the attempt to form a one-party regime involved the elimination of rivals who had been viable power contenders. Such attempts were rarely successful, and these civilian regimes were generally overthrown by the military either quite soon after the establishment of a one-party regime or in anticipation of it, sometimes in the context of widespread popular discontent in which civilian sectors invited military intervention. Sometimes immediately, sometimes following an interlude of a military-installed civilian regime, military rule was then established. The only successful attempts, in terms of regime survival, to form a one-party regime by coercion have been in Kenya and Zambia, which have differed from the others in that they have established one-party competitive structures into which the opposition has been more or less absorbed. The heavy-handed means by which Odinga has been prevented from making an electoral comeback in KANU in Kenya and by which Kapwepwe and Nkumbula were prevented from presenting an electoral challenge to Kaunda in Zambia demonstrate the limits of this process of absorption. Nevertheless, banning opposition parties in this context of the formation of a competitive one-party regime represents a more co-optive approach to dealing with the opposition than has been employed elsewhere.

Finally, where a one-party regime was not imposed, the attempt to maintain and work within the framework of a multi-party competitive regime failed to provide a viable basis for post-independence rule. Subsequent multi-party elections intensified political rivalries. The outcomes of the elections were contested and no elite faction was able to salvage victory. With the breakdown of the existing regime, the military overthrew the civilian government and established military rule.

This analysis thus casts doubt on two common assumptions about the effects of the introduction of elections in Africa: first, that mass electoral participation either would make no difference or would be deconsolidating and destabilizing; and second, that elections had no legitimacy. With regard to the first, this chapter has argued that electoral participation played an important role in influencing overall patterns of political change in Africa and that, at least for French Africa, a higher rate of voting was part of a pattern that enhanced political cohesion and resulted in greater stability. Further, the role of mass electoral participation must be seen primarily as a resource for the political elite, that was an outcome of cohesion or fractionalization rather than as a mass resource that produced "demand inflation" and put "intolerable" pressure on the government. (See Heeger, 1974: 78–79, who makes a similar point.) To the extent that level of participation had any effect on stability independent of its relationship with the cohesion of the political elite as expressed by party dominance, that effect seems to have been positive.

With regard to the second assumption, it was found that the degree to which a party was able to consolidate its power under the rules of the transferred electoral system affected post-independence stability. The transferred electoral system defined the rules of competition, and winning a total victory within those rules was apparently perceived as legitimate to a greater extent than might have been supposed. Those countries in which the political elite was able to form a broad coalition within the dominant party and to defeat the opposition decisively in the course of the electoral process were generally those that had regime continuity in the post-independence period. This is obviously not to say that elections have remained the legitimate means of forming governments in Africa but, rather, that the legitimacy of elections as devices for adjusting elite claims in such cases in the pre-independence period may have been greater than has sometimes been recognized.

5. Elections in Authoritarian Regimes

A central element in the establishment of authoritarian rule in Africa was the elimination of multi-party, competitive elections. Yet electoral policy was not uniform in the two types of authoritarian regimes that characterized post-independence Africa—the one-party regime and the military regime. The policy of military governments has generally been to eliminate elections. In the one-party regimes, however, elections per se were not eliminated; they were, rather, transformed into some form of controlled election. Although "departicipation" (Kasfir, 1976b) took place in virtually all countries in the sense that the classical electoral arena was shut down, in some cases a limited popular mobilization, in the form of controlled one-party elections, was continued.

Why have one-party regimes bothered to hold controlled elections? Hermet (1978: 13) has observed that holding an election in a particular form is never a gratuitous act; rather, it involves both costs and benefits. What benefits can those who organize elections anticipate from them? What are the "motives-cum-functions" (Schmitter, 1978: 149) that help to explain their existence and continuation? As Schmitter (1978: 149) has suggested, even a controlled election must have some motives or at least potential functions; it must be *intended* to contribute to sustaining political domination in some way. One must then look at the form and structure of an election to see what it is "designed to do" (Lowi, 1976: 243).

In addressing these issues, it is necessary to distinguish two types of one-party regimes according to the type of election held in each. The two types coincide with differences in colonial ruler: in ex-French colonies with one-party regimes, elections have taken the form of plebiscites; in ex-British colonies with one-party regimes, they have taken the form of one-party competitive elections. Though similar in many respects, the two types of election function in somewhat different ways.

The Plebiscitary Pattern

The pattern of electoral transformation characteristic of the one-party states of ex-French Africa involves the elimination of competitive elections and the introduction in their place of non-competitive, one-party elections. These elections can be quite strictly called plebiscites. The voter has no choice among candidates and can vote only for or against the official candidates on the one-party list. With official returns reporting nearly unanimous voting for the unopposed candidates, plebiscitary elections are a means of symbolic ratification of government policy and candidates.[1]

Three aspects of these elections are striking. The first is the remarkable degree to which they are held on a regular basis in accordance with the constitutionally defined interval (see Table 18). The second is the high rate of turnover of members of parliament associated with these elections. Finally, these elections appear to involve a substantial amount of popular mobilization in support of the official candidates. Close to half of the total population (or virtually the entire eligible population) is generally reported as having voted, and official returns in most of these countries typically show well over 90 percent of the voters supporting the official candidates. For comparative purposes it may be noted that in the United States about 60 percent of the electorate has voted in recent presidential

1. The word *plebiscite* has been used in two senses. The first is the standard notion of a referendum, a consultation of the people by the leaders on an issue in which the people have an accept/reject, aye/nay choice. When an election to public office becomes a plebiscite, there is no real choice at all and rejection is rare indeed. (In the remarkably honest elections in Congo-Brazzaville in 1973, a couple of candidates failed to gain a majority of "yes" votes, but were seated anyway [*Africa South of the Sahara,* 1978–79].) The second connotation of *plebiscite,* used particularly by Bendix, refers to the direct relationship between the state and the citizens, and the avoidance or elimination of intermediate organizations. In this sense the plebiscite is part of an illiberal principle which rejects the role of voluntary associations to represent interests in civil society before the state (see Bendix, 1964: 82ff.). Both features were prominent characteristics of Bonapartism and are part of the regimes under discussion here.

Table 18. *Reported Results of Plebiscitary Elections for Assembly*

Country	Election	Turnout[a]	Affirmative vote[b]	Affirmative vote as percent of registered
Ivory Coast	1965	99.9%	100 %	99.9%
	1970		99.9	
	1975	99.4	99.9	99.3
Guinea	1963	99.5		
	1968	99.7	99.9	99.7
	1974	99.8	100	99.8
Mauritania	1966		96.3	
	1971		100	93.8
	1975	94.0	99.9	
Senegal	1968	92.6	100	92.6
	1973	97.4	100	97.4
Gabon	1967			99.4
	1969		100[c]	
	1973		99.6	
Cameroun	1965[d]	97.1	99.9	97.1
	1970	96.7	98.0	
	1978	98.6	99.9	98.7
Niger	1965	98.5	100	98.5
	1970	97.1	100	97.1
Chad	1962	86.9	99.6	86.6
	1963	94.7	98.4	93.2
	1969	96.2	99.7	96.3
Mali	1964	88.9	99.9	88.8

[a]Voters as percent of registered voters.
[b]Percent of actual votes.
[c]The results have been reported as "virtually" or "almost" unanimous (see *Africa Independent*, 1972: 234; *Africa Research Bulletin*, 1969: 1322).
[d]East Cameroun only.

elections. Even allowing for substantial over-reporting in the official figures, it seems clear that in tropical Africa sizable numbers of people are mobilized in a ritual act of voting on election day.[2] One of the few available commentaries on these elections suggests that "all efforts are mobilized to insure a high turnout" (Zolberg, 1964: 270).

2. For instance, Zuccarelli has estimated that in Senegal in 1968 the UPS vote may have been inflated by 10 to 15 percent. Correcting for this "zealousness" of local officials produces a result of 77 to 82 percent of those registered voting for the UPS (see Schumacher, 1975: 26).

The effort expended to mobilize the population, the resources diverted to the elections and electoral campaigns, the extensive coverage in the local media, and the high rate of legislative turnover are indications that these elections are taken seriously by the government. This fact suggests that they must be understood as more than mere drama or a sham. For what purpose, then, do African leaders mobilize the population and rotate legislators on a regular basis in this way?

In providing a regular opportunity for mobilizing mass participation, plebiscitary elections may contribute to three goals. They may serve as an occasion for communication between the political leadership and the people; they may enhance national integration and identity; and they may generate legitimacy for the state.

First, then, the election campaign and on occasion the election outcome itself can serve as a channel of communication. Election campaigns are useful devices through which the leadership can publicize the goals and programs of the party and can undertake a substantial propaganda campaign (see Zolberg, 1964: 272). Information also flows in the other direction. The electoral campaign is a time for candidates to make new contact with the masses and get a feeling of grass-roots sentiments. It is an opportunity to sound out opinion at the local and intermediate levels and to get some feedback in a political system in which feedback may be otherwise very limited. The results of the elections may provide useful information about the ability of the government and of specific individuals to mobilize support and also about sources of opposition. For instance, the results of the 1968 elections in Senegal and the plebiscitary presidential elections in Tanzania in 1975, while showing overwhelming affirmative voting, also revealed notable regional deviations from the general pattern. These provided quite clear information about the presence and source of opposition (see Martin, 1978; Schumacher, 1975: 26).

Plebiscites may also serve to integrate citizens into the political system by providing an occasion for affirming or reaffirming their sense of identity with it. This function of plebiscites has received substantial attention among analysts of one-party elections in the Soviet Union (see Milnor, 1969; Swearer, 1961). In these discussions it is emphasized that each step in the election process, from the nomination stage through the campaign to the election itself, involves the mobilization of party cadres and grass-roots participation. In this way, it is argued, elections impart a sense of identity and national integration through generalized participation, which is, of course, reinforced by the accompanying propaganda and campaign speeches. In this context the formal act of voting has been described as "comparable in purpose to such civic rituals as singing the national anthem or saluting a country's flag" (Swearer, 1961: 149). As Meyer has suggested, election day "is thus a day of dedication and rededication, the occasion for solemn confessions of faith and loyalty. The importance of such Holy Days for any political system should not be underestimated" (Meyer, 1965, in Milnor, 1969: 118).

The African one-party elections of course do not involve the same degree of grass-roots organization as the Soviet elections. The parties are notoriously weak and their organizational, ideological, and financial resources are extremely limited. The extent to which plebiscitary elections in Africa succeed in imparting a sense of national identity and integration remains a question that can only be resolved empirically, but it seems reasonable to infer that one reason elections are retained in Africa is their apparent or potential contribution to reinforcing national identity and national integration. In the campaigns, which form an important part of plebiscites, people are encouraged to attend rallies and meetings. In getting people out in this manner, the campaigns make the citizens more aware of the government and raise national consciousness. Campaigning is based on a national, rather than an ethnic, appeal, and an effort is made to impart a feeling of being a participant in a single nationwide event and to build a sense of identification with the nation.

The contribution of the mobilization and propaganda of a campaign in a plebiscitary election to the goal of integration is not limited to its appeal to ethnic groups. An attempt is also made to mitigate class conflict and to incorporate potentially dissident groups, as can be seen in this report of the 1971 presidential election in Cameroun:

> [C]onsiderable effort was put into the election campaign: of particular concern were the votes of young people, who tend to be critical of the President's policy of close relations with France and who could easily become a disaffected group since the economy has not expanded sufficiently to accommodate the new generation of educated Cameroonians. (*Africa Contemporary Record*, 1970–71: B253)

The mass mobilization that is a fundamental feature of plebiscitary elections also has the purpose of demonstrating massive support for the candidates and, through them, for the state and its policies. In a plebiscitary election, of course, there is only an appearance of the possibility of rejecting official candidates, while the real purpose is to ratify them. In making a show of the support that can be mobilized behind the state, its candidates, and its policies, these elections are designed to generate legitimacy as they seek to establish a direct and apparently consensual tie between rulers and ruled (Hermet, 1978: 16). As a mechanism for legitimation, plebiscites retain both the ideological principle that elections are a fair way to make political decisions and the ideal which stands behind elections, that legitimacy emanates from the masses. It is interesting and perhaps ironic that on a symbolic level plebiscitary elections do a better job than classical elections of demonstrating the idea that legitimacy emanates from mass support. In regimes with classical elections, a low voter turnout and a failure of the winning candidate to gain an electoral majority may challenge the idea of government by the people. In one-party elections, mobilization and demonstration of mass support becomes the goal, while the election becomes the mechanism for achieving that goal. Unlike multi-party elections, one-party elections assure a majority and automatically bestow (or at least involve the reporting of) overwhelming support to a candidate. Nor does the fact that these elections are "rigged" necessarily prevent them from playing this role. As Swearer maintains for the Soviet Union:

> The popular mandate, though rigged, has its vigor as a legitimizer of the Soviet leadership and its policies. Even a one-party regime feels the need for popular endorsement, no matter how artificially that endorsement is obtained. This, one suspects, is not only to legitimize the leadership in the mass mind and to help identify the people with its policies, but also to reassure the leadership of its popularity and infallibility. In this sense elections serve as a plebiscite giving the regime a blank check to run the state. It also fulfills the psychological needs of the leadership. (Swearer, 1961: 145)

Aside from the mobilization of mass participation, plebiscitary elections provide a periodic, legitimate, institutionalized opportunity for changing officeholders. In the national elections which are of interest here, the relevant offices are those of members of parliament. The weakness of national assemblies and their role as rubber stamps have been widely noted for countries throughout Africa; yet, not only are these assemblies retained but the turnover of their members at election time is very high. In plebiscitary elections, of course, the decisions regarding the removal and replacement of members of parliament are made through the nominating process, and nomination is similar to appointment. Removal from or nomination to the legislature may take place for a variety of reasons, and a knowledge of the nominating process and a close analysis of the legislative changes would contribute to understanding the distribution of power, the kinds of political bargaining that occur, and the coalitions that form. Unfortunately, no studies of this topic are available.

In an effort to carry out a preliminary inquiry on this topic, data were examined on members of the national assemblies of six countries which held plebiscitary elections between 1960 and 1970.[3] These elections brought about a high level of turnover in the national assemblies, and few changes were made between elections. In the 1965 election in Mali and in the 1970 election in Niger, nearly a third of the assembly was changed; in Senegal in 1968 the proportion rose to about one-half; and the greatest turnover occurred in Mauritania in 1965, when turnover reached 85 percent. For purposes of comparison it is interesting to remember that in the United States turnover in Congressional elections during most of the twentieth century has been between 3 and 6 percent (Polsby, 1968: 146).

Some variations have occurred in this pattern of the use of elections for appointment to and removal from office. For example, the 1960 election in the Ivory Coast had the principal result of removing nearly half of the one hundred members of the national assembly. Of the forty-eight vacancies that appeared in this way, only eighteen were filled, and the total size of the assembly was thus reduced to seventy. Over the next few years, twenty-two others were removed from office without the pretext or legitimating device of an election. Some of these were removed for plotting against the government, though a couple were reinstated after having been

3. The lists of deputies for these six countries—Ivory Coast, Mali, Mauritania, Niger, Senegal, and Upper Volta—were presented in most of the annual issues of *Le Guid'Ouest Africain*. It should be noted that this source simply lists the deputies for each year, and it is assumed in the following analysis that all those changes that took place in an election year took place in connection with the elections.

acquitted of the charge. By the time new elections were held, in 1965, the assembly had been reduced in size from seventy to only fifty-one members, since none of the dismissed members had been replaced. If the 1960 elections served mainly to dismiss certain individuals, the 1965 elections were used in exactly the opposite way. Only five incumbents were not returned, and the election served primarily to select new members. In addition to filling all the vacancies, fifteen new seats were created, so that nearly half of the total of eighty-five were new members. The election thus became a kind of distributive or patronage ritual. In the 1970 elections, new seats were again added, increasing the total size to its original hundred. Unlike the 1965 election, however, removals as well as new appointments were made through electoral channels and about a fifth of the old assembly was replaced. The 1975 election was once again used as a distributive mechanism when twenty additional seats were created, bringing the total size of the assembly to one hundred and twenty members. Other countries have also found it advantageous to increase the size of the legislature as a means of creating opportunities for making new appointments. In Mali in 1965, the assembly was increased from seventy to eighty members; in Guinea in 1974, from one hundred to one hundred and fifty; and in Mauritania in 1975, from fifty to seventy.

As advantageous as it may sometimes be to use plebiscitary elections as an opportunity to dispense political offices, this use of elections has not always been made, as the 1960 election in the Ivory Coast demonstrated. Niger and Upper Volta likewise held elections in which the emphasis was not on new appointments and the dispensing of rewards but on removal from office. The most extreme case was the 1964 election in Upper Volta. Twenty incumbents in the seventy-two-member assembly were dropped and none of these positions was filled. The only other change occurred about two years earlier, when the assembly, which originally had seventy-five members, was reduced by three. Thus, the election was the principal occasion for removing deputies from office, and it was not used as an opportunity for making new legislative nominations. The Upper Volta election is the purest case of election *qua* purge.

The election in Niger in 1964 represents another case in which less than maximum use was made of the opportunity elections provide for making new appointments. Here too, the total size of the assembly was reduced. Unlike the case of Upper Volta, however, the election was not the main mechanism for effecting this reduction, nor was it used exclusively for dismissing deputies. More members (one-third of the assembly) were removed nonelectorally, about two years before the election, than were removed by means of the election. With all these vacancies, the 1964 election itself provided the occasion for more new nominations (25) than for dismissals (16). Nevertheless, not all the seats were filled, and the size of the assembly was reduced from sixty to fifty. A more conventional case of legislative turnover, as noted above, was the 1970 election in Niger, in which about 30 percent of the deputies were removed and replaced.

Plebiscitary elections, then, are an important mechanism for making, and also for legitimating, changes in legislative personnel. From the information presently available, it is difficult to analyze this personnel turnover in greater detail. Of those legislators who left office, we do not know how many simply retired, how many may have been appointed to other, perhaps more important, positions, or how many may have been ousted for their opposition or their inability to play a minimally effective role in controlling constituency politics. Among those who were newly nominated, we do not know how many were being rewarded for loyalty, how many were co-opted, or how many may have owed their nomination to the rising power of a new faction within the party which became capable of controlling the nomination to some of the legislative seats.

Nevertheless, it seems clear, from the active use made of plebiscitary elections to dispense, withhold, and remove from office, that they are a form of patronage ritual. Nomination to the legislature or removal from it is an important way to reward political friends and pay political debts, to co-opt potential opposition leaders, and to punish—or threaten to punish and thereby keep in line—those who stray from the path of political loyalty. From this point of view it can be seen that plebiscitary elections are a technique for forming a coalition of support and preventing the emergence of a political opposition in an effort to enhance the decision-making capabilities of the state and to insulate it from unwanted pressures from civil society. The insignificance of the office in question (assembly seat), in that little power and policy responsibility is associated with it, does not detract from this function. Rather, this feature is necessary for the insulation of decision-makers and is offset by the high status, perquisites, upward mobility, and material advantages that the office confers. The fact that new legislative appointments are made almost exclusively in conjunction with these elections (whereas dismissals are sometimes made between elections) indicates that the form of an election and the publicity and notoriety that accompany it may enhance the status of the office involved.

These elections, then, are a mechanism for building a dominant coalition. In his analysis of plebiscitary elections in Cameroun, Bayart has emphasized their role in articulating multiple clientele systems and transforming "various segments of the national elite into an homogeneous and dominant social class" (1978: 79). Noting the lively competition for nomination, he adds: "At stake is the internal ordering of the future ruling class" (1978: 80).

In sum, the holding of plebiscitary elections can be seen as an attempt to enhance or maintain a given type of domination or pattern of collective allocations. It has the purpose of legitimating the state and its policies, building popular support for and identity with both the state and the party, and managing factional elite relationships.

One-Party Competitive Elections

The second principal type of electoral transformation is the transition to one-party competitive elections. In the period before 1975 this pattern appeared in the legislative elections (but not presidential elections, which have been plebiscitary) in the one-party regimes of former British East Africa: Tanzania, Kenya, and Zambia. It may be noted that one-party competitive elections appeared briefly in Rwanda,[4] were about to be introduced by Obote in Uganda when Amin's coup put that country on a different course, and have more recently been introduced in Malawi and Zaire.

Some degree of competition exists in these elections, in that voters can choose among two or more candidates, all of whom belong, of course, to the single party. The specific mechanism varies somewhat. In Tanzania, the party selects two competing candidates to stand in each constituency, and the voters select one of the two in

4. Rwanda had an electoral system different from the single-member constituencies in the other cases of one-party competitive elections. In Rwanda there were multi-member constituencies in which the party nominated in 1965 four times as many candidates and in 1969 two times as many candidates as there were seats (see *Rwanda Carrefour d'Afrique,* nos. 46, 48, 90–91).

the general election. In Kenya, a competitive primary is held in which voters select the official candidate, who then stands unopposed and is declared the winner (without further plebiscitary voting) on election day. Any number of candidates are allowed to stand; the average in 1969 was nearly four per seat (Hyden and Leys, 1972: 397). In Zambia a competitive primary is held to select the three candidates who will run in the election. In these situations, then, electoral choice is not eliminated, but it is restricted to candidates within the single party who are running on the program of the party. Voters have a choice among candidates but not among policy alternatives.

Like the countries with plebiscitary elections, those that have introduced one-party competitive elections have tended to hold elections at regular intervals. The officially reported participation that accompanies one-party elections, however, is considerably lower than that reported in the plebiscitary elections, as measured both by rate of registration and by turnout, which ranges from about half to three-quarters of those registered, according to figures which are generally regarded as reasonably accurate (see Table 19).

Not only do one-party competitive elections, like plebiscitary elections, result in high rates of personnel turnover, but to a significant degree these decisions are made by vote of the electorate. In Tanzania, for instance, where significant turnover results from the fact that a sizable number of members of parliament do not stand for reelection, a great many more of those who do stand are not returned in the election. In 1965, 45 percent of the incumbents who ran were defeated in the election—a pattern repeated in other elections and other countries. Again, it is interesting to note that this figure is many times higher than that for the United States Congress. In one-party competitive elections, the threat of nonreelection is thus a real one.

The one-party competitive election in Africa differs from the plebiscitary election, then, in two features: it tends to be accompanied by less manipulation of the symbols of popular support—in that official figures seem generally to be an accurate reflection of rate of participation rather than a manipulated symbol of support and legitimacy—and, of course, voters are given a choice, albeit a severely constrained one, among candidates. Given the similarities and differences, the two types of elections seem to be designed with

Table 19. *Turnout and Turnover in One-Party Competitive Elections*

Country	Year of election	Turnout[a]	Turnover[b]	Percent nominated incumbents who lost[c]
Kenya	1969[d]	47%	58%	54%
	1974[e]		49	50
Tanzania	1965	73	80[f]	45
	1970	72	70[f]	33
	1975	82	64[g]	42[h]
Zambia	1973	43	68	29
	1978	65	66[i]	45[i]
Malawi	1978	55[j]	46	66

[a]Voters as percent of registered voters.
[b]Percent of first-term members of parliament.
[c]Excluding unopposed constituencies.
[d]Based on 147 of 158 constituencies.
[e]This was actually a party primary before the one-party regime was institutionalized.
[f]In 1965 and 1970 the total number of elected seats was increased.
[g]This includes as first-term members of parliament twelve who had held appointed seats in the previous assembly. If they are considered instead as returned, the figure is 51 percent. It may be noted that, contrary to the two earlier elections in Tanzania, the total number of seats was reduced in 1975.
[h]Previously elected incumbents only.
[i]Based on 122 of 125 constituencies.
[j]Estimate reported in *Africa Research Bulletin* (July, 1978).

many of the same purposes and are intended to serve much the same functions, but with some variations.

Because some choice-making is retained, the competitive one-party election is a more effective vehicle than is the plebiscitary election for upward communication from the grass roots to the political center. Since all candidates must stand on the platform of the party and cannot distinguish themselves on broad issues, competition on the basis of servicing the local community, both in terms of patronage politics of competing clientele networks and in the provision of material benefits and services to the local community, is heightened. Most studies of one-party competitive elections have noted the saliency of personality and local "pork-barrel" benefits as election issues (Cliffe, 1967: 237ff., 336; Prewitt and Hyden, 1967: 296; Hyden and Leys, 1972: 402, 416; Barkan and Okumu, 1978: 101). Unsatisfactory records by the incumbents in this regard are a major reason for the relatively high rate of failure to be reelected (Hyden and Leys, 1972: 416; Barkan and Okumu, 1978: 101–2).

Thus, while plebiscitary elections almost completely eliminate demand-making, restricting it to the very diffuse act of withholding support either through apathy or by a somewhat more decisive abstention, one-party competitive elections are a fairly effective channel for the expression of local, grass-roots demands.

Of course, because there is no organized opposition and because very little discussion of general issues of national policy takes place, these local demands remain unaggregated claims for distribution. As with plebiscitary elections, there is little opportunity to express opposition to the government except through abstention, although occasionally the defeat of an incumbent is a clear signal of more generalized opposition rather than a reflection of the record of the incumbent in servicing the local community. In 1969 in Kenya, for instance, of the nineteen ministers and assistant ministers who were defeated in the elections, almost all were from the western part of the country, where the banned KPU had been strong. This pattern of nonreelection clearly reflected more general opposition and hostility to the government in that part of the country (Hyden and Leys, 1972: 396).

The removal of issues of national policy and overall political orientation from the competitive arena has usually meant that one-party elections have not functioned as channels for downward communication from the political center to the masses. In the absence of campaign discussion about these issues, one-party competitive elections have generally been relatively ineffective vehicles for propagandizing national goals and winning support for national policies. Major national figures often fail to use the campaigns as opportunities to address public rallies (Hyden and Leys, 1972: 402), and campaign speeches are notable for the almost total absence of any discussion of national policy issues (Cliffe, 1967: 237; Hyden and Leys, 1972: 402). The contrast with plebiscitary elections in this regard is revealed in the observation that only the plebiscitary presidential election of Tanzania, and not the competitive assembly election occurring concurrently in the same country, was at all issue-oriented and directly involved political education (Kjekshus, 1974: 368). This aspect of the one-party competitive election is often congruent with the type of authoritarianism of which it is a part—one which seeks only passive acceptance rather than active support and mobilization (Linz, 1964: 255, and 1975: 269ff.). In Tanzania, however, where an attempt has been made to enlist mass energies for socialist transformation, this disadvantage of one-party competitive elections has been noted with great concern. Electoral studies of that country have reported that with the emphasis on local issues, elections have done little to build support for the establishment of a socialist state (Hyden and Leys, 1972: 419; Saul, 1972). It is not clear, however, to what extent one-party competitive elections are by their structure necessarily ill-suited to the task of propagandizing and mobilizing for national goals. Particularly interesting is the attempt in the Tanzanian election of 1975 to remedy the situation. In that year an election manifesto was published which spelled out the national goals and objectives of the party in detail (Martin, 1978: 123). In the nomination process, prospective candidates had to demonstrate their mastery of the content of the manifesto, and in the campaign meetings candidates could address only issues in the manifesto. They were no longer allowed to promise their constituencies special favors, and the role of members of parliament was modified so that they became defined as elected "animators" (Martin, 1978: 123–24). The result of these changes was that "to an unprecedented extent, Tanzanian elections have been characterized by intensive political mobilisation and education campaigns" (Martin, 1978: 123).

The contribution of one-party competitive elections to promoting national integration and identity is hard to assess. Like the plebiscitary election, the one-party competitive election has been seen as a kind of dedication ceremony binding the voters to the political center and heightening national consciousness by emphasizing participation in a single, national act. Some analyses, especially of Tanzania, have emphasized this function, pointing to the universal use of Swahili in the campaign to promote the idea of cultural homogeneity throughout the country and to regulations, generally respected, prohibiting appeals to race, ethnic group, or religion in the campaign (Cliffe, 1967: 241, 338; Mushi, 1974: 99).

Nevertheless, any potential for strengthening national integration and identity seems limited by the lack of emphasis on national issues, the absence (in most cases) of the use of elections for propagandizing, rationalizing, and explaining national goals and policies, and the emphasis instead on local, pork-barrel, patronage politics. To some extent, the elections represent not so much a single national event but so many local elections (Cliffe, 1967: 302). Furthermore, within this context, the importance of particularistic, ascriptive ties in patterns of voting and support have been widely noted, even in cases where there has been little overt electioneering about these issues (Bienen, 1974: 99ff., 107–8; Hyden and Leys, 1972: 401; Cliffe, 1967: 306ff.). Cliffe (1967: 336) has argued that the "heightened particularistic demands unleashed by the elections" may not only limit the integration-identity function of elections, but may in fact erode national identity and integration. This may happen in two ways. First, the emphasis on local distributive issues may lead to competitive bidding among particularistic groups and, second, it may lead in some areas to a heightened feeling of neglect by the central authorities and thus to alienation from the national political system.

Yet the emphasis on local issues that seems to characterize most of these one-party competitive elections may at the same time have the potential for promoting integration. First, the greater emphasis on demands for material benefits—either in the form of government services and development projects for the local community or in the form of jobs and spoils for patron-client networks—may, to the extent that these demands are met, tie the beneficiaries into the political system and give them a greater stake in it. These distributive benefits may be regarded as side payments which do not affect the overall orientation of public policy or undermine a system of domination which may more fundamentally benefit other groups. This, of course, is the co-optation mechanism of the political machine, in which voters are attracted to the material benefits of patronage politics and their attention is diverted from the larger, more fundamental questions of politics. As Saul (1972: 205) has commented: "As crumbs are distributed in this manner, the underlying structure of exploitation and privilege (domestic and international) tends to pass unnoticed." It is a co-optation mechanism in the electoral sphere which has parallels in other areas. It is similar to the effect of a land reform which distributes small plots to peasants, thereby giving them a stake in a system of private property in which their life chances may remain dismal. It also resembles the distribution of immediate benefits to workers, sometimes in the form of a wage increase, fringe benefits, or profit-sharing arrangements, sometimes in the form of certain organizing or trade-union rights, in a way that turns their attention away from class struggle and radical politics and gives them an incentive for cooperation (Collier and Collier, 1979).

A related way in which one-party competitive elections can contribute to integration is as a mechanism for sorting out rival factional relationships and for linking the periphery to the center through clientele networks. For Barkan and Okumu, this is the main function of one-party competitive elections in Kenya:

> By using the electoral process to facilitate public definition of the roles which members of clientelist linkage structures are supposed to play, the government . . . has created a more durable set of linkages between the periphery and the center of the Kenyan political system than would otherwise exist. . . . This fusion of clientelist structures and electoral process [may constitute] a unique blend of "traditional" and "modern" procedures through which central government authority can be maintained. (1978: 106)

The potential legitimating role of the one-party competitive election is distinct from that of plebiscitary elections. The retention of a choice-making component of electoral participation in the former, even though severely constrained, points to a different basis for legitimacy-building. One-party competitive elections have the potential for legitimating a ruling class and the state not so much through manipulation and demonstration of a massive show of support, as in plebiscitary elections, but through "rituals of choice" that project an aura of popular rule. Here there is greater emphasis on the idea of selection by the people and the notion of representative government that accompanies leadership selection. In most of these elections, the focus on local issues and servicing the local community enhances the idea of the elected leader as a delegate who represents the locality. Studies of Tanzania and Kenya have suggested that this concept of representation has become an important and widely held value (Cliffe, 1967: 338).

Competitive elections may legitimate not only through the projection of an image of popular government but also, it has been suggested, because, to a greater degree than plebiscitary elections, they impose on voters a share of responsibility for political outcomes (policy) and make the voters accomplices "who will be far more likely to support than to rebel against laws and policies for which they, themselves, can be said to be partially responsible" (Ginsberg and Weissberg, 1978; see also Hermet, 1978: 14). Elections have the potential for legitimating, then, because they are mechanisms for obtaining the consent of the governed. This cre-

ation of the myth of government by consent is an important function that has been emphasized by analysts of classical elections as
well. Denying that elections produce a mandate based on substantive issues and popular opinion, Lowi (1976: 256) has stated: "The
primary purpose of the electoral process in the United States is to
provide consent rather than to produce political knowledge [about
popular preferences]." This view of elections was held by at least
some of the delegates to the Constitutional Convention in 1787,
such as Elbridge Gerry, who favored elections as a means of building support and obtaining consent, thus strengthening the government, even though he feared popular influence in government (Ginsberg and Weissberg, 1978).

Some analysts have suggested that elections legitimate and build
support by "anaesthetizing" the electorate (Hermet, 1978: 13; Saul,
1972: 204). The vote symbolizes equality and popular control of
government, thus masking the lack of real influence and often the
continuation and even strengthening of inequality and class domination. In the absence of political competition concerning the basic
issues of the distribution of power and allocation of resources
throughout society and with the focus instead on local distributive
issues, the result is to insulate the state and the privileged from mass
pressure (Saul, 1972: 204). Again, this point has been emphasized
as well by analysts of classical elections. Analyzing the United
States, Edelman has argued that competition in a two-party system
can often be seen as ritualized conflict between nearly indistinguish-
able adversaries. This conflict "engages the interest of a large segment of the population and legitimizes the electoral result and the
succeeding administration. . . . [It does not] offer a reliable or major means of influencing instrumental payoffs through subsequent
legislative, administrative, and judicial decision-making; but it does
permit group influence in these processes to operate without
significant interference by mass publics who are affected by the
decisions" (Edelman, 1971: 23). This view is echoed by Katznelson
and Kesselman, who suggest that inauthentic participation, in
which candidates agree on existing structural arrangements and do
not challenge the distribution of power and in which participants
have no real opportunity to effect changes in their interest, is a form
of institutional control that reinforces structural inequality. "By
diverting energies of subordinates into system-supporting activity,

inauthentic participation can be used by authorities as evidence of the legitimate, democratic, open, and responsive nature of the political system" (Katznelson and Kesselman, 1975: 17).

Available studies of one-party competitive elections in Africa seem to indicate that these elections do in fact build support and legitimacy for the government in the ways discussed above. A survey study in Kenya suggests that voters have in fact come to view servicing the local community, rather than making decisions about the larger issues of national policy, as the most important role for a member of parliament.[5] Furthermore, one-party competitive elections do seem to have imparted a sense of genuine popular influence upon the choice of leaders and upon government in general. Summing up the findings of a survey conducted in Tanzania, Prewitt and Hyden (1967: 296; see also Cliffe, 1967: 242, 338) have concluded with respect to the 1965 elections: "The voters seem relatively efficacious and self-confident about their power to alter the composition of the leadership class," a view repeated with respect to the 1970 elections (Hyden and Leys, 1972: 413). These findings have emerged in analyses of popular opinion in Kenya as well, where voters are said to feel efficacious and aware of their ability to replace an unresponsive incumbent. As a result, "they definitely feel that elections make leaders more responsive" and political leaders have come to be viewed as competent, effective, and legitimate (Stockton, cited in Bienen, 1974: 127). Finally, commenting on the 1965 and 1970 elections in Tanzania, Hyden and Leys (1972: 413) say that there is little doubt that the elections produced a new sense of trust in the government. A survey carried out in Kenya reveals high levels of support, trust, and satisfaction with the government (Hopkins, cited in Bienen, 1974: 122–124). In one of the strongest comments on the degree to which the 1965 election in Tanzania succeeded in building support and legitimacy, Cliffe has suggested that the mass support generated by the election could explain the subsequent adoption of radical policies that may have been opposed by power-

5. Barkan and Okumu (1978: 103–4). In this study, 64 percent of those expressing an opinion thought the most important activity of a member of parliament was to "tell government what people in district want" or "obtain projects and benefits for the district," whereas only 6 percent thought the most important activity was to "take active part in the debates of the National Assembly and pass bills." (See also Hyden and Leys, 1972: 416; Mbise and Moris, 1974; Barkan, 1979b: 83.)

ful interests (Cliffe, 1967: 337; see also Saul, 1972: 206). In general, then, reports seem to indicate that one-party elections have been reasonably successful in building support and legitimacy.

Finally, a main function of most elections—classical as well as controlled—involves personnel turnover, the renewal of a segment of the political elite. The relatively high rate of turnover in plebiscitary elections was noted above. The picture is similar for one-party competitive elections, in which turnover has ranged from about one-half to two-thirds of the assembly.

The primary difference between plebiscitary elections and one-party competitive elections in personnel turnover is that in the latter the personnel choices have been less controlled at the center. This can be seen at two points in the electoral process. The first is at the time of nomination. Observers of one-party competitive elections in Africa seem to agree that the nominating process is surprisingly open. In Kenya qualifications for nomination have been particularly nonrestrictive, with the notable exception that in 1969 former members of the recently banned KPU were not allowed to stand, under the provision that required membership in KANU for at least six months. Aside from this rather glaring exception, recruitment in Kenya at this level was quite open, as any number of candidates could stand and the Executive Committee of KANU, with which final approval of candidates rested, rejected only 5 of 616 candidates in 1969 (Hyden and Leys, 1972: 396). In 1974 the party played an even more minimal role in this regard (Barkan and Okumu, 1978: 102).

Observers of Tanzanian elections also report an open process of nomination although the role of the party is greater than in Kenya. Since only two candidates may stand in each constituency, it is the task of the district conferences of the party to rank the contenders. The final selection and confirmation of the two candidates is made by the National Executive Committee (NEC) of the party. Though the NEC is not required to select the two top choices of the district conferences, it did so in over 90 percent of the constituencies in both 1965 and 1970 (Harris, 1967: 33; Hyden and Leys, 1972: 408). Despite the greater role of the party in Tanzania, selection of candidates has been regarded as relatively open (Cliffe, 1967: 231, 258; Saul, 1972: 198–99). "The possibility of manipulation of selection and party elections by the district-level leaders was limited. Generally where local activists were at all sophisticated or politically conscious, they would tend to resist such influence. . . . An added safeguard was provided by the fact that at least in 1965 the district and regional level meetings . . . were open to the public" (Cliffe, 1967: 231). Further evidence of the openness of the nomination process is the fact that some "obviously powerful party leaders" were not recommended at the district level and few of these were restored by the NEC (Cliffe, 1967: 258).

In Zambia, too, the role of the party nomination process is greater than it is for Kenya. Nomination takes place in two steps. In the first, local party officials decide which of many aspirants may stand in the primary; in the second, the Central Committee of the party confirms the candidacy of the primary winners, about one quarter of whom the party rejected in the 1973 and 1978 elections (*Africa Contemporary Record* 1973–74; *African Index*, Dec. 1–15, 1978). Though this rate of rejection is considerably higher than in either Kenya or Tanzania, it should also be remembered that uniquely in Zambia the electoral process consists of two popular competitive contests, the primary and the election itself.

The point, then, for all three countries is not that there is no manipulation of the process of nomination at all but that such manipulation is apparently quite limited. A relevant standard of comparison might be not some ideal type of "free" election but classical elections, the empirical cases to which "controlled" elections are contrasted. In the opinion of Cliffe, in the 1965 election in Tanzania "there was less manipulation of the selection process by the political leadership than in, say, an average congressional election in the U.S.A." (Cliffe, 1967: 334).

The second point at which the personnel choice is open rather than subject to central control is in the final selection of members of parliament by popular vote. Some irregularities have clearly occurred in these elections, though it might be noted that these have generally not been ascribed to central control, and in some cases election petitions were subsequently successful in court. As a result of at least a substantial lack of central interference, not only have a high percentage of incumbent members of parliament been removed from office by popular vote (as mentioned above), but ministers, assistant ministers, and party officials have also gone down to electoral defeat (Cliffe, 1967: 268, 303; Barkan and Okumu, 1978: 102, 103; *Africa Contemporary Record* 1973–74: B330). Because the final choice among candidates is made by popular vote, the personnel function of these elections is less centrally controlled and manipulated than would otherwise be the case.

Though the personnel choices are less subject to outright and purposive manipulation from the center, this does not mean that these elections are necessarily less co-optive. The electoral regime, along with the civil service (see Bienen, 1974: 39ff.), is a major point of state-society contact. A large part of the constituency work of the state is the task of members of parliament and the clientele network to which they are linked.[6] The electoral system is a mechanism for determining the local strength and relative degree of popular support of competing factions or clientele networks and for linking the state to that group. Personnel selection through electoral choice thus performs a co-optive function which is less manipulable but which contains an automatic mechanism for involving leaders who are best able to attract popular support. A more open system of recruitment may co-opt by minimizing the autonomous accumulation of support. This pattern of co-optation has been emphasized by Barkan and Okumu:

> The main function of elections in Kenya is to recruit talented political entrepreneurs into a national system of clientelist networks which link the periphery to the centre, *and* contain their activities so that the entrepreneurs pose no challenge to the regime. Election to the National Assembly does not confer the opportunity to participate in the formulation nor, increasingly, the deliberation of public policy. Election confers the opportunity to join a national patriarchy and gain access to a share of the resources that the patriarchy commands. (1978: 97–99)

Such co-optation was also observed in the one-party competitive elections introduced in 1977 in Zaire, where the resulting substantial turnover "mainly served to broaden the regime's support within the ranks of the elite by co-opting a number of disestablished civilian power brokers" (*Africa Contemporary Record*, 1977–78).

In order for elections to play a co-optive role, sufficient tangible benefits must be associated with an office which in other contexts is viewed as empty and meaningless. The material, status, and career benefits conferred in this way have been noted by a number of

---

6. This point has been emphasized and analyzed in detail by Barkan (1979b), who also notes that in Tanzania this role of members of parliament has recently been limited (see above).

analysts.[7] Additional evidence can be seen in the large number of aspirants to membership in the assembly. In Kenya there were averages of 4.1 and 4.7 candidates in each constituency in 1969 and 1974, respectively (Barkan and Okumu, 1978: 100; *Africa Research Bulletin*, 1974: 3395). In Tanzania there was an average of 7.5 aspirants per constituency in 1965, rising to 10.7 and 10.9 in 1970 and 1975, respectively (Martin, 1978: 110), out of which the party selected the two candidates.

Mass participation in one-party competitive elections may potentially serve many of the same functions as in plebiscitary elections. The one-party competitive election, however, is a somewhat riskier game. As in classical models of risk-taking, the possible pay-offs may be greater as well as the risk. Participation, as Saul (1972) has suggested, is a complex dialectical phenomenon which can express genuine participation from below and control from above. Participation in one-party competitive elections is somewhat more genuine than it is in plebiscitary elections. More popular demands get expressed and there is less centralized control over the personnel decisions involved. Yet, precisely because of the lower level of manipulation, the pay-offs for legitimacy may be greater, as may be the co-optive flexibility of the regime.

Nonelectoral Military Regimes

For present purposes the crucial point about regimes set up by military governments is that they have been nonelectoral. While civilians have almost universally set up regimes with some form of electoral mechanism as one of the major points of state-society contact and as a potential legitimating device, military governments have set up regimes with few, if any, legitimating institutions. Whereas the pattern of the one-party regime, both plebiscitary and competitive, has been to transform elections and electoral participation, the typical pattern of the military regime has been to suspend elections and thus to control electoral participation as a political resource simply by eliminating it. In contrast to the other

7. Under the terms of the leadership code, the material benefits have been limited in Tanzania, whereas in other countries a major perquisite is the opportunity for private accumulation (see Barkan, 1979b).

two regime types, in which elections and the limited mobilization they involve are a means of giving the appearance of legitimacy, military regimes deny themselves this minimal potential mechanism of legitimacy. They have immediate rationales for rule, which tend to consist of an evocation of the shortcomings of the overthrown regime and the specific reasons for military intervention, but few attempts are made to forge institutional bases for legitimacy.[8] For control they rely on coercion as well as on their ability to use specific policy outputs to placate those in a position to oppose them politically.[9] This pattern of control is, of course, also characteristic of the civilian regimes discussed above. The difference is the more limited extent to which military regimes even begin to address (far less answer successfully) the question of legitimation and the basis for long-term rule. Nevertheless, the military regimes have not been uniform in this respect, and like the one-party-regimes, the cases tend to fall into two groups, which again correspond to the grouping by former colonial ruler.

Among the former British colonies, the lack of an attempt to legitimate military regimes and to establish a basis for long-term rule has been the most extreme. This is not to deny that some of these regimes have been very long-lived but, rather, to suggest the temporary, transitional nature of these military regimes. Whereas a civilian regime makes a claim to legitimate constitutional rule, however ineffective that claim may be and however dictatorial or fictional the constitution, one of the first acts of a military regime is,

8. Horowitz (1979: 27) has suggested that military regimes represent the institutionalization of "illegitimate" power.

9. See, for example, Kasfir's (1976a: 71) account of the specific measures undertaken by Amin in an attempt to gain the support of various civilian sectors following the coup, and Decalo's (1976b: 235) assessment of Eyadema's need to adopt popular policies in Togo. Easton has distinguished between specific support, which derives from approval of specific policy outputs, and diffuse support, which involves the acceptance and legitimacy of the political system. The former, he asserts, is "insufficient." "No regime or community could gain general acceptance and no set of authorities could expect to hold power if they had to depend exclusively or even largely on outputs to generate support as a return for specific and identifiable benefits" (Easton, 1965: 269). The preponderant reliance by military regimes on specific support (in addition to coercion) rather than diffuse support has been noted in Latin America as well (Cardoso, 1973: 174; O'Donnell, 1979). Uganda presents an interesting case. Amin's establishment of councils of elders (Kasfir, 1976a: 72–73) was clearly an attempt to establish legitimacy; yet, while it went beyond a specific output, it stopped short of a full-fledged "legitimacy formula" and an attempt to establish constitutional rule.

typically, to suspend the constitution, thereby making its transitional nature true almost by definition. Among the former British colonies, the military have ruled without the establishment of any potentially legitimating apparatus. In addition to suspending the constitution and dissolving the national assembly, political parties and political activities have been banned until the return to legitimate, constitutional, civilian rule which is held out for the future. Though they may be long-lived, these regimes see themselves as transitional. When civilian rule is reintroduced, it is discontinuous with the military rule that preceded it. While civilians may hold many important roles in military regimes and there may be significant consultation with civilian sectors, there is nonetheless a substantial change of personnel as the military "go back to the barracks" and civilian politicians take their place.[10] The return to civilian rule has also represented a dramatic regime break as no-party, nonelectoral rule is replaced by a multi-party electoral regime. This pattern of regime change occurred in Ghana in 1969, in Sierra Leone in 1968, and in Ghana and Nigeria in 1979.

The former colonies of France and Belgium have tended to follow a pattern that contrasts somewhat with this pattern of a fairly long (with the exception of Sierra Leone) period of outright military rule without the establishment of any minimal legitimating apparatus, followed by a discontinuous return to multi-party constitutional rule. In Francophone Africa, the typical pattern of military regimes has been either to retain the single party that existed before the coup (as in the Central African Republic, Burundi, and Congo-Brazzaville) or to move quite rapidly, usually within a couple of years, to establish a new party. (The major exception to this pattern is Mali, where the military rulers did not set up a single party until several years had passed.) The parties that have existed under military regimes have for the most part been weak, typically not having even the minimal electoral and mobilizational tasks of the single

10. See, for instance, Bienen's (1976) description of the "important" roles of civilians—even civilian politicians—in the Nigerian military regime. Although it may therefore be more accurate to refer to the Nigerian regime as mixed than as military, it remains true that the 1979 events represent a discontinuous process of the exit of the military regime and the introduction of a civilian democratic regime. This discontinuous view of the alternation between military and civilian regimes in former British Africa is consistent with Bienen's (1978: 62) report that "politicians played important roles under a military regime . . . while maintaining hostility to the very idea of a military regime."

parties in plebiscitary regimes (see Decalo, 1973: 117). It is none-theless striking that for many of these countries, articles that chron-icle the annual events and political developments of African coun-tries, even those by particularly well-informed specialists (such as those that appear in *Africa Contemporary Record* and *Africa South of the Sahara*), frequently refer to the party. Often reserved for the party are tasks such as the formulation of a new constitution and the nomination of the head of state.

The retention or creation of a party in these military regimes reflects a process of gradual transformation of the military regime into a more civilian one based on civilian institutions and a concern with the problems of legitimacy and constitutional rule. These re-gimes have tended to promulgate a new constitution, sometimes ratified by popular referendum, and in some cases this has been accompanied by the transformation of the military regime into a plebiscitary regime similar to those discussed above. Zaire was the first country in which such a transformation was undertaken; in 1970 a national assembly was set up and regular plebiscitary elec-tions were instituted. A similar transformation took place in the Congo (Brazzaville) during the period following 1973. It was sub-stantially suspended under Opango (*Africa Contemporary Record,*

Table 20. *Pattern of Change from Military Toward Civilian and Constitutional Regimes*

ANGLOPHONE AFRICA	
Period of No-Party Military Rule	Pattern of Change
Ghana, 1966–1969	Military exit and establishment of multi-party electoral regime
Ghana, 1972–1979	Military exit and establishment of multi-party electoral regime
Nigeria, 1966–1979	Military exit and establishment of multi-party electoral regime
Sierra Leone, 1967–1968	Military exit and establishment of multi-party electoral regime, but first civilian president not elected and subsequent formation of one-party regime
Uganda, 1971–1979	Military government ousted by invading Tanza-nian and exile forces; multi-party elections held after transitional period

Table 20. *Continued*

	Single party founded	New constitution	Constitutional referendum	Presidential plebiscite	Plebiscitary assembly election
Period of military rule					
Zaire, 1965–1970	1967	1967 1978		1970 1977	1970 1977
CAR[b], 1966–1979	former party retained	1976			
Burundi, 1966–	former party retained	1974	1974		
Togo, 1967–1980	1969	1972 1980	1972 1980	1972 1980	1980
Congo, 1968–1973	1969[c]	1973	1973	—[d]	1973
Mali, 1968–1979	1976	1974	1974	1979	1979
Benin[e], 1972–1979	1975	1977		—[f]	1979
Rwanda, 1973–	1975	1978	1978	1978	
Niger, 1974–					
Chad, 1975–					
Mauritania, 1978–					

FRANCOPHONE AFRICA[a]

[a]Unlike other Francophone countries, Upper Volta ended its period of military rule (1966–1978) with the introduction of multi-party elections, though the former military head of state was elected president.
[b]The military regime in the CAR was overthrown under the leadership of Dacko, the former civilian head of state. In the beginning of 1981, Dacko was elected president in multi-party competitive elections.
[c]The party established in 1969 has been described as the "re-named" or "reconstituted" single party which existed before the coup.
[d]Head of single party automatically assumes presidency.
[e]Benin had a number of shorter-lived military regimes before the one that came to power in 1972.
[f]President elected by members of parliament.

1977–78), who assumed power in 1977, after the assassination of Ngouabi, but was reinstituted with the 1979 referendum and elections following Opango's ouster and the assumption of power by Nguesso, a military man, but perhaps more importantly a key party leader. More recently, this transformation to civilian rule was introduced with the 1979 one-party plebiscitary elections to the assembly in Mali and Benin and with similar elections in Togo in 1980.

Although other countries have so far stopped short of completing this transformation to a one-party plebiscitary regime, they have (with the exception of Niger, which as of 1980 had taken no steps toward transformation of the military regime),[11] generally maintained or established a single party and introduced a new one-party constitution as a first step. The one-party preferences on the part of the military of ex-French Africa could already be detected following the coups of 1963, the earliest (along with that in Zaire) on the continent. In all three of these cases, a military regime was not established, but a new civilian regime was introduced by means of a one-party or one-list election. In subsequent years, the back-to-the-barracks policy was replaced by this transformation policy that combined military rule with one-party trappings. Throughout French-speaking Africa, only in Upper Volta[12] has a military regime been succeeded by a democratic regime based on multi-party elections, though in this case the military head of state did not return to the barracks but was elected President, following the pattern of continuity of the head of state in the French-speaking areas. It may also be noted that the attempt of Ghanaian military leaders in 1977 and 1978 to introduce Union Government, a constitutional no-party regime with an institutionalized role for the military, was in some ways closer to the Francophone than the Anglophone pattern. This attempt was frustrated, however, by popular opposition (a referendum, arranged to approve and accept this formula, failed to produce a convincing mandate), and in the end Ghana followed a more typical pattern for ex-British Africa.

Conclusion

The authoritarian regimes that were quickly established across Africa in the years after independence had the purpose of limiting political pluralism and eliminating opposition in an attempt to consolidate the supremacy of the ruling elite. In order to limit pluralism, authoritarian regimes limit mobilization (Linz, 1972: 26). The electoral policies of virtually all the post-independence regimes have

11. It is too soon to detect the pattern of transition of military regime in Mauritania, and no stable regime has managed to come to power so far following the coup in Chad.

12. In Benin, in addition to a great variety of other constitutional formulae attempted by the military in the course of the chaotic events of the first decade of independence, the military twice attempted to hold multi-party elections. Both, however, were annulled (see Decalo, 1976b).

effectively disenfranchised the masses, in the sense of eliminating or constraining the role of elections as potential mechanisms of demand-making, as well as denying the masses a role or severely limiting their role in selecting their leaders. This demobilization or departicipation has eliminated a political resource, in the form of popular support, for potential opposition elites.

Although demobilization was nearly universal in post-colonial Africa, civilian regimes overwhelmingly opted to retain some form of election. The choice of electoral policy was influenced by the benefits that might be expected as well as by political heritage. The distinct patterns of party dominance, political opposition, and electoral participation that emerged in the period of decolonization meant that African leaders had different political resources and faced different political challenges as their countries became independent. These differences led to different choices regarding mobilization and control in the new nations. The choices may also have been influenced by the cultural heritage of the colonial ruler. It is an important measure in terms of the cultural and political heritage that we can understand why the new rulers in former British colonies chose overwhelmingly to retain some competitive or semi-competitive form of election while in the former French colonies they did not, or why in some former French colonies (those in which a dominant party emerged out of the competitive electoral politics of decolonization) the rulers continue to mobilize high levels of support infrequently but on a regular basis in plebiscitary elections, whereas in others (those in which no clearly dominant party emerged and the military intervened in the context of debilitating rivalry among elite factions) they have been much more cautious about introducing the plebiscitary mobilization of support even when they have taken the first step of establishing a formal single-party system.

Of the intended benefits that induce the elite to retain some form of election and accept its cost,[13] the most important are the legitimacy function of gaining support or mass acceptance of the way in which the state makes authoritative decisions and allocations and the personnel function of patronage and coalition-management.

---

13. In terms of the financial cost alone of these elections, Mushi (1974: 114) has reported that a conservative estimate of the cost of the 1970 elections in Tanzania is nine to ten million shillings, "for a poor country, a colossal sum."

The other roles played by elections discussed above can perhaps be subsumed under these two headings.

It is widely accepted that legitimacy in post-colonial Africa is low and the system of domination is maintained through coercion and through apathy or lack of political consciousness. Yet, this is no reason to assume that African leaders are not concerned about the problems of legitimacy, for it is equally widely asserted by analysts representing most traditions of scholarship that acceptance and legitimacy, rather than coercion, are the preferred bases of supremacy. As Habermas (1975: 96) has said, "Because the reproduction of class societies is based on the privileged appropriation of socially produced wealth, all such societies must resolve the problem of distributing the surplus social product inequitably yet legitimately." The importance of legitimacy for the long-term survival of a ruling class has been emphasized particularly by Gramsci and Althusser. Gramsci (1971: 12, 56) defines two types of supremacy. The first, called *dictatorship* or *domination*, is based on coercion. The second, called *hegemony* or *leadership,* is based on the widespread acceptance throughout society of the values of the dominant class. The first consists of control of the state only; the second consists of control over civil society as well. This distinction is similar to Althusser's (1971: 143) distinction between the two types of state apparatus: the repressive state apparatus (including the government, the bureaucracy, the legal system, and the armed forces and police) and the ideological state apparatus (including the party system and the political system in general, the trade unions, and many other institutions that are often considered part of civil society rather than of the state).

The subtypes of authoritarian regimes discussed in this chapter can be thought of as involving different strategies for maintaining supremacy. All place heavy reliance on coercion or on the "repressive state apparatus." What distinguishes them are the different potentially hegemonic structures or "ideological state apparatuses" that are set up. The main theme of this chapter has been the various ways in which African states have attempted to address the question of legitimacy and have begun to set up structures of legitimation as a basis for more durable rule. These regimes are distinguished by the ways in which they attempt to mobilize mass support as a way of generating legitimacy.

The plebiscitary alternative involves the most vigorous policy of support mobilization to manipulate the symbols of legitimacy. The mobilization strategy is what Purcell (1973: 30) has called "low subject mobilization," in which "citizens are mobilized on a temporary basis to ratify the decisions of the authoritarian elite and to demonstrate support for the regime. Much of the time, however, the regime does not encourage participation." Elections serve as an infrequent but symbolically important occasion for mobilizing a very large proportion of the population into the passive role of approving official candidates in an effort to demonstrate support and enhance the apparent legitimacy of the state.

In the one-party competitive regimes, the type of mobilization might be called *modified subject mobilization*. Mobilization in these cases has what Almond and Verba have referred to as some "participant" qualities in that, even though all candidates are officially approved, the citizen is given a choice among candidates. The citizen thus may have some limited influence on leadership selection, and, as with Almond and Verba's concept of the "competent citizen," participation involves the explicit threat to incumbents of not being reelected (1963: 214). In one-party competitive elections, less of the population is generally mobilized, and in symbolic terms it appears less important to report massive mobilization in official election returns. The attempt to generate legitimacy depends less on the appearance of massive support and more on the sense of participant influence and popular choice.

The military regimes that have been established in Africa generally follow a policy of suspension of elections and little or no support mobilization. The military in former British Africa have tended to regard the military regime as temporary or transitional and have not really addressed the question of legitimacy structures through which to maintain their rule. As a result, regime change in ex-British Africa has taken the form of a discontinuous exit from power on the part of the military and the setting up of a civilian government, usually based on a legitimacy formula of multi-party democratic rule.[14] The military rulers of former French Africa, on the other hand, have been more likely to begin, sooner or later, to respond to the need for a legitimacy formula. Regime change in these countries seems to be following a pattern of gradual transformation of the

14. In Sierra Leone, the multi-party democratic regime gradually gave way to a one-party regime.

military regime toward a one-party plebiscitary regime rather than the more discontinuous introduction of a multi-party democratic regime.

The second main potential function of elections is in relation to personnel turnover. In providing an occasion for selection for and removal from a coveted position, elections may be seen as an attempt to create and renew the political class by offering an opportunity to co-opt, reward, and sanction friends or opponents. Schmitter's description of the role of elections in Salazar's Portugal is applicable to Africa. He suggests that the principal function of controlled elections is "to articulate a dominant coalition between segments of a divided political elite and conflicting factions of the superordinate economic class; and to disarticulate any potential rival coalition between elements of a dispersed political counterelite and components of subordinate economic classes" (1978: 156).

In the case of plebiscitary elections, these personnel decisions are more centralized than they are in the one-party competitive elections, where the process seems more open and the final choice is decided in a generally free vote. Analyses of both types of election, however, suggest that this kind of coalition-management is an important aspect of elections in Africa (see especially Bayart, 1978, and Barkan and Okumu, 1978). Additional studies are needed that will analyze the specific personnel outcomes of the two types of election in terms of the coalition-building and opposition-dispersing tasks.

A caveat is in order at this point. This discussion has proceeded from the point of view of the political elite and the function of elections in maintaining political domination or supremacy. Given the fact that the choice of electoral system is a policy decision, this is appropriate. That is not to say, however, that controlled elections in Africa are simply "functional" for the state or reinforce and bolster the system of domination. The degree to which elections succeed in performing any of these functions is open to empirical investigation. This is why it is more accurate to refer to "motives" or "intended benefits," which help to explain why these elections are introduced and retained, than to "functions," which would refer to the role actually played by elections in the political system. The electoral systems discussed clearly contain within them contradictions which may be "dysfunctional" for stable rule and which may provide openings for undermining the political order rather than perpetuating the status quo. The patently fraudulent claim of popular sovereignty that accompanies them, particularly the plebiscitary elections, may serve to alienate voters rather than to elicit their consent and enhance legitimacy. The limited demand-making permitted, particularly in one-party competitive elections, may produce types of demands that contradict the overall policy orientation of the state. Elections provide only a limited resource for co-optation, and co-optation as a resource for dealing with potential opposition may have its limits. These contradictions indicate the existence of political openings and room to maneuver. A more dialectical view of the role of elections in both maintaining and undermining the system of domination is called for (see Bayart, 1978: 84). It is important to keep in mind, however, that civilian leaders have not totally abandoned elections but, rather, continue to hold them in some form on a regular basis. Furthermore, in French-speaking Africa there seems to be some tendency for military governments to reintroduce plebiscitary elections as the preferred mechanism for achieving a civilian and "constitutional" regime. Though clearly insufficient, some form of popular approval or acclamation as expressed through voting seems to be a necessary component of any attempt to establish political legitimacy in the twentieth century. The costs of maintaining these elections cannot be explained without reference to these expected benefits.

Finally, a concluding observation about the African single party may be made. The field of African studies has long since passed beyond the assessments of parties made in the early 1960s which emphasized their similarities either to a "mass," "revolutionary-centralizing," or "solidarity" model on the one hand or to a "patron," "elite," or "pragmatic-pluralist" model on the other and which dwelt on the role of these parties in "mobilizational" or "reconciliational" systems (Hodgkin, 1961: 68; Morgenthau, 1964: 336ff.; Coleman and Rosberg, 1964: 5; Apter, 1965: 199, 397). The subsequent recognition of the weakness of African parties (Zolberg, 1966a; Bienen, 1967; Wallerstein, 1966) led some analysts to deemphasize the party almost to the point of denying that it had any role in African politics at all. (This was reflected in the suggestion—well received among some students of Africa—that it was most appropriate to characterize even those countries that maintained parties as "no-party" states (see, for instance, Wallerstein, 1966: 214; Barkan and Okumu, 1978: 91). Yet the extent to which the existence of parties remains a feature of African re-gimes is striking, as is the extent to which parties have been rein-troduced by the military in many countries. As for elections, one may ask: why have African leaders bothered to maintain parties at all?

Instead of the above models, Bienen (1970, 1971) has suggested that it is more relevant to draw analogies from the model of the political machine. While this approach is fruitful for highlighting certain features, African parties of course do not generally have the political power and organizational strength that this model implies. It might, therefore, be usefully supplemented with yet another "model," that of the authoritarian party, which explicitly links the party to the broader type of regime of which it is a part. Linz (1964: 314) has described the authoritarian party in terms that sound very familiar to students of Africa:

> The authoritarian party is not a well organized ideological organization which monopolizes all access to power. . . . A considerable part of the elite has no connection with the party and does not identify with it. Party membership creates few, if any, duties. Ideological indoctrination is often minimal, the conformity and loyalty required may be slight. . . . The party is often ideologically and socially heterogeneous. Far from branching out into many functional organizations, in an effort to control the state apparatus and penetrate other spheres of life. . . , it is a skeleton organization of second-rate bureaucrats.

The authoritarian party is a "minimal organisational facade" (Schmitter, 1978: 157) which is consistent with authoritarian rule characterized by low levels of mobilization and politicization of civil society. In this context, the party provides the necessary min-imal linkage between the state and society, occupies (with the mo-tive of monopolizing) political space "with minimal and barely sufficient effectiveness" (Schmitter, 1978: 156), and serves as a vehicle for periodic elections (where they are held). In this way, the party performs a number of tasks that contribute to the political supremacy of the ruling group. As a component of a fictive regime, one which is substantially separated from the structure of effec-tive power, the authoritarian party is a device for insulating the decision-making apparatus from pressures from civil society and perhaps even for generating support for the state. As Portes (1977: 194) has described the PRI in Mexico: "The PRI has not been a center of decision-making . . . but rather a source of services which allow those in control of the state to make decisions and pursue policies."

A few recent studies of African politics have begun to revive the discussion of the role of these "weak" authoritarian parties. Commenting on the effectiveness of the UPS of Senegal as an instrument of state control, O'Brien (1978: 181, 186) reports that "the UPS is a remarkably efficient organization in its own unedifying way. . . . It does quite effectively incorporate enough of existing rural leadership . . . to make political life difficult or in many areas virtually impossible for organized opposition." It is an important vehicle of patronage, jobs, and the dispensing of governmental favors, and all in all is a "formidable agency of national political power" (1978: 186–87). Campbell (1978: 86) has made a similar point regarding the PDCI in the Ivory Coast: "The apparent insubstantiality of civil society in the Ivory Coast is thus largely a product of governmental action designed to disarm or neutralize popular political activity and to marginalize and minimize such activity where it cannot be suppressed completely. The absence of grass-roots political activity and control within the Ivorian single party, the PDCI , is of central importance in this regard." Writing in the late 1970s, he agrees with Zolberg's much earlier assessment of the party as "the most important instrument of government control, and 'auxiliaire d'autorité'" (1978: 87). Even for Kenya, where the extreme weakness of the party has received particular attention (Barkan and Okumu, 1978; Tamarkin, 1978; Bienen, 1974), the legitimacy and recruitment functions of KANU have been noted: "The weak and emasculated party has been turned into a useful agent for the consolidation of the regime" (Tamarkin, 1978: 308). Finally, following a comment on the weakness of the parties that have been set up under military rule, Decalo (1973: 117) continues: "The mere creation of such civil-military channels of communication with their marginal, upward political mobility possibilities and outlets to patronage have, however, solidified army rule." In sum, then, it seems that one's expectations about the African party must be adjusted and its role must remain an empirical question, the answer to which may be useful in understanding the mechanisms of political domination in Africa.

6. Conclusion: Patterns of Change in Tropical Africa

This book has explored patterns of national regime change in tropical Africa from the introduction of electoral, multi-party politics in the period of decolonization through the first decade and a half of independence. To orient the analysis, two contrasting images of the possible effects of the introduction of mass electoral participation were presented in Chapter 1. On the one hand, the spread of mass participation has been said to result in demands antithetical to the interests of the dominant classes. On the other hand, mass participation has been said to serve as a political resource for political elites, who can use it to bolster their own power position. How do the African cases fit these contrasting images?

It would be difficult to argue that the introduction of mass electoral participation anywhere in Africa led to a situation in which the masses achieved a significant degree of political power with which they could threaten elite interests. The extension of mass electoral participation during the pre-independence period can better be understood as part of a new set of rules for structuring elite competition and as a resource for political leaders. Furthermore, the introduction of mass electoral politics took place under the aegis, and sometimes under the heavy hand, of the colonial powers. It must be seen as part of the process of decolonization, which, as Wasserman (1976: 133) has suggested for the case of Kenya, "represents the adaptive, cooptive, pre-emptive process of integrating a potentially disruptive nationalist party into the structures and requisites of the colonial political economy."

Although the introduction of mass participation did not result in a major challenge from below, there was important variation among cases in the degree to which it enhanced or inhibited the ability of an emerging elite to consolidate its rule. This book has tried to show that in some cases mass participation served as a resource that an elite faction was able to use in order to assume a position of sufficient dominance to establish continuous rule in the post-independence period. In other cases, mass participation reinforced the diffusion of power among elite factions, resulting in greater instability of rule and greater regime experimentation in the post-independence period.

These contrasting effects of the introduction of mass electoral participation seemed to depend on the cause of its emergence and the context into which it was introduced. It is insufficient to view mass participation simply as an input to the political system which is the product of social mobilization and other factors in the environment of politics; the consequences of participation may depend on political factors, such as patterns of party competition and the particular arrangement of political structures, involving, in the African context, the role and importance of local political leaders and the implications for the bandwagon and fragmentation processes that accompanied the expansion of the electorate.

With this understanding of the effects of the introduction of mass electoral participation, the subsequent transformation or elimination of participation in the post-independence period can be seen not so much as a way of closing effective channels of mass participation, but as a response to issues of intra-elite competition and the problem of consolidating rule. As other analysts have also suggested, there was little evidence of "over-participation," of "too many" demands on the government, or of a significant threat to the elite emanating from the masses in this way (see Heeger, 1974; Hayward, 1973; Austin and Tordoff, 1972). Post-independence electoral policy varied according to colonial inheritance and the nature of intra-elite politics, but in each case it reflected an attempt to deprive rival elite factions of the important political resource of popular support and thus to limit pluralism, concentrate power, and, where some form of controlled election was retained, to establish a structure for mobilizing support and potentially laying a (limited) basis for legitimacy.

This study has shown that differences in experiences with electoral politics during the period of decolonization affected the patterns of political change and the emergence of different types of authoritarian regimes in the post-independence period. These relationships may be summarized as follows.

In those countries with leading parties which fared particularly well in the multi-party competitive elections introduced in the period of decolonization, these parties generally managed to eliminate the opposition and form one-party regimes in the course of the elections—either through complete electoral victory or through the merger of a weaker party with a clearly dominant one. Two kinds of one-party regimes tended to be formed, however, and this difference appeared to result from differences in former colonial ruler as well as differences in the degree to which the parties mobilized the population electorally. In the first type, primarily found in ex-French Africa, all electoral competition was eliminated, and plebiscitary regimes based on continued support mobilization were established. In the second, primarily found in ex-British Africa, electoral competition was retained within the framework of a one-party system.

In those countries where the major party did not fare as well in the multi-party elections of the pre-independence period, military rule was generally instituted, though it is possible to distinguish alternative intermediate steps. In the ex-French African colonies, coercive means were used to establish a one-party regime, whereas in the ex-British and ex-Belgian colonies, a multi-party regime was initially retained. Neither of these subpatterns tended to produce a viable solution to the problem of a lack of consolidation of power, however, and the regimes tended to be overthrown and military regimes ultimately established.

Modal Patterns of Political Change

These sequences of political change, from the pre-independence experiences to the emergence of distinct types of authoritarian regime, may be summarized in terms of five modal patterns followed by the countries under consideration. These patterns may be distinguished by looking first at three initial, interrelated conditions that have had important effects on post-independence politics: the degree of party dominance, the level of electoral participation, and colonial ruler. To derive the patterns, it is necessary to dichotomize pre-independence party dominance and electoral participation in order to assign high and low scores on these variables.[1] The five patterns and the countries to which they refer are presented in Figure 3. It must be emphasized that since these patterns refer to probabilistic relationships explored in the preceding chapters, it is obviously not the case that all the countries come out "correctly" at each step in the pattern. Some follow the pattern perfectly and may be taken as representative countries exemplifying the pattern. Others follow a sequence except for one deviation, and a few either switch from one pattern to another or cannot be described in terms of these patterns. (This is the case most notably for Rwanda.)

Pattern I includes those ex-French African countries in which dominant parties during the pre-independence period mobilized the population to build sufficient electoral support so that the party could either eliminate opposition parties through total electoral victory or absorb the opposition through mergers. One-party regimes in these countries were thus formed before independence. After independence, this policy of support mobilization was continued in the plebiscitary regimes that were established. These regimes survived the post-independence period under consideration.

The countries in Pattern II are primarily those former French colonies that had low levels of party dominance and generally low levels of participation. None of these countries had a one-party regime at the time of independence, but within the next few years all attempted to form one coercively through some type of ratification election. These elections took three forms: either one-party or one-list elections; competitive elections involving a simple-majority list system, in which the whole country was redefined as a single constituency, thus assuring the total victory of the dominant party; or, in Ghana—the one non-French African country in this pattern—a referendum on the issue of the formation of a one-party regime. This attempt to legitimate the formation of a one-party regime through an election was generally unsuccessful. It tended to

---

1. For these purposes, the variables were dichotomized at the means of the distribution of all twenty-six cases. In the case of electoral participation, however, the mean did not represent a natural break in the distribution. Therefore, instead of the arithmetic mean, the nearest natural break was used. This point (which was only two-tenths of a percentage point from the mean) in only one case changed the scoring from that based precisely at the mean.

Figure 3. Modal patterns of political change, 1945–75.

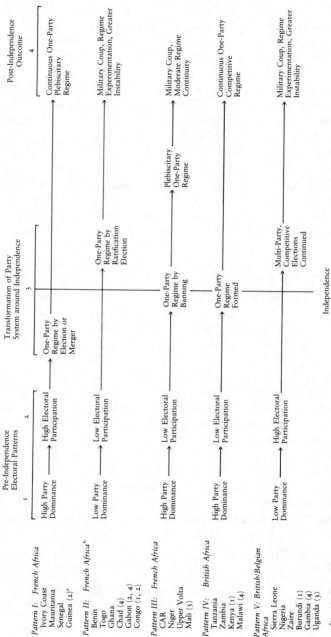

intensify existing tensions and cleavages, and in all cases except Chad, the military ousted the government within a year or two. With the exception of the 1960 coup in the Congo (Zaire), the first coups in tropical Africa occurred among these countries. In general, these military interventions did not result in the establishment of long-term military rule but were followed by the installation of a new civilian government. These new regimes tended in turn to be overthrown in a second coup, usually followed by the establishment of longer-term military rule. The post-independence history of these countries has thus tended to be relatively unstable, characterized by a fairly high degree of regime experimentation and a relatively high incidence of unsuccessful coup attempts in addition to the incidence of actual military take-overs. Benin is the extreme example of this pattern, with six coups from 1963 to 1972 and a variety of civilian arrangements alternating with military governments, producing five different constitutions and ten different presidents in the decade and a half after independence (Decalo, 1976b: 39). The deviations from this general pattern occurred in Gabon and Chad. In Gabon, the French intervened after the first coup and restored the ousted civilian government to power. The government has managed to retain power and set up a plebiscitary regime. In Chad the first coup did not follow the initial formation of a one-party regime but came thirteen years later; the intervening years, however, were a period of rebellion and civil war which might be traced to the formation of a one-party regime and the banning of the Muslim PNA (Morrison et al., 1972: 209; *Africa Research Bulletin*, 1975: 3594).

Cameroun and the Congo follow the modal sequences less closely than the other former French colonies. The Congo in a sense switched into Pattern II, while Cameroun switched out of it. Having started the sequence with relatively high levels of party dominance and electoral participation (characteristic of Pattern I), the Congo has experienced post-independence regime changes and instability similar to the countries in Pattern II, with the slight variation that the first military coup did not follow a ratification election.[2] Rather,

2. The Congo appears to resemble the Pattern II countries even more closely when other factors are taken into account. The high participation rate is shared by Gabon in this grouping: these two colonies have by far the smallest populations in French Africa and as a result tend to have uncommonly high scores on almost all per-capita indicators. In addition, the Congo's high score on party dominance must be seen in part as an artifact of dichotomizing: the score was near the mean and the lowest of all the French African colonies that were scored high.

the mere announcement of a one-party election triggered mass rioting and one of the few popular coups that have taken place on the continent. Cameroun, on the other hand, having started the sequence with low levels of party dominance and electoral participation, has had in the post-independence period a plebiscitary regime characteristic of the countries in Pattern I.

A word should be added about the inclusion of Ghana in Pattern II, which otherwise includes only former French colonies. Despite the tendency of many analysts to group Nkrumah's Ghana in the same category as the "party states" of former French West Africa, i. e., Pattern I (see, for instance, Zolberg, 1966a), to the extent that Ghana was a maverick among the former British colonies the present analysis suggests that it makes more sense in many ways to group this case during this period with the French African colonies having weaker, less dominant, and less mobilizing parties, i.e., Pattern II. Nkrumah's rhetoric, aspirations, and international posture and prestige may have been more similar to the more charismatic founding fathers of French Africa (primarily those in the Pattern I countries), but in terms of political structure Ghana resembled the Pattern II French African colonies more closely than it did either the "party-states" of Pattern I or other British African colonies, given its combination of low levels of both party dominance and electoral participation and its coercive move from that position to a one-party regime deviod of competitive elements. Since the overthrow of Nkrumah, however, the cycle of military intervention and restoration of civilian rule through multi-party elections has in a sense brought Ghana back to its British colonial heritage.

Pattern III represents an intermediate sequence for ex-French Africa. The major party in each country achieved a high level of dominance in terms of the dichotomized variable, but in fact party dominance was lower than for the parties in Pattern I (with the exception of Guinea, which, like the cases in Pattern III, also had low participation—indeed, Guinea might alternatively be characterized as having switched from Pattern III to I). These parties did not mobilize the vote and attract additional support by means of which they could establish one-party regimes by election or merger. Instead, with the exception of Mali, where a one-party regime was formed by election in 1959 following a change in electoral law which facilitated party consolidation (see Foltz, 1965: 114), the countries in this pattern, like those in Pattern II, formed a one-party regime by coercion. The tactic adopted was the straightforward banning of opposition parties, either before or within a couple of months of independence. When it was time for the next scheduled election, an attempt was made to set up a plebiscitary regime similar to those in the countries that followed Pattern I. These plebiscitary regimes remained in power for varying lengths of time, but eventually all have been overthrown by the military, again like the Pattern II countries. In contrast to Pattern II, however, the first decade and a half of independence was a period of relative "stability," for these military governments retained power throughout the period to 1975. During the post-independence period, therefore, these countries had only two heads of state—one civilian and one military.[3] Furthermore, they had fewer coup attempts and plots against the government than Pattern II countries.

Pattern IV includes those ex-British African colonies in which the British introduced an institutionalized form of multi-racial politics in order to guarantee the (over)representation of European settler interests. As a result, party alignments tended to coincide with racial cleavages, so that, compared to other colonies in British Africa, relatively little competition developed among Black African parties, the more usual pattern being a dominant African party opposing a party representing European settlers. Furthermore, the British delayed the introduction of elections and the extension of the suffrage in these colonies. Electoral participation, therefore, remained relatively low, first, because there were fewer elections in these "late" decolonizers and hence fewer opportunities for the dominant party to build an extensive organization and mobilize the vote, and, second, because with relatively little intra-African party competition, a high proportion of constituencies were not contested and, following the British practice, no voting took place in such constituencies. By independence, the special arrangements for the representation of European settlers had been dropped and the dominant African parties moved to establish a one-party regime.

Whereas among the ex-French African colonies the major difference is between those that formed a one-party regime by coercion and those that were able to do so by noncoercive, more legitimate

3. A partial exception is Upper Volta. Though there was substantial regime experimentation with a formula for transforming the military regime into a civilian and constitutional one, the political personae remained remarkably unchanged throughout the post-independence period (and until the coup in 1980), and Upper Volta shared the continuity in political leadership of the other countries in this pattern.

means, among the ex-British African colonies the major difference is between those that formed a one-party regime by any means and those that did not, though once again those one-party regimes tended to be formed from positions of relative strength and high levels of party dominance. In Tanzania and Malawi a one-party regime was formed by the electoral victory of the respective parties, which had no effective African opposition at all. In Zambia an attempt was made over eight years of multi-party politics to eliminate the opposition in elections, but as this goal continued to elude party leaders, a one-party regime was finally established by banning the opposition. In Kenya, despite a relatively low level of party dominance during the period of decolonization, a one-party regime was initially formed by the merger of the second largest party into the largest. Uniquely among the African countries, the one-party regime was neither given de jure status nor retained through more informal, coercive means, and a splinter group was allowed to establish an opposition party. Three years later that party was banned, and this final coercive move to a one-party regime was made from a position of somewhat greater party dominance than the low score for the pre-independence period indicates. One-party competitive regimes were established in all of these countries, though in Malawi electoral competition was not introduced until after the post-independence period under consideration, during which the British practice of simply declaring the electoral victory of the sole candidates in uncontested constituencies throughout the country was followed.

Pattern V includes the countries of nonsettler British Africa as well as two former Belgian colonies, Burundi and Zaire. These countries had low party dominance in the period before independence, and as a result of party competition, electoral participation was relatively high. Although Zaire and Nigeria had low turnout compared to the other countries in this group, this difference is in good measure due to the fact that universal suffrage had not been introduced in these countries before independence, as it had been elsewhere in Africa.[4] The franchise in Zaire was limited to manhood

4. The only other country (aside from Sierra Leone—see Chapter 2, footnote 3) which did not have universal suffrage by the independence election was Tanzania, but this fact does not distort the low score on participation for that country. In the first election with universal suffrage, turnout in Tanzania did not even approach the 23 percent cutoff point.

suffrage, but nonetheless the rate of participation came within three percentage points of the cutoff—a very high rate of participation among those eligible to vote. In the Northern Region of Nigeria, which has about half the total population, the franchise was also limited to manhood suffrage. Nigeria would rank "high" on the dichotomous participation variable if only half the Northern population were considered (23 percent) or if the Northern vote were doubled (24 percent). In all of these countries, multi-party regimes were initially retained in the post-independence period and competitive elections were held. In each case, however, the election became a focus for intense political conflict, resulting in a military take-over. Like the countries in Pattern III, the post-independence history of these countries has generally been marked by frequent regime change and experimentation and high levels of instability.

The two major deviations from this pattern are The Gambia and Uganda. The Gambia, the smallest country among the twenty-six considered here and one which lacks an army, has never had a military coup. It continues to have the only surviving multi-party regime in tropical Africa. In Uganda, multi-party elections were never held in the post-independence period. Rather, the opposition was banned and an attempt was underway to switch into the pattern of one-party competitive regimes being followed by Uganda's neighbors, a process which was interrupted by the military coup of Idi Amin.

Recent Developments

Although these patterns are intended to summarize the sequences of political change experienced by African countries to 1975, that year does not represent a sharp breaking point and as of 1980 the patterns delineated above continue to fit quite well. Nevertheless, a few new trends in the latter half of the 1970s may be noted. Generally, those countries with the most unstable post-independence regime history have, after a period of maneuvering and jockeying for power, managed to establish somewhat more long-lived regimes, often in part as a result of the removal from the political scene of the major power contenders. This can be seen in Benin, where, following the removal from the political stage of the dominant trio of political leaders and the rapid series of regime changes noted above, a military regime was set up which has survived, as of 1980, for eight years. Recently, most of these military regimes have at least initiated some steps toward a return to civilian rule. In French Africa, as noted in Chapter 5, these changes tend to take the form of a gradual conversion of the military regime to a one-party regime. In former British Africa, as well as in Upper Volta, return to civilian rule has involved the restoration of the multi-party competitive regime, a regime type that has not, except in The Gambia, exhibited much staying power in tropical Africa.[5] Despite the hiatus in political activity that has accompanied military rule in these countries, it is not clear for either of these patterns of change that the basic political alignments and parameters of political conflict and cleavage which preceded and to a significant extent precipitated military rule have been either overcome or superseded. The persistence of these cleavages is perhaps most visible where multi-party competitive regimes have been introduced. The new parties in Nigeria and Upper Volta bear a close resemblance to their predecessors of the 1950s and early 1960s. In Ghana an attempt at Union Government, which would have prevented the reemergence of the old political cleavages, failed, and once again the parties and alignments look quite familiar to students of the earlier period. The fate of these new experiments in multi-party competitive politics will reflect the problems that the elites have faced all along: how to establish channels for forming a ruling coalition from among a diverse and divided elite and how to integrate the masses in a way that not only co-opts them and their potential for opposition but also neutralizes them as a political resource and power base for alternate factions and rival power contenders. It will be interesting to see if this new generation of multi-party regimes fares any differently from the first. It may be noted that two previous attempts to reintroduce multi-party regimes were not successful in terms of long-term survival. The earlier attempt in Ghana (1969–1972) lasted only a few years before the military overthrew the government and established a military regime. In Sierra Leone, the multi-party regime was transformed into a one-party regime through a process of intimidation, harassment, and erosion of the opposition (the formerly ruling SLPP), in a unique development among the former British colonies. The process of adjusting intra-elite claims under the one-party regime of Sierra

5. In November 1980, after this chapter was written, a military coup toppled the multi-party regime in Upper Volta.

Leone and under the multi-party regimes of Nigeria and Ghana will be interesting to watch in the next few years, as will the impact of the greater degree of "populism" to which democratic regimes often give rise.

For many of the countries that have had relatively unstable post-colonial histories and military intervention, then, the current period seems to be characterized by a reintroduction, through one means or another, of some type of civilian regime. In addition to the changes initiated or overseen by the military governments, in two other cases, Uganda and the CAR, the military regimes were forcibly overthrown. The year 1979 constituted something of a watershed in this process, with the introduction of civilian regimes in seven countries (Nigeria, Ghana, Mali, Benin, Uganda, the CAR, and, in effect, also the Congo), following a similar development in Upper Volta the year before. It is impossible to predict the future of these civilian regimes. What the change seems to indicate is the weakness of military regimes and a continuing pattern of regime experimentation in those countries in which a relatively cohesive political elite did not emerge in the course of the politics of decolonization.

Countries with relatively stable one-party regimes during the first decade and a half of independence are beginning to face new challenges, and the possibility of course exists that differences among countries will erode as more of these gradually succumb to military intervention. So far, among the Pattern I and Pattern IV countries, this has occurred only in Mauritania, which was to some extent overwhelmed by external events. Among the others, the most prominent challenge, of course, is the change in top leadership, specifically the question of the leadership succession from the founding father to a new head of state. Up to 1980, Kenya and Senegal were the only countries among these to have experienced this succession, and so far a regime change has not been precipitated.

Another change among the one-party regimes has been an increase in the use of controlled electoral competition. None of the Pattern IV countries has retreated from its one-party competitive position, and competitive elections have been introduced in some additional countries in the period since 1975. This change has occurred in Zaire, in the Ivory Coast, and in Malawi, which as a Pattern IV country "should" have been holding such elections all

along; also, as mentioned above, Obote had been about to introduce competitive one-party elections in Uganda when he was overthrown by Amin. In addition, a competitive one-party dominant
system was recently instituted in Senegal. In this case, controlled
electoral competition does not take place within the single party
but, rather, among the clearly dominant ruling party and a carefully
selected set of initially two, and more recently three, opposition
parties. In the 1978 elections, which took place under the three-
party system, the dominant Parti Socialiste (formerly the UPS) won
82 percent of the votes (and the same percentage of seats, under a
system of proportional representation), all of the remaining seats
going to one of the two opposition parties. In each of these countries
interest in the election seemed to be high (except perhaps in the
Ivory Coast) and the competition lively. The changes seem to be
intended to increase legitimacy, broaden the base of support, and
rejuvenate the political leadership (see *Africa Contemporary
Record*, 1977–78). In Malawi this occurred in the context of a
regime which had previously had a more minimal legitimating and
support-eliciting apparatus than the other civilian regimes in tropical Africa. In Senegal and the Ivory Coast it occurred in the context
of a party that was perceived as being in need of rejuvenation,
particularly with the approach of the issue of presidential succession. In Zaire it occurred in the context of a crisis in the economic
policies and political support of the leadership, culminating in the
invasions into Shaba province by exiles from across the Angolan
border. These changes in regime, then, reflect concrete policy decisions made by the elite to shore up its rule.

Beyond the Patterns

Two sets of speculative questions may be raised about the way in
which the analysis of these patterns could be extended backward to
include additional historical variables and about the implications of
the patterns for future directions of change. It is evident that the
groups of countries identified with the five patterns correspond
closely to geographical zones within colonial groupings. The first
pattern includes those ex-French African countries along the upper
Guinea coast, the coast of the western "hump" of Africa. The
second, with the exception of Chad, includes those countries of
ex-French Africa, as well as Ghana, which lie along the Gold Coast.

The third includes noncoastal ex-French Africa. The fourth includes ex-British East and Central Africa, and the fifth includes ex-British West and ex-Belgian Africa.

How does one explain this correspondence between geographic groupings and these distinct political patterns? One possibility is diffusion among neighbors, especially within the colonial sub-groups, and also, of course, simultaneous diffusion from metropole to a number of colonies. In addition, there may be distinctive factors associated with these geographical groupings acting as internal causes for each country within the group.[6] For instance, geograph-ical grouping corresponds to the historical conditions of European penetration. In the coastal countries, particularly in West Africa, penetration was early, relatively great, and very uneven, producing a coastal-interior split with respect to many aspects of West-ernization (urbanization, religion, education, economy). The inte-rior countries had less European penetration, are very poor, have limited possibilities for economic development, and are generally sparsely settled, with substantial areas of arid desert. Although Pattern IV countries are all in East or Central Africa, it is clear that the basic common trait of these cases is that they were British colonies with multi-racial politics. Though this analytical definition is more accurate than the geographical definition, which would also have included Uganda, the use of the geographical definition helps account for the diffusion, aborted by the Amin coup, of a one-party competitive system to Uganda. Pattern V corresponds least well to a geographic definition and may more accurately be described as including the areas of nonsettler politics and indirect colonial rule.

This discussion is obviously preliminary. Work needs to be done to understand the prior conditions to which these geographical and colonial groupings really correspond and to disentangle the logic or mechanisms that relate such prior conditions to the political pat-terns that have been described. Such an analysis might involve a further elaboration along the lines of the suggestive groupings of countries according to differences in the nature of European pene-tration, economic domination, integration into the world capitalist system, and emerging patterns of class differentiation proposed by Samir Amin (1972).

6. Here again, as in the analysis of colonial subgroups presented in Chapter 3, the task, in the terms of Przeworski and Teune (1970), is to substitute explanatory factors for the names of these geographic and colonial groupings.

Finally, what, if any, effects will these different patterns of political change and particularly these different regime types have on future developments in Africa? Regime types were distinguished according to their institutionalized, formal mechanisms for the attempted legitimation of the state. As Wriggins (1969: 39) has stated: "With legitimacy much is simple; without it, everything is difficult." It would seem, then, that regime may have an impact on the capacity of the state to act effectively in certain areas of public policy. This topic has not yet been carefully analyzed by scholars concerned with Africa, perhaps because differences in legitimacy are still largely incipient. Nevertheless, it would be interesting to begin to explore the different kinds of organizational, symbolic, and coercive resources that the various types of regimes bring to the task of building and executing long-term development policies, of whatever type.

Evidence from Latin America, where the interplay between regime characteristics and policy performance has been more extensively studied, points to the importance of certain resources that may be available to one-party regimes. Scholars who have compared the one-party dominant regime of Mexico with the recent experiences of Argentina, Brazil, Chile, and Uruguay have pointed to the continuity of political institutions that may be provided even by a relatively weak one-party system; the use of symbolic resources that may play a critical role in contexts in which payoffs based on material resources are in short supply; the possibly greater political flexibility and co-optive capacity of party structures, as opposed to administrative structures directed by military elites, in responding to opposition and crisis; and the greater insulation of the state from civil society compared with many multi-party regimes. The greater ability and flexibility afforded by the Mexican regime in meeting political challenges and in avoiding political stalemate and crisis has clearly enhanced the capacity of the state not only to survive but to pursue successfully a model of rapid economic growth. This enhanced capacity has been double-edged. On the one hand, it has had the effect of partially concealing the nature of class domination and of facilitating pursuit of an economic model that has embodied a pattern of an extremely skewed distribution of resources throughout society. On the other hand, given this type of class domination, which is in many ways similar to that of Brazil, Argentina, Chile, and Uruguay, the Mexican one-party regime has allowed that country to avoid the type of harshly repressive military regime that has clearly facilitated the pursuit of fairly similar economic models in the other four countries. When state violence and disregard for human rights are as flagrant and widespread as they have been in the Southern Cone of South America, these differences in regime, despite the fact that they do not correspond to differences in class domination, assume considerable importance (O'Donnell, 1978; Kaufman, 1977; Eckstein and Evans, 1978; Davis, 1976; Stevens, 1977; Collier, forthcoming).

In Africa, as well, there may be an important relationship between type of regime and the capacity it affords the state. This relationship, of course, is not limited to capitalist states but is also evident in the attempt to pursue a socialist alternative in Tanzania. It is for this reason that the importance of the attempts by political elites to establish supremacy through regimes with these characteristics should not be minimized, and the one-party regimes of Africa should be understood in this light. This is not to say that the one-party regimes in Africa have become hegemonic or that these states are strong, with high capacity; rather, as Zolberg (1966a) emphasized, the states are weak, large "residual" areas of policy are outside the purview of the state, and there are substantial internal and international constraints on policy choice. The patterns of change described above refer merely to the very beginning of a differentiation of African countries according to regime which, if continued, may lead to similar kinds of differences in the means or modes of supremacy observable in somewhat older states, such as those in Latin America.

This study has described only the first step in the appearance and evolution of different regime types in Africa. The patterns that emerged must be seen against the background of the specific period in which they took place, the period of decolonization and the first decade and a half of independence—an analytically distinctive period in which national elites came to assume power, attempted to establish control of their new states, and first had the opportunity to create new political institutions unhampered by the constraints of colonial rule. It was a critical period of state-building and attempted consolidation of elite control of the state. The types of regimes established were a reflection of the ways in which the rules of multi-party, mass electoral politics in the period of decolonization facilitated or hampered the emergence of a relatively cohesive political class in the different colonial contexts. The choice of post-independence regime must also be seen as an attempt to establish a more effective mode of domination or supremacy. The move to establish some form of authoritarian regime had the purposes of limiting pluralism, of building a coalition, of co-opting or routing any opposition, and, where some form of election was maintained, of establishing a mechanism for politically incorporating the masses, eliciting their support, and legitimating the state.

The issues that have arisen with the decision to establish some form of electoral mechanism in independent Africa are quite similar to those which have arisen elsewhere. With regard to Europe, Bendix points out that:

> Napoleon III demonstrated the possibilities of plebiscitarian rule, and leaders of the established elites became increasingly torn between their fears of the consequences of rapid extensions of the suffrage to the lower classes and their fascination with the possibilities of strengthening the powers of the nation-state through the mobilization of the working class in its service. These conflicts of strategy produced a great variety of transitional compromises in the different countries. The starting points for these developments were the provisions of the *Ständestaat* and the postrevolutionary *régime censitaire*, and the end points were the promulgations of universal adult suffrage. But the steps taken and the paths chosen from the one point to the other varied markedly from country to country and reflected basic differences in the dominant values and character of each social structure. (Bendix, 1964: 94–95)

Because of the political and ideological context in which the African countries became independent in the mid-twentieth century, the new independent states acquired the most advanced form of electoral franchise, and it was not possible to use the same techniques of limiting the suffrage to mediate the potential impact of mass participation that had been employed in Europe in the previous century. Yet the African elites may also be viewed as torn between the possibilities and fears of mass participation, and different types of African regimes reflect different approaches to mass participation. This study has shown that where one party was clearly able to capture the electorate and form a one-party regime, the plebiscitary or mobilizational possibilities have been the strongest. Where a more fractionalized elite emerged from the period of multi-party electoral politics, a more restrictive approach has predominated under the military rule that has characterized those countries. The various policies toward elections in the post-independence period can be seen as different mixes of the mobilizational and restrictive approaches to mass participation. These differences represent alternative approaches to the establishment of supremacy, and they may assume greater importance as economic change and the differentiation and politicization of civil society proceed.

The process of mass incorporation into the political system represents a drama, taking place across the African continent, of which we have witnessed only the opening scene. The process is clearly a dialectical one. On the one hand, it contains within it opportunities for control and conquest, for the legitimation of a system of domination, and for the pre-emptive co-optation of key leaders and groups. These themes have been the focus of this book. On the other hand, it contains opportunities for politicization and, under certain circumstances, for real changes in the distribution of power. The ongoing interaction between these two tendencies will be a key issue in the future of African politics.

Appendix I
Variables Used in the Analysis

List of Variables

Pre-Independence Political Variables

    Percent of population voting in independence election

    Number of territory-wide elections

    Number of territory-wide elections with universal suffrage

    Number of territory-wide elections in which over 20 percent of population voted

    Number of years from first territory-wide election to universal suffrage

    Party dominance factor, derived from the following components:

        Percent of the vote for the leading party in independence election

        Number of parties with legislative representation at independence

        Percent of legislative seats won by leading party in independence election

        Percent of legislative seats held by leading party at independence

        Legislative fractionalization following independence election

        Legislative fractionalization at independence

        Number of important parties in pre-independence period

        Number of important opposition parties

        Number of parties in ruling coalition at independence

Post-Independence Political Variables

    Type of one-party regime formation

    Elite instability, independence to 1975

    Number of coups, independence to 1975

Social and Economic Variables

    GDP per capita, 1958

    Population, 1967

    Mass-social-mobilization and elite-social-mobilization factors, derived from the following components:

Number of wage-earners as percent of economically active population, 1963
Percent of labor force in subsistence agriculture, 1967
Primary school enrollment per capita, 1953
Secondary school enrollment per capita, 1950
Number in higher education as percent of age group, 1961
Percent literate, 1950
Percent of population in cities over 20,000, 1955
Communications factor, derived from the following components:
Radios per capita, 1964
Newspaper circulation per capita, 1964
Telephones per capita, 1966
Commercial vehicles per capita, 1966
Cars per capita, 1966
Percent of population speaking major vernacular language
Primacy of the first relative to the second major vernacular language
(ratio of percent of population speaking each)
Number of languages spoken

Description and Sources of Variables

Political Variables

With the exception of elite instability (discussed below), the political data employed in this study were gathered and scored by the author. This scoring was based on a wide variety of monographic, historical, and political studies, as well as periodicals, serials, and international yearbooks.

Party Dominance. A composite measure of party dominance was formed on the basis of the component variables listed above. Maximum-likelihood factor analysis was used as a technique for data reduction in order to combine the separate measures into a single index for data analysis.[1] From this analysis a single factor emerged which explained 67.3 percent of the variance.

Several comments are called for regarding the component variables that make up the party-dominance index. A number of these variables are based on the distribution of legislative seats. For the French colonies, the indices were relatively easy to construct, as these colonies had held straightforward direct elections based on a common roll since 1956. In the British colonies,

---

1. This use of factor analysis for the purpose of data reduction is obviously quite distinct from some earlier uses of factor analysis in which researchers mechanically analyzed large bodies of data, proceeding almost as if they hoped that factor analysis could draw theory out of data (for critiques of this earlier approach, see Young, 1969; and Burrowes, 1972). The goal here is simply to derive, from a set of conceptually and statistically interrelated variables, a summary variable that can conveniently be used in data analysis.

the wide variety of electoral arrangements made it difficult to decide which seats to count in constructing an index of dominance. First of all, the electoral principle tended to be introduced in the legislative council first in the form of indirect elections, and different regions within the same colony proceeded to direct elections at different times. In addition, the British had various arrangements by which legislative seats were reserved for special groups—usually chiefs and racial minorities (European or Asian). The problem thus arose of deciding which seats to count in constructing the index. For instance, in calculating the simple percentage of legislative seats held by the major party, was it appropriate to include the seats it won in indirect elections or those nominated seats it held? If seats were reserved, should those be included in the calculation?

Three kinds of indirect election can be distinguished among the various electoral arrangements in the British colonies: (1) indirect election by a nonelected body; (2) indirect elections by an already constituted, elected body; and (3) a multistage indirect election in which delegates to an electoral college were elected by popular vote. Three different kinds of arrangements whereby seats were "reserved" can also be distinguished: (1) election of reserved seats by a special roll of voters; (2) multistage elections where a special roll—generally a communal group—selects competing candidates for reserved seats, who are then voted upon by all the voters in the election; and (3) the system of reserving seats for candidates from a given communal group but permitting all parties to nominate these candidates, who then stand in an election in which all the voters participate.

It seemed appropriate that the index of party dominance should reflect the strength of the leading party in terms of its ability to bring about mergers and realignments and to win popular electoral support. It should not reflect its strength derived from nomination by the colonial government, nor should it reflect a lack of strength in arenas it was not meant to enter, as in seats reserved for chiefs. The following kinds of seats were therefore not counted in calculating either the number of seats held by the leading party or the total number of seats: nominated seats; seats indirectly elected by a nonelected body; and reserved seats voted on only by a roll of special voters.

In East Africa, the British also had "special" or "national" seats which were voted on by the popularly elected members of the legislature. These are included in the indices where relevant, since they reflect the kind of capacity to consolidate power in which we are interested. Likewise, indices based on the distribution of seats at independence, rather than on the results of an election, involve the activities of a party in terms of mergers, splits, realignments, and aisle-crossing, and these are also included.

It is clear from the previous discussion that the party-dominance indices rely heavily on electoral statistics. Although there may be problems with electoral statistics, I agree with Zolberg's judgment that electoral performance is the most reliable criterion available for assessing the relative dominance of the leading party (Zolberg, 1966a: 35).

The final three components of the party-dominance factor were constructed on the basis of the work of Thomas Hodgkin. In the appendix to his *African Political Parties* (1961), Hodgkin listed what he judged to be the politically important parties that had existed during, but not necessarily throughout, the period 1945–60 in each African country. The number of important parties, judged by a prominent analyst of African politics, is another index of party consolidation or fractionalization over that period. Two variables were constructed on this basis: the total number of parties listed by Hodgkin, and his assessment of the number of important opposition parties in 1960. A third variable constructed from data in the Hodgkin appendix is the number of parties in the governing coalition in 1960.

Electoral Participation. The figure for electoral participation to which most frequent reference is made in the analysis is that for the percent of the population voting in the independence election. In all cases except Sierra Leone, this election preceded independence. In Sierra Leone the last pre-independence election was held four years before independence under a restricted franchise, whereas the last pre-independence election scored for the other countries was held not more than one or two years prior to independence, and almost all of these were held on the basis of universal suffrage. Hence, the most comparable election for Sierra Leone was the one that occurred just after independence, and it was used in scoring this variable.

The other participation and electoral variables were derived from standard histories and monographs on colonial Africa and are discussed in Chapter 2. Territory-wide elections refer to those in which there was voting throughout most of the territory; that is, the election was not restricted to urban areas, the Crown Colony, etc., and indirect elections based on selection by an already constituted body were not included, but indirect elections based on a multi-tiered system with popular voting at the base level were.

One-Party Regime Formation. The problem of defining a one-party regime is complex. For instance, is there an important difference between a one-party regime and a dominant-party regime, and how can the distinction between them be consistently coded across countries; that is, at what point does an opposition cease to be significant? Also, to what extent is it important to consider the ways in which one-party regimes have been instituted? In some cases, it was done from a base of a broadly popular party with little opposition; in others, it occurred in a situation of substantially less power and popular support.

With respect to the first of these questions, I decided to use the control of 100 percent of the seats in the legislature as defining the existence of a one-party regime. This is a relatively conservative criterion that excludes the cases which have been called dominant-party regimes and which have often been treated together with one-party regimes. However, any other criterion would have produced virtually insurmountable problems of consistency across cases, as it is extremely difficult, especially with the unevenness in quantity and quality of information available for the African countries, to determine at what point a single party had effective control over the legislature or had no effective opposition from another party. It may be noted that, as with pre-independence party-dominance measures, I did not count reserved seats in the calculations for the establishment of a one-party regime. Thus, Malawi was considered to have had a one-party regime at a time when members of a European party still held reserved seats in the legislature. In cases when one or two independents, not representing an opposition party, held seats in the legislature, as in Tanzania, the Ivory Coast, and Mauritania, I counted the countries as having one-party regimes.

The question of the manner in which a one-party regime was formed was considered important, and I constructed a variable that scores the types of formation, rather than relying only on the more commonly analyzed dichotomy of whether or not a one-party regime was formed. This variable is discussed in Chapter 4. For the purposes of this variable, the short-lived one-party regime formed by merger in Kenya in 1964 was not counted; Kenya was scored in terms of the events of 1969 as having formed a one-party regime by banning and coercion.

Elite Instability. This is an updated version of the variable presented in Donald Morrison et al., *Black Africa: A Comparative Handbook* (1972). It is based on the sum of the weighted scores of the following events (weights are indicated in parentheses): coups (5), attempted coups (3), and plots (1). These events were coded by Morrision et al. for the period from independence to 1969. Robert Jackman (1978) extended the scoring to 1975 and was generous enough to share his data with me. In addition, I constructed a simple additive index of the number of successful coups over the same period.

Social and Economic Variables

All these variables were collected as part of the African National Integration Project at Northwestern University and were kindly supplied in machine-readable form by Donald Morrison. Most have been published in the *Black Africa* handbook. Since these variables were used primarily as controls for correlations among political variables that refer to the pre-independence period, data from the 1950s were used when available. For total population, however, the figure for 1967, given in the African National Integration Project data, was employed. Earlier estimates for the 1950s were available, but since these were based on extrapolations of data from the late 1960s it was decided to use the 1967 data.

For the communications and social-mobilization measures, maximum-likelihood factor analysis was again used as a data-reduction technique to derive a small number of usable indicators. In the analysis of the seven social-mobilization variables, the factor analysis produced two factors which together explained 61 percent of the variance. As indicated in Chapter 3, literacy and primary school enrollment had the highest loadings on one of the factors (.81 and .80, respectively). The highest loading on the other factor was for higher education (.99). The two factors thus seemed to reflect the emergence of social groups on two levels: the emergence of a somewhat socially mobilized population that had acquired some degree of literacy and education, and the emergence of a highly educated elite. The two factors were thus labeled *mass* and *elite social mobilization*.

The analysis of the communications variables also produced two factors. The highest loadings on the first factor were for cars, commercial vehicles, and telephones per capita (.94, .83, and .78, respectively), and this factor accounted for 46.7 percent of the variance. The second factor accounted for an additional 29 percent. Since newspaper circulation had a loading of .9995 on that factor, that variable was used to represent the factor.

Appendix II
Correlations and Partial Correlations for All Cases, Former French Africa and Former British Africa*

	Party dominance with electoral participation			Party dominance with type of one-party regime formation			Electoral participation with type of one-party regime formation		
	All	Fr.	Brit.	All	Fr.	Brit.	All	Fr.	Brit.
Zero-order correlation	−.05	.25	−.74	.64[a]	.52[a]	.87[a]	.02[b]	.44[b]	−.84[b]
First-order partial: Control variable									
GDP per capital	−.04	.31	−.74	.64	.52	.88	.03	.54	−.85
Population	−.14	.27	−.86	.60	.54	.87	−.05	.59	−.93
No. languages	−.15	.24	−.82	.62	.53	.87	−.04	.44	−.93
First language, % speakers	−.09	.24	−.72	.61	.53	.86	−.01	.44	−.83
First language, primacy ratio	−.12	.19	−.66	.60	.49	.82	−.04	.40	−.80
Communications	−.10	.31	−.89	.64	.52	.93	−.00	.50	−.86
Newspaper circulation	−.08	.23	−.76	.60	.52	.85	−.01	.44	−.86
Elite social mobilization	.01	.45	−.76	.64	.55	.85	.02	.49	−.86
Mass social mobilization	−.18	.26	−.72	.58	.39	.87	−.08	.50	−.83
Electoral participation				.64	.47	.69			
Party dominance							.06	.37	−.60

*Pearson product-moment correlations.

[a]The nonparametric rho is equal to .65, .66, and .75 for all the cases and the French and British subgroups, respectively.

[b]Rho is equal to −.02, .30, and −.75 for all the cases and the French and British subgroups, respectively.

	Party dominance with elite instability, coups			Electoral participation with elite instability, coups		
All	Fr.	Brit.	All	Fr.	Brit.
−.50, −.54	−.41, −.54	−.61, −.68	−.05, −.04	−.12, −.20	.05, .19
−.50, −.55	−.42, −.56	−.61, −.69	−.04, −.01	−.05, −.12	.03, .19
−.48, −.50	−.41, −.54	−.57, −.63	−.01, −.02	−.20, −.28	.11, .34
−.50, −.53	−.45, −.58	−.60, −.69	−.02, −.00	−.13, −.22	.12, .32
−.50, −.56	−.44, −.58	−.56, −.67	−.04, −.04	−.13, −.22	−.05, .14
−.48, −.53	−.39, −.55	−.54, −.62	−.02, −.01	−.08, −.20	−.12, .03
−.49, −.53	−.41, −.54	−.62, −.69	.08, .08	−.02, −.10	.34, .46
−.47, −.56	−.43, −.53	−.49, −.62	−.03, −.04	−.14, −.16	−.05, .15
−.48, −.53	−.39, −.55	−.50, −.61	−.12, −.08	−.23, −.23	−.03, .15
−.45, −.57	−.34, −.49	−.65, −.66	.02, −.03	−.11, −.20	.08, .12
−.50, −.54	−.39, −.51	−.85, −.82			
			−.08, −.08	−.02, −.08	−.74, −.65

Table (*continued*)

	Type of one-party regime formation with elite instability, coups		
	All	Fr.	Brit.
Zero-order correlation	−.44, −.45	−.47, −.52	−.35, −.57
First-order partial: Control variable			
GDP per capita	−.44, −.46	−.49, −.54	−.30, −.58
Population	−.42, −.42	−.43, −.49	−.30, −.54
No. languages	−.43, −.44	−.48, −.52	−.33, −.56
First language, % speakers	−.43, −.46	−.48, −.52	−.25, −.60
First language, primacy ratio	−.42, −.43	−.46, −.53	−.21, −.47
Communications	−.45, −.46	−.47, −.51	−.53, −.74
Newspaper circulation	−.41, −.48	−.48, −.53	−.15, −.49
Elite social mobilization	−.45, −.45	−.49, −.52	−.17, −.48
Mass social mobilization	−.39, −.46	−.40, −.47	−.38, −.53
Electoral participation	−.44, −.45	−.47, −.49	−.57, −.77
Party dominance	−.18, −.17	−.34, −.33	.48, .09

Bibliography

Africa Independent: A Study of Political Developments. 1972. Keesing's Research Report no. 6. New York: Charles Scribner's Sons.

Alexandre, Pierre. 1970. "Chiefs, Commandants and Clerks: Their Relationship from Conquest to Decolonisation in French West Africa." In Michael Crowder and Obaro Ikime, eds., *West African Chiefs*. New York: Africana Publishing.

Allen, Christopher. 1978. "Sierra Leone." In John Dunn, ed., *West African States: Failure and Promise*. Cambridge, England: Cambridge University Press.

Almond, Gabriel A., and Sidney Verba. 1963. *The Civic Culture*. Princeton: Princeton University Press.

Althusser, Louis. 1969. *For Marx*. London: Penguin Press.

———. 1971. *Lenin and Philosophy and Other Essays*. New York: Monthly Review Press.

Amin, Samir. 1972. "Underdevelopment and Dependence in Black Africa: Origins and Contemporary Forms." *Journal of Modern African Studies* 10, no. 4 (December): 503–524.

Amon d'Aby, F. J. 1951. *La Côte d'Ivoire dans la cité africaine*. Paris: Larose.

Andreski, Stanislav. 1968. *The African Predicament: A Study in the Pathology of Modernisation*. London: Michael Joseph.

Apter, David E. 1963. *Ghana in Transition*. New York: Atheneum.

———. 1965. *The Politics of Modernization*. Chicago: University of Chicago Press.

———. 1967. *The Political Kingdom in Uganda*. Princeton: Princeton University Press.

Austin, Dennis. 1958. "Institutional History of Gold Coast/Ghana." In Hansard Society for Parliamentary Government, *What Are the Prob-*

lems of Parliamentary Government in West Africa? Report of a conference held by the Hansard Society for Parliamentary Government, September 1957. Oxford.

———. 1964. "Elections in an African Rural Area." In William John
Hanna, ed., *Independent Black Africa*. Chicago: Rand McNally.

———. 1966. *Politics in Ghana, 1946–1960*. London: Oxford University
Press.

———. 1970. *Elections in Ghana 1969*. New Delhi: Indian Council for
Africa.

———. 1975. "Introduction." In Dennis Austin and Robin Luckham, eds.,
Politicians and Soldiers in Ghana, 1966–1972. London: Frank Cass.

Austin, Dennis, and William Tordoff. 1972. "The Newly Independent
States." In Geraint Parry, ed., *Participation in Politics*. Manchester:
University of Manchester Press.

Ballard, John A. 1966. "Four Equatorial States." In Gwendolen M. Carter,
ed., *National Unity and Regionalism in Eight African States*. Ithaca,
N.Y.: Cornell University Press.

Banks, Arthur S. 1971. *Cross-Polity Time-Series Data*. Cambridge: MIT
Press.

Barkan, Joel D. 1979a. "Comparing Politics and Public Policy in Kenya and
Tanzania." In Joel D. Barkan and John J. Okumu, eds., *Politics and
Public Policy in Kenya and Tanzania*. New York: Frederick A. Prae-
ger.

———. 1979b. "Legislators, Elections, and Political Linkage." In Joel D.
Barkan and John H. Okumu, eds., *Politics and Public Policy in Kenya
and Tanzania*. New York: Frederick A. Praeger.

Barkan, Joel D., and John J. Okumu. 1978. "'Semi-Competitive' Elections,
Clientelism, and Political Recruitment in a No-Party State: The Kenyan Experience." In Guy Hermet, Richard Rose, and Alain Rouquié,
eds., *Elections without Choice*. New York: John Wiley.

Barker, Jonathan S., and John S. Saul. 1974. "The Tanzania Elections in
Post-Arusha Perspective." In University of Dar es Salaam Election
Study Committee, *Socialism and Participation: Tanzania's 1970 National Elections*. Dar es Salaam: Tanzania Publishing House.
tional Elections. Dar es Salaam: Tanzania Publishing House.

Barrows, Walter L. 1976. "Ethnic Diversity and Political Instability in
Black Africa." *Comparative Political Studies* 9, no. 2 (July): 139–170.

Bates, Margaret L. 1962. "Tanganyika." In Gwendolen M. Carter, ed.,
African One-Party States. Ithaca, N.Y.: Cornell University Press.

Bayart, Jean-François. 1978. "Clientelism, Elections, and Systems of In-
equality and Domination in Cameroun." In Guy Hermet, Richard
Rose, and Alain Rouquié, eds., *Elections without Choice*. New York:
John Wiley.

Bebler, Anton. 1973. *Military Rule in Africa: Dahomey, Ghana, Sierra
Leone, and Mali*. New York: Frederick A. Praeger.

Beer, Samuel H., and Adam B. Ulam, eds. 1962. *Patterns of Government: The Major Political Systems of Europe*. Second edition. New York: Random House.

Bendix, Reinhard. 1964. *Nation-Building and Citizenship*. New York: John Wiley and Sons.

———. 1967. "Tradition and Modernity Reconsidered." *Comparative Studies in Society and History* 9, no. 3 (April): 292–346.

Bennett, George, and Carl Rosberg. 1961. *The Kenyatta Election: Kenya 1960–1961*. London: Oxford University Press.

Bienen, Henry. 1967. *Tanzania: Party Transformation and Economic Development*. Princeton: Princeton University Press.

———. 1968. *The Military Intervenes: Case Studies in Political Development*. New York: Sage Publications.

———. 1970. "One-Party Systems in Africa." In Samuel P. Huntington and Clement H. Moore, eds., *Authoritarian Politics in Modern Society*. New York: Basic Books.

———. 1971. "Political Parties and Political Machines in Africa." In Michael F. Lofchie, ed., *The State of the Nations: Constraints On Development in Independent Africa*. Berkeley and Los Angeles: University of California Press.

———. 1974. *Kenya: The Politics of Participation and Control*. Princeton: Princeton University Press.

———. 1976. "Transition from Military Rule: The Case of Western State Nigeria." In Henry Bienen and David Morell, eds., *Political Participation under Military Regimes*, Sage Contemporary Social Science Issues, no. 26. Beverly Hills: Sage Publications.

———. 1978. *Armies and Parties in Africa*. New York and London: Africana Publishing.

Bienen, Henry, and David Morell, eds. 1976. *Political Participation under Military Regimes*. Sage Contemporary Social Science Issues, no. 26. Beverly Hills: Sage Publications.

Binder, Leonard, et al. 1971. *Crises and Sequences in Political Development*. Princeton: Princeton University Press.

Birmingham, W. B., and G. Jahoda. 1955. "A Pre-Election Survey in a Semi-Literate Society." *Public Opinion Quarterly* 19, no. 2 (Summer): 140–152.

Black, C. E. 1967. *The Dynamics of Modernization*. New York: Harper and Row.

Blake, Robert. 1967. *Disraeli*. New York: St. Martin's Press.

Boggs, Carl, Jr. 1971. "Gramsci's 'Prison Notebooks,'" Parts 1 and 2. *Socialist Revolution* 2, no. 5 (September–October): 79–118; 2, no. 6 (November– December): 29–56.

Bowles, Samuel, and Herbert Gintis. 1980. "The Crisis of Liberal Democratic Capitalism: The Case of the United States." Amherst, Mass.: University of Massachusetts (mimeo.).

Bretton, Henry L. 1966. *The Rise and Fall of Kwame Nkrumah*. New York: Praeger Publishers.

Brokensha, David. 1970. "An African Party at the Grassroots: The Convention People's Party in Larteh Town in 1960's." In Wilfred Cartey and Martin Kilson, eds., *The Africa Reader: Colonial Africa*. New York: Vintage Books.

Buell, Raymond Leslie. 1965. *The Native Problem in Africa*. London: Frank Cass.

Burns, Sir Alan. 1966. *Parliament as an Export*. London: George Allen and Unwin.

Burrowes, Robert. 1972. "Theory Si, Data No! A Decade of Cross-National Research." *World Politics* 25, no. 1 (October): 120–144.

Butler, David, and Austin Ranney. 1978. *Referendums*. Washington, D.C.: American Enterprise Institute for Public Policy Research.

Byrd, Robert O. 1963. "Characteristics of Candidates for Election in a Country approaching Independence: The Case of Uganda." *Midwest Journal of Political Science* 7 (February): 1–27.

Campbell, Bonnie. 1978. "Ivory Coast." In John Dunn, ed., *West African States: Failure and Promise*. Cambridge, England: Cambridge University Press.

Campbell, Peter. 1965. *French Electoral Systems and Elections since 1789*. Hamden, Conn.: Archon Books.

Cardoso, Fernando Henrique. 1973. "Associated Dependent Development: Theoretical and Practical Implications." In Alfred Stepan, ed., *Authoritarian Brazil: Origins, Policies, and Future*. New Haven: Yale University Press.

———. 1977. "The Consumption of Dependency Theory in the United States." *Latin American Research Review* 12, no. 3, pp. 7–24.

———. 1979. "On the Characterization of Authoritarian Regimes in Latin America." In David Collier, ed., *The New Authoritarianism in Latin America*. Princeton: Princeton University Press.

Cardoso, Fernando Henrique, and Enzo Faletto. 1969. *Dependencia y desarrollo en América Latina*. Mexico City: Siglo Veintiuno Editores. (Also published in English in 1979 as *Dependency and Development in Latin America*, Berkeley and Los Angeles: University of California Press.)

Carter, Gwendolen M., ed. 1962. *African One-Party States*. Ithaca, N.Y.: Cornell University Press.

———. 1963. *Five African States*. Ithaca, N.Y.: Cornell University Press.

———. 1966. *National Unity and Regionalism in Eight African States*. Ithaca, N.Y.: Cornell University Press.

Cartey, Wilfred, and Martin Kilson, eds. 1970. *The Africa Reader: Colonial Africa*. New York: Vintage Books.

Cartwright, John. 1970. *Politics in Sierra Leone*. Toronto and Buffalo: University of Toronto Press.

————. 1978. *Political Leadership in Sierra Leone*. London: Croom Helm.

Cavarozzi, Marcelo José. 1975. "The Government and the Bourgeoisie in Chile: 1938–1964." Doctoral dissertation, University of California, Berkeley.

Clark, G. Kitson. 1965. *The Making of Victorian England*. London: Methuen.

Clegg, E. M. 1957. *The Franchise in Rhodesia and Nyasaland*. Royal Institute of International Affairs, Department of Race Relations, Occasional Paper no. 1. Oxford.

Cliffe, Lionel. 1967. *One Party Democracy: The 1965 Tanzania General Elections*. Nairobi: East African Publishing House.

Clignet, Remi P., and Philip J. Foster. 1964. "French and British Colonial Education in Africa." *Comparative Education Review* 8 (October): 191–198.

Cohen, Sir Andrew. 1959. *British Policy in Changing Africa*. Evanston: Northwestern University Press.

Cohen, Dennis L. 1970. "The Convention People's Party of Ghana: Representational or Solidarity Party?" *Revue Canadienne des Etudes Africaines* 4, no. 2 (Spring): 173–194.

Coleman, James S. 1960. "Conclusion: The Political Systems of the Developing Areas." In Gabriel A. Almond and James S. Coleman, eds., *The Politics of the Developing Areas*. Princeton: Princeton University Press.

————. 1964a. "Economic Growth and Political Reorientation." In Melville J. Herskovits and Mitchell Harwitz, eds., *Economic Transition in Africa*. Evanston: Northwestern University Press.

————. 1964b. "Nationalism in Tropical Africa." In William John Hanna, ed., *Independent Black Africa*. Chicago: Rand McNally.

————. 1965. *Nigeria: Background to Nationalism*. Berkeley and Los Angeles: University of California Press.

Coleman, James S., and Carl G. Rosberg, Jr., eds. 1964. *Political Parties and National Integration in Tropical Africa*. Berkeley and Los Angeles: University of California Press.

Collier, David, and Ruth Berins Collier. 1977. "Who Does What, to Whom, and How: Toward a Comparative Analysis of Latin American Corporatism." In James M. Malloy, ed., *Authoritarianism and Corporatism in Latin America*. Pittsburgh: University of Pittsburgh Press.

Collier, David, and Richard E. Messick. 1975. "Prerequisites versus Diffusion: Testing Alternative Explanations of Social Security Adoption." *American Political Science Review* 69, no. 4 (December): 1299–1315.

Collier, Ruth Berins. 1978. "Parties, Coups and Authoritarian Rule: Patterns of Political Change in Tropical Africa." *Comparative Political Studies* 11, no. 1 (April): 62–93.

————. Forthcoming. "Popular Sector Incorporation and Regime Evolution in Brazil and Mexico." In Sylvia Ann Hewlett and Richard S.

Weinert, eds., *Brazil and Mexico: Patterns in Late Development*. Philadelphia: Institute for the Study of Human Issues.

Collier, Ruth Berins, and David Collier. 1979. "Inducements versus Constraints: Disaggregating Corporatism." *American Political Science Review* 73, no. 4 (December): 967–986.

Congressional Quarterly Weekly Report. (Various issues.)

Corley, T. A. B. 1961. *Democratic Despot: A Life of Napoleon III*. London: Barrie and Rockliff.

Cornevin, Robert. 1969. *Histoire du Togo*. Paris: Editions Berger-Levrault.

Corradi, Juan Eugenio. 1978. "The Politics of Silence: Discourse, Text, and Social Conflict in South America." *Radical History Review* 18, no. 1 (Fall): 38–57.

Cowan, L. Gray. 1958. *Local Government in West Africa*. New York: Columbia University Press.

———. 1962. "Guinea." In Gwendolen M. Carter, ed., *African One-Party States*. Ithaca, N. Y.: Cornell University Press.

Crowder, Michael. 1964. "Indirect Rule—French and British Style." *Africa* 34, no. 3 (July): 197–205.

———. 1965. "Independence as a Goal in French West African Politics: 1944–1960." In William Lewis, ed., *French-Speaking Africa*. New York: Walker and Company.

———. 1968. *West Africa under Colonial Rule*. Evanston: Northwestern University Press.

———. 1970. "Colonial Rule in West Africa: Factor for Division or Unity?" In Marion E. Doro and Newell M. Stultz, eds., *Governing in Black Africa*. Englewood Cliffs, N.J.: Prentice-Hall.

Crowder, Michael, and Obaro Ikime. 1970. Introduction to Michael Crowder and Obaro Ikime, eds., *West African Chiefs*. New York: Africana Publishing.

Dahl, Robert A. 1971. *Polyarchy: Participation and Opposition*. New Haven: Yale University Press.

Davis, Charles L. 1976. "The Mobilization of Public Support for an Authoritarian Regime: The Case of the Lower Class in Mexico City." *American Journal of Political Science* 20 (November): 653–670.

Decalo, Samuel. 1973. "Military Coups and Military Regimes in Africa." *Journal of Modern African Studies* 11, no. 1 (March): 105–128.

———. 1975. *African Historical Dictionary: Dahomey*. Metuchen, N.J.: Scarecrow Press.

———. 1976a. *African Historical Dictionary: Togo*. Metuchen, N.J.: Scarecrow Press.

———. 1976b. *Coups and Army Rule in Africa: Studies in Military Style*. New Haven: Yale University Press.

———. 1977. *African Historical Dictionary: Chad*. Metuchen, N.J.: Scarecrow Press.

Delavignette, Robert L. 1970. "French Colonial Policy in Black Africa, 1945 to 1960." In L. H. Gann and Peter Duignan, eds., *Colonialism in Africa 1870–1960. Vol 2. The History and Politics of Colonialism 1914–1960.* Cambridge, England: Cambridge University Press.

de Lusignan, Guy. 1969. *French-Speaking Africa since Independence.* New York: Frederick A. Praeger.

Deschamps, Hubert. 1970. "France in Black Africa and Madagascar between 1920 and 1945." In L. H. Gann and Peter Duignan, eds., *Colonialism in Africa 1870–1960. Vol. 2. The History and Politics of Colonialism 1914–1960.* Cambridge, England: Cambridge University Press.

De Schweinitz, Karl, Jr. 1970. "Growth, Development, and Political Modernization." *World Politics* 22 (July): 518–540.

Deutsch, Karl W. 1961. "Social Mobilization and Political Development." *American Political Science Review* 55, no. 3 (September): 493–514.

Dowse, Robert E. 1969. "The Military and Political Development." In Colin Leys, ed., *Politics and Change in Developing Countries.* Cambridge, England: Cambridge University Press.

Dumont, René. 1969. *False Start in Africa.* Translated by Phillis Nauts Ott. Second edition. New York: Frederick A. Praeger.

Duvall, Raymond, and Mary Welfling. 1973. "Determinants of Political Institutionalization in Black Africa: A Quasi-Experimental Analysis." *Comparative Political Studies* 5 (January): 387–417.

Duverger, Maurice. 1951. *Political Parties.* New York: John Wiley.

Easton, David. 1965. *A Systems Analysis of Political Life.* New York: John Wiley.

Eckstein, Susan, and Peter Evans. 1978. "Revolution as Cataclysm and Coup: Political Transformation and Economic Development in Mexico and Brazil." *Comparative Studies in Sociology* 1: 129–155.

Edelman, Murray. 1967. *The Symbolic Uses of Politics.* Urbana: University of Illinois Press.

———. 1971. *Politics as Symbolic Action.* Chicago: Markham Publishing.

Eisenstadt, S. N. 1964. "Modernization and Conditions of Sustained Growth." *World Politics* 16 (July): 576–594.

———. 1966. *Modernization: Protest and Change.* Englewood Cliffs, N.J.: Prentice-Hall.

Elias, T. O. 1962. *Ghana and Sierra Leone: The Development of Their Laws and Constitutions.* London: Stevens and Sons.

———. 1967. *Nigeria: The Development of Its Laws and Constitution.* London: Stevens and Sons.

Emerson, Rupert. 1960. *From Empire to Nation.* Boston: Beacon Press.

———. 1966. "Paradoxes of Asian Nationalism." In Immanuel Wallerstein, ed., *Social Change: The Colonial Situation.* New York: John Wiley and Sons.

Engels, Friedrich. 1959. "The Origin of the Family, Private Property and the State." In Lewis S. Feuer, ed., *Basic Writings on Politics and Philosophy: Karl Marx and Friedrich Engels*. Garden City, N.Y.: Anchor Books.

Feit, E. 1968. "Military Coups and Political Development: Some Lessons from Ghana and Nigeria." *World Politics* 20 (January): 179–193.

Finer, S. E. 1962. *The Man on Horseback: The Role of the Military in Politics*. New York: Frederick A. Praeger.

———. 1967. "The One-Party Regimes in Africa: Reconsiderations." *Government and Opposition* 2 (July–October): 491–509.

First, Ruth. 1972. *Power in Africa*. Middlesex, England: Penguin Books.

Fisher, Humphrey J. 1969. "Elections and Coups in Sierra Leone, 1967." *Journal of Modern African Studies* 7, no. 4 (December): 611–636.

Fitch, Bob, and Mary Oppenheimer. 1966. *Ghana: End of an Illusion*. New York: Monthly Review Press.

Flanigan, William, and Edwin Fogelman. 1971. "Patterns of Democratic Development: An Historical Comparative Analysis." In John V. Gillespie and Betty A. Nesvold, eds., *Macro-Quantitative Analysis*. Beverly Hills: Sage Publications.

Foltz, William J. 1965. *From French West Africa to the Mali Federation*. New Haven: Yale University Press.

France, Ambassade de, Service de Presse et d'Information. 1961. *The Republic of the Congo*. New York.

Frank, Thomas M. 1960. *Race and Nationalism: The Struggle for Power in Rhodesia–Nyasaland*. New York: Fordham University Press.

French West Africa. 1925–1945. *Journal Officiel de l'Afrique Occidentale Française*.

Gailey, Harry A. 1964. *A History of the Gambia*. London: Routledge and Kegan Paul.

Gamson, William A. 1968. *Power and Discontent*. Homewood, Ill.: Dorsey Press.

Gann, L. H., and Peter Duignan, eds. 1970. *Colonialism in Africa 1870–1960*. Vol. 2. *The History and Politics of Colonialism 1914–1960*. Cambridge, England: Cambridge University Press.

Gardinier, David E. 1963. *Cameroon: United Nations Challenge to French Policy*. London: Institute of Race Relations, Oxford University Press.

Gauze, Rene. 1973. *The Politics of Congo–Brazzaville*. Stanford: Hoover Institution Press.

Gellar, Sheldon. 1973. "State-Building and Nation-Building in West Africa." In S. N. Eisenstadt and Stein Rokkan, eds., *Building States and Nations*. Beverly Hills: Sage Publications.

Geras, Norman. 1978. "Althusser's Marxism: An Assessment." In *Western Marxism: A Critical Reader*. London: Verso.

Gerschenkron, Alexander. 1966. *Economic Backwardness in Historical Perspective*. Cambridge, Mass.: Belknap Press.

Gerteiny, Alfred G. 1967. *Mauritania.* New York: Frederick A. Praeger.

Gertzel, Cherry. 1970. *The Politics of Independent Kenya 1963–68.* Nairobi: East Africa Publishing House.

Ginsberg, Benjamin, and Robert Weissberg, 1978. "Elections as Legitimizing Institutions." In Jeff Fishel, ed., *Parties and Elections in an Anti-Party Age: American Politics and the Crisis of Confidence.* Bloomington: Indiana University Press.

Glass, D. V. 1950. "Gregory King's Estimate of the Population of England and Wales, 1695." *Population Studies* 3 (March): 338–374.

Gonidec, P. F. 1971. *La République du Tchad.* Paris: Editions Berger-Levrault.

Gramsci, Antonio. 1971. *Selections from the Prison Notebooks.* New York: International Publishers.

Great Britain, Central Office of Information. 1964. *Constitutional Development in the Commonwealth.* Reference Pamphlet no. 5. London: Her Majesty's Stationery Office.

Great Britain, Colonial Office. (Various dates.) *Colonial Reports: Gambia, 1954 and 1955, 1960 and 1961; Northern Rhodesia, 1959, 1962; Uganda, 1960, 1961.* London: Her Majesty's Stationery Office.

Green, Reginald Herbold. 1971. "Political Independence and the National Economy: An Essay on the Political Economy of Decolonisation." In Christopher Allen and R. W. Johnson, eds., *African Perspectives.* Cambridge, England: Cambridge University Press.

Green, Reginald Herbold, and Ann Seidman. 1968. *Unity or Poverty? The Economics of Pan-Africanism.* Baltimore: Penguin Books.

Grew, Raymond, ed. 1978. *Crises of Political Development in Europe and the United States.* Princeton: Princeton University Press.

Guerard, Albert. 1943. *Napoleon III.* Cambridge, Mass.: Harvard University Press.

Gupta, Anirudha. 1965–1966. "The Zambian National Assembly: Study of an African Legislature." *Parliamentary Affairs* 19 (Winter): 48–55.

Gurr, Ted Robert. 1972. *Polimetrics: An Introduction to Quantitative Macropolitics.* Englewood Cliffs, N.J.: Prentice-Hall.

Gutteridge, William F. 1969. *The Military in African Politics.* London: Methuen.

Habermas, Jurgen. 1975. *Legitimation Crisis.* Boston: Beacon Press.

Hailey, Lord Malcolm. 1957. *An African Survey Revised 1956.* London: Oxford University Press.

Hakes, Jay E. 1970. "Election Year Politics in Kenya." *Current History* 58, no. 343 (March): 154–159, 177.

———. 1973. *Weak Parliaments and Military Coups in Africa: A Study in Regime Instability.* Sage Research Papers in the Social Sciences, Comparative Legislative Studies Series, vol. l, no. 90–004. Beverly Hills: Sage Publications.

Hall, Bud, and Steve Lucas. 1974. "The Election as an Exercise in Political Communication." In University of Dar es Salaam, Election Study Committee, *Socialism and Participation: Tanzania's 1970 National Elections.* Dar es Salaam: Tanzania Publishing House.

Hall, Richard. 1965. *Zambia.* London: Pall Mall Press.

Hamilton, William B., ed. 1964. *The Transfer of Institutions.* Durham, N.C.: Duke University Press.

Hanham, H. J. 1959. *Elections and Party Management: Politics in the Time of Disraeli and Gladstone.* London: Logmans, Green.

Hansard Society for Parliamentary Government 1958. *What Are the Problems of Parliamentary Government in West Africa?* Report of a conference held by the Hansard Society for Parliamentary Government, September 1957. Oxford.

Harris, Belle. 1967. "The Electoral System." In Lionel Cliffe, ed., *One Party Democracy: The 1965 Tanzania General Elections.* Nairobi: East African Publishing House.

Hayward, Fred M. 1973. "Political Participation and Its Role in Development: Some Observations Drawn from the African Context." *Journal of Developing Areas* 7, no. 4 (July): 591–612.

Heeger, Gerald. 1974. *The Politics of Underdevelopment.* New York: St. Martin's Press.

Hermet, Guy. 1978. "State-Controlled Elections: A Framework." In Guy Hermet, Richard Rose, and Alain Rouquié, eds., *Elections without Choice.* New York: John Wiley.

Hill, Frances. 1974. "Elections in the Local Context." In University of Dar es Salaam, Election Study Committee, *Socialism and Participation: Tanzania's 1970 National Elections.* Dar es Salaam: Tanzania Publishing House.

Hodgkin, Thomas. 1957. *Nationalism in Colonial Africa.* New York: New York University Press.

———. 1961. *African Political Parties.* Middlesex, England: Penguin Books.

Hooker, James R. 1971. "Malawi's General Election: The People's Will Expressed without Benefit of Polls." *American University Fieldstaff Reports,* Central and Southern African series 15, no. 5: 1–6.

Horowitz, Irving Louis. 1979. "The Norm of Illegitimacy—Ten Years Later." In Bogdan Denitch, ed., *Legitimation of Regimes.* Beverly Hills: Sage Publications.

Hoselitz, Bert F. 1964. "Advanced and Underdeveloped Countries: A Study in Development Contrasts." In William B. Hamilton, ed., *The Transfer of Institutions.* Durham, N.C.: Duke University Press.

Huntington, Samuel P. 1969. *Political Order in Changing Societies.* New Haven: Yale University Press.

———. 1970. "Social and Institutional Dynamics of One-Party Systems."

In Samuel P. Huntington and Clement H. Moore, eds., *Authoritarian Politics in Modern Society*. New York: Basic Books.

Huntington, Samuel P., and Joan M. Nelson. 1976. *No Easy Choice: Political Participation in Developing Countries*. Cambridge, Mass.: Harvard University Press.

Hyden, Goran, and Colin Leys. 1972. "Elections and Politics in Single-Party Systems: The Case of Kenya and Tanzania." *British Journal of Political Science* 2, no. 4 (October): 389–420.

Jackman, Robert W. 1976. "Politicians in Uniform: Military Governments and Social Change in the Third World." *American Political Science Review* 70, no. 4 (December): 1078–1097.

———. 1978. "The Predictability of Coups d'Etat: A Model with African Data." *American Political Science Review* 72, no. 4 (December): 1262–1275.

Jennings, Sir William Ivor. 1958. *Problems of the New Commonwealth*. Durham, N.C.: Duke University Press.

Johnson, John J. 1964. *The Military and Society in Latin America*. Stanford: Stanford University Press.

Johnson, R. W. 1978. "Guinea." In John Dunn, ed., *West African States: Failure and Promise*. Cambridge, England: Cambridge University Press.

Johnson, Willard. 1970. *The Cameroon Federation: Political Integration in a Fragmentary Society*. Princeton: Princeton University Press.

Joll, James. 1978. *Antonio Gramsci*. New York: Penguin Books.

Jones, Griff. 1964. *Britain and Nyasaland*. London: George Allen and Unwin.

Jordan, Robert S. 1969. *Government and Power in West Africa*. London: Faber and Faber.

Kalck, Pierre. 1971. *Central African Republic: A Failure in De-Colonisation*. London: Pall Mall Press.

Kamarck, Andrew M. 1971. *The Economics of African Development*. Revised edition. New York: Frederick A. Praeger.

Kasfir, Nelson. 1976a. "Civilian Participation under Military Rule in Uganda and Sudan." In Henry Bienen and David Morell, eds., *Political Participation under Military Regimes*, Sage Contemporary Social Science Issues, no. 26. Beverly Hills: Sage Publications.

———. 1976b. *The Shrinking Political Arena: Participation and Ethnicity in African Politics, with a Case Study of Uganda*. Berkeley and Los Angeles: University of California Press.

Katznelson, Ira, and Mark Kesselman. 1975. *The Politics of Power: A Critical Introduction to American Government*. New York: Harcourt Brace Jovanovich.

Kaufman, Robert R. 1977. "Mexico and Latin American Authoritarianism." In José Luis Reyna and Richard S. Weinert, eds., *Author-

itarianism in Mexico. Philadelphia: Institute for the Study of Human Issues.

Keehn, Norman H. 1974. "Building Authority: A Return to Fundamentals." *World Politics* 26 (April): 331–352.

Kenworthy, Eldon. 1970. "Coalitions in the Political Development of Latin America." In Sven Groennings et al., eds., *The Study of Coalition Behavior.* New York: Holt, Rinehart and Winston.

Kenya. (N.d.) *Annual Report of the National Assembly for the Years 1965 and 1966.* Nairobi: The Government Printer.

———. (N.d.) *Annual Report of the National Assembly for the Year 1967.* Nairobi: The Government Printer.

———, Constitution of. 1963. Kenya Gazette Supplement no. 105. Nairobi: The Government Printer.

Kenya National Assembly. (Various dates.) *Official Reports.* Vol. XIV, 1968; Vol. XVII, Part I, 1969; Vol. XIX, 1970; Vol. XXIV, 1971. Nairobi: The Government Printer.

Kenya National Assembly, House of Representatives. (Various dates.) *Official Reports.* Vol. III, Part I, 1964; Vol. VII, 1965; Vol. IX, Part II, 1966. Nairobi: The Government Printer.

Kenya National Assembly, Senate. (Various dates.) *Official Reports.* Vol. I, 1963, Vol. III, Part I, 1964; Vol. IV, Part I, 1965. Nairobi: The Government Printer.

Kilson, Martin. 1963. "Authoritarian and Single-Party Tendencies in African Politics." *World Politics* 15, no. 2 (January): 262–294.

———. 1966a. *Political Change in a West African State: A Study of the Modernization Process in Sierra Leone.* Cambridge, Mass.: Harvard University Press.

———.1966b. "Nationalism and Social Classes in British West Africa." In Immanuel Wallerstein, ed., *Social Change: The Colonial Situation.* New York: John Wiley and Sons.

———. 1970. "The Emergent Elites of Black Africa, 1900 to 1960." In L. H. Gann and Peter Duignan, eds., *Colonialism in Africa 1870–1960.* Vol. 2. *The History and Politics of Colonialism, 1914–1960.* Cambridge, England: Cambridge University Press.

Kitchen, Helen, ed. 1964. *A Handbook of African Affairs.* New York: Frederick A. Praeger.

Kjekshus, Helge. 1974. "Socialism and Participation: Some Concluding Remarks." In University of Dar es Salaam, Election Study Committee, *Socialism and Participation: Tanzania's 1970 National Elections.* Dar es Salaam: Tanzania Publishing House.

Kornhauser, William. 1959. *Politics of Mass Society.* New York: Free Press.

Kraus, Jon. 1965. "Ghana's New 'Corporate Parliament.'" *African Report* 10, no. 8 (August): 6–11.

———. 1970. "Arms and Politics in Ghana." In Claude E. Welch, Jr., ed., *Soldier and State in Africa: A Comparative Analysis of Military Intervention and Political Change.* Evanston: Northwestern University Press.

———. 1971. "Political Change, Conflict, and Development in Ghana." In Philip Foster and Aristide R. Zolberg, eds., *Ghana and the Ivory Coast.* Chicago: University of Chicago Press.

Laclau, Ernesto. 1977. *Politics and Ideology in Marxist Theory.* London: New Left Books.

Lambert, Jacques. 1967. *Latin America: Social Structures and Political Institutions.* Berkeley and Los Angeles: University of California Press.

Landry, Adolphe. 1945. *Traité de Démographie.* Paris: Payot.

Lasswell, Harold D., and Abraham Kaplan. 1950. *Power and Society: A Framework for Political Inquiry.* New Haven: Yale University Press.

Lee, J. M. 1969. *African Armies and Civil Order.* New York: Frederick A. Praeger.

Legum, Colin, ed. 1966. *Africa: A Handbook to the Continent.* New York: Frederick A. Praeger.

———. 1969. *Africa Handbook.* Middlesex, England: Penguin Books.

Lemarchand, René. 1964. "Congo (Leopoldville)." In James S. Coleman and Carl G. Rosberg, Jr., eds., *Political Parties and National Integration in Tropical Africa.* Berkeley and Los Angeles: University of California Press.

———. 1966. "Political Instability in Africa: The Case of Rwanda and Burundi." *Civilisations* 16, no. 3: 307–337.

———. 1970a. *Rwanda and Burundi.* New York: Frederick A. Praeger.

———. 1970b. "The Coup in Rwanda." In Robert I. Rotberg and Ali Mazrui, eds., *Protest and Power in Black Africa.* New York: Oxford University Press.

Lerner, Daniel. 1958. *The Passing of Traditional Society: Modernizing the Middle East.* New York: Free Press.

———. 1964. "The Transformation of Institutions." In William B. Hamilton, ed., *The Transfer of Institutions.* Durham, N.C.: Duke University Press.

Le Vine, Victor. 1964. *The Cameroons: From Mandate to Independence.* Berkeley and Los Angeles: University of California Press.

———. 1970. "The Coups in Upper Volta, Dahomey, and the Central African Republic." In Robert I. Rotberg and Ali Mazrui, eds., *Protest and Power in Black Africa.* New York: Oxford University Press.

Le Vine, Victor, and Roger P. Nye. 1974. *African Historical Dictionary: Cameroon.* Metuchen, N.J.: Scarecrow Press.

Lewis, W. Arthur. 1965. *Politics in West Africa.* Toronto: Oxford University Press.

Leys, Colin, ed. 1969. *Politics and Change in Developing Countries.* Cambridge, England: Cambridge Univerisity Press.

———. 1974. *Underdevelopment in Kenya.* Berkeley and Los Angeles: University of California Press.

———. 1978. "Capital Accumulation, Class Formation, and Dependency—The Significance of the Kenyan Case." In Ralph Miliband, ed., *The Socialist Register 1978.* London: Merlin Press.

Linz, Juan J. 1964. "An Authoritarian Regime: Spain." In Erik Allardt and Yrjo Littunen, eds., *Transactions of the Westermarck Society.* Vol. X, *Cleavages, Ideologies, and Party Systems.* Helsinki: Academic Bookstore.

———. 1972. "Notes Toward a Typology of Authoritarian Regimes." Paper delivered at the annual meeting of the American Political Science Association, Washington, D.C.

———. 1975. "Totalitarian and Authoritarian Regimes." In Fred I. Greenstein and Nelson Polsby, eds., *The Handbook of Political Science,* Vol. 3. Reading, Mass.: Addison Wesley.

Lipset, S. M. 1959a. *Political Man: The Social Bases of Politics.* Garden City, N.Y.: Doubleday.

———. 1959b. "Some Social Requisites of Democracy." *American Political Science Review* 53 (March): 69–105.

Lofchie, Michael F. 1970. "Representative Government, Bureaucracy, and Political Development: The African Case." In Marion E. Doro and Newell M. Stultz, eds., *Governing in Black Africa.* Englewood Cliffs, N. J.: Prentice-Hall.

———. 1971a. "Political Constraints on African Development." In Michael F. Lofchie, ed., *The State of the Nations: Constraints on Development in Independent Africa.* Berkeley and Los Angeles: University of California Press.

———, ed. 1971b. *The State of the Nations: Constraints on Development in Independent Africa.* Berkeley and Los Angeles: University of California Press.

———. 1972. "The Uganda Coup: Class Action by the Military." *Journal of Modern African Studies* 10, no. 1 (May): 19–35.

Low, D. A. 1962. *Political Parties in Uganda 1949 –1962.* University of London, Institute of Commonwealth Studies, Commonwealth Papers VIII. London: Athlone Press.

Lowi, Theodore J. 1976. *American Government: Incomplete Conquest.* Hinsdale, Ill.: Dreyden Press.

McFarland, Daniel Miles. 1978. *African Historical Dictionary: Upper Volta.* Metuchen, N.J.: Scarecrow Press.

Mackenzie, W. J. M. 1957. "The Export of Electoral Systems." *Political Studies* 5, no. 3 (October): 249–257.

Mackenzie, W. J. M., and Kenneth Robinson, eds. 1960. *Five Elections in Africa.* Oxford: Clarendon Press.

McKinlay, R. D., and A. S. Cohan. 1975. "A Comparative Analysis of the Political and Economic Performances of Military and Civilian Regimes: A Cross-National Aggregate Study." *Comparative Politics* 8, no. 1 (October): 1–30.

———. 1976. "Performance and Instability in Military and Nonmilitary Regime Systems." *American Political Science Review* 70, no. 3 (September): 850–864.

Mackintosh, J. P. 1962. "Electoral Trends and the Tendency to a One-Party System in Nigeria." *Journal of Commonwealth Political Studies* 1 (November): 194–210.

McKown, Roberta E. 1975. "Domestic Correlates of Military Intervention in African Politics." *Journal of Political and Military Sociology* 3, no. 2 (Fall): 191–206.

McKown, Roberta E., and Robert E. Kauffman. 1973. "Party System as a Comparative Analytic Concept in African Politics." *Comparative Politics* 6 (October): 47–72.

Mair, Lucy. 1962. *The Nyasaland Election of 1961.* London: Athlone Press.

Maitland-Jones, J. F. 1973. *Politics in Ex-British Africa.* London: Weidenfeld and Nicolson.

Malawi. 1977. *The Malawi Government Directory.* Zomba: The Government Printer.

Mamdani, Mahmood. 1976. *Politics and Class Formation in Uganda.* New York: Monthly Review Press.

Markovitz, Irving Leonard. 1977. *Power and Class in Africa.* Englewood Cliffs, N. J.: Prentice-Hall.

Marshall, T. H. 1965. *Class, Citizenship, and Social Development.* Garden City, N. Y.: Anchor Books.

Martin, Denis. 1978. "The 1975 Tanzanian Elections: The Disturbing Six Percent." In Guy Hermet, Richard Rose, and Alain Rouquié, eds., *Elections without Choice.* New York: John Wiley.

Martins, Luciano. 1978. "Notes on the State's Role and Its 'Relative Autonomy' in Brazil." Paper presented at the Mexico-Brazil Conference, Columbia University.

Matthews, Ronald. 1966. *African Powder Keg: Revolt and Dissent in Six Emergent Nations.* London: The Bodley Head.

Mazrui, Ali A. 1976. "Soldiers as Traditionalizers: Military Rule and the Re-Africanization of Africa." *World Politics* 28, no. 2 (January): 246–272.

Mbise, Ismael R., and John R. Moris. 1974. "A Study in Contrasts: The Election in Arusha and Meru." In University of Dar es Salaam, Election Study Committee, *Socialism and Participation: Tanzania's 1970 National Elections*. Dar es Salaam: Tanzania Publishing House.

Merrington, John. 1978. "Theory and Practice of Gramsci's Marxism." In *Western Marxism: A Critical Reader*. London: New Left Review Press.

Milbraith, Lester. 1965. *Political Participation*. Chicago: Rand McNally.

Milbraith, Lester, and M. L. Goel. 1977. *Political Participation: How and Why Do People Get Involved in Politics?* Chicago: Rand McNally.

Milcent, Ernest. 1962. "Senegal." In Gwendolen M. Carter, ed., *African One-Party States*. Ithaca, N.Y.: Cornell University Press.

Milnor, A. J. 1969. *Elections and Political Stability*. Boston: Little, Brown.

Moore, Clement H. 1965. "One-Partyism in Mauritania." *Journal of Modern African Studies* 3, no. 3 (October): 409–420.

Moore, D. C. 1961. "The Other Face of Reform." *Victorian Studies* 5 (September): 7–34.

Morgenthau, Ruth Schachter. 1964. *Political Parties in French-Speaking West Africa*. Oxford: Clarendon Press.

———. 1965. "African Elections: Tanzania's Contribution." *Africa Report* 10, no. 12 (December): 12–15.

Morris, H. F., and James S. Reed. 1966. *Uganda: The Development of Its Laws and Constitution*. London: Stevens and Sons.

Morris-Jones, W. H. 1969. "Political Recruitment and Political Development." In Colin Leys, ed., *Politics and Change in Developing Countries*. Cambridge, England: Cambridge University Press.

Morrison, Donald G., Robert C. Mitchell, John N. Paden, and Hugh Michael Stevenson. 1972. *Black Africa: A Comparative Handbook*. New York: Free Press.

Morrison, Donald G., and Hugh Michael Stevenson. 1971. "Political Instability in Independent Black Africa: More Dimensions of Conflict Behavior within Nations." *Journal of Conflict Resolution* 15, no. 3 (September): 347–368.

———. 1972. "Integration and Instability: Patterns of African Political Development." *American Political Science Review* 66 (September): 902–927.

Mulford, David C. 1964a. *The Northern Rhodesia General Election 1962*. Nairobi: Oxford University Press.

———. 1964b. "Northern Rhodesia: Some Observations on the 1964 Elections." *Africa Report* 9, no. 1 (February): 13–17.

———. 1967. *Zambia: Politics of Independence*. London: Oxford University Press.

Mushi, S. S. 1974. "Elections and Political Mobilization in Tanzania." In University of Dar es Salaam, Election Study Committee, *Socialism and Participation: Tanzania's 1970 National Elections*. Dar es Salaam: Tanzania Publishing House.

Myrdal, Gunnar. 1968. *Asian Drama*. New York: Pantheon.

Needler, Martin C. 1968. *Political Development in Latin America*. New York: Random House.

Nelson, Joan M. 1969. *Migrants, Urban Poverty, and Instability in Developing Nations*. Center for International Affairs, Harvard University, Occasional Papers in International Affairs, no. 22. Cambridge, Mass.

Nettl, J. P., and Roland Robertson. 1968. *International Systems and the Modernization of Societies*. New York: Basic Books.

Newbury, C. B. 1964. *The West African Commonwealth*. Durham, N.C.: Duke University Press.

Ng'weno, Hilary. 1974. "The 1974 Elections" (Kenya). *JOE Election Review* (October): 5–10.

Nordlinger, Eric A. 1968. "Political Development: Time Sequences and Rates of Change." *World Politics* 20 (April): 494–520.

———. 1977. *Soldiers in Politics: Military Coups and Governments*. Englewood Cliffs, N.J.: Prentice-Hall.

Nun, José. 1969. *Latin America: The Hegemonic Crisis and the Military Coup*. Berkeley: Institute of International Studies, University of California.

O'Brien, Donal Cruise. 1965. "The Limits of Political Choice in French West Africa: 1956–1960." *Civilisations* 15, no. 2: 206–220.

———. 1978. "Senegal." In John Dunn, ed., *West African States: Failure and Promise*. Cambridge, England: Cambridge University Press.

O'Connell, James. 1970. "The Fragility of Stability: The Fall of the Nigerian Federal Republic." In Robert I. Rotberg and Ali Mazrui, eds., *Protest and Power in Black Africa*. New York: Oxford University Press.

O'Connor, James R. 1973. *The Fiscal Crisis of the State*. New York: St. Martin's Press.

O'Donnell, Guillermo A. 1973. *Modernization and Bureaucratic-Authoritarianism: Studies in South American Politics*. Berkeley: Institute of International Studies, University of California.

———. 1977. "Corporatism and the Question of the State." In James M. Malloy, ed., *Authoritarianism and Corporatism in Latin America*. Pittsburgh: University of Pittsburgh Press.

———. 1978. "Reflections on the Patterns of Change in the Bureaucratic-Authoritarian State." *Latin American Research Review* 13, no. 1: 3–38.

———. 1979. "Tensions in the Bureaucratic-Authoritarian State and the Question of Democracy." In David Collier, ed., *The New Authoritarianism in Latin America*. Princeton: Princeton University Press.

Okumu, John J. 1979. "Party and Party-State Relations." In Joel D. Barkan and John J. Okumu, eds., *Politics and Public Policy in Kenya and Tanzania*. New York: Frederick A. Praeger.

Oppenheim, Felix E. 1975. "The Language of Political Inquiry: Problems of Clarification." In Fred I. Greenstein and Nelson Polsby, eds., *The Handbook of Political Science,* vol. 3. Reading, Mass.: Addison Wesley.

Organski, A. F. K. 1965. *The Stages of Political Development.* New York: Alfred A. Knopf.

Ostheimer, John M. 1973. *Nigerian Politics.* New York: Harper and Row.

Pachai, Bridglal. 1966. "Constitutional Progess in Malawi." *Africa Quarterly* 6, no. 1 (April–June): 4–17.

Palmer, R. R. 1959. *The Age of the Democratic Revolution.* Princeton: Princeton University Press.

———. 1960. *A History of the Modern World.* Second edition, revised with the collaboration of Joel Colton. New York: Alfred A. Knopf.

Panter-Brick, S. F. 1972. "Note sur l'Article de T. Yannopoulos et Denis Martin." *Revue Française de Science Politique* 22, no. 4 (August): 883–886.

Parry, Geraint, ed. 1972a. *Participation in Politics.* Manchester: University of Manchester Press.

———. 1972b. "The Idea of Political Participation." In Geraint Parry, ed., *Participation in Politics.* Manchester: University of Manchester Press.

Peagram, R. C. 1962. "A Report on the General Elections to the National Assembly of Uganda Held on 25th April, 1962." Entebbe: The Government Printer.

Pettman, Jan. 1974. "Zambia's Second Republic—The Establishment of a One-Party State." *Journal of Modern African Studies* 12, no. 2 (June): 231–244.

Pflanze, Otto. 1963. *Bismarck and the Development of Germany.* Princeton: Princeton University Press.

Pike, John G. 1968. *Malawi: A Political and Economic History.* New York: Frederick A. Praeger.

Pinson, Koppel S. 1954. *Modern Germany.* New York: Macmillan.

Polsby, Nelson. 1968. "The Institutionalization of the U.S. House of Representatives." *American Political Science Review* 62, no. 1 (March): 144–168.

Portes, Alejandro. 1977. "Legislatures under Authoritarian Regimes: The Case of Mexico." *Journal of Political and Military Sociology* 5, no. 2 (Fall): 185–201.

Post, Ken. 1964. *The Nigerian Federal Election of 1959.* London: Oxford University Press.

———. 1968a. "The Distribution of Power in West African Political Systems." Paper delivered at the African Studies Center Colloquium on Decision-Making and the Development Process in Africa, University of California, Los Angeles.

————. 1968b. *The New States of West Africa.* Second edition. Baltimore: Penguin Books.

————. 1970. "British Policy and Representative Government in West Africa, 1920 to 1951." In L. H. Gann and Peter Duignan, eds., *Colonialism in Africa 1870–1960.* Vol. 2. *The History and Politics of Colonialism, 1914–1960.* Cambridge, England: Cambridge University Press.

Post, Ken, and George D. Jenkins. 1973. *The Price of Liberty.* Cambridge, England: Cambridge University Press.

Post, Ken, and Michael Vickers. 1973. *Structure and Conflict in Nigeria 1960–1966.* London: Heinemann.

Pratt, Cranford. 1976. *The Critical Phase in Tanzania, 1945–1968: Nyerere and the Emergence of a Socialist Strategy.* Cambridge, England: Cambridge University Press.

Prewitt, Kenneth, and Goran Hyden. 1967. "Voters Look at the Elections." In Lionel Cliffe, ed., *One Party Democracy: the 1965 Tanzania General Elections.* Nairobi: East African Publishing House.

Price, J. H. 1967. *Political Institutions of West Africa.* London: Hutchinson Educational.

Pride, Richard A. 1970. *Origins of Democracy: A Cross-National Study of Mobilization, Party Systems, and Democratic Stability.* Sage Professional Papers, Comparative Politics Series, no. 01–012. Beverly Hills: Sage Publications.

Provizer, Norman. 1977. "The National Electoral Process and State Building: Proposals for New Methods of Election in Uganda." *Comparative Politics* 9, no. 3 (April): 305–326.

Przeworski, Adam. 1975. "Institutionalization of Voting Patterns, or Is Mobilization the Source of Decay?" *American Political Science Review* 69, no. 1 (March): 49–67.

————. 1980. "Some Problems in the Study of the Transition to Democracy." Revised version of a paper presented at the Conference on Prospects for Democracy: Transitions from Authoritarian Rule, Woodrow Wilson Center, Washington, D.C., Sept. 25–26, 1979.

Przeworski, Adam, and Henry Teune. 1970. *The Logic of Comparative Social Inquiry.* New York: John Wiley and Sons.

Purcell, Susan Kaufman. 1973. "Decision-Making in an Authoritarian Regime: Theoretical Implications from a Mexican Case Study." *World Politics* 26 (October): 28–54.

Rae, Douglas W. 1967. *The Political Consequences of Electoral Laws.* New Haven: Yale University Press.

Rasmussen, Thomas. 1969. "Political Competition and One-Party Dominance in Zambia." *Journal of Modern African Studies* 7, no. 3 (1969): 407–424.

Rathbone, Richard. 1973. "Businessmen in Politics: Party Struggle in Ghana, 1949–57." *Journal of Development Studies* 9, no. 3 (April): 391–402.

————. 1978. "Ghana." In John Dunn, ed., *West African States: Failure and Promise*. Cambridge, England: Cambridge University Press.

République de Congo, Ministère de l'Information. *Qu'est-ce que le Congo.* Document no 3. Brazzaville.

Riggs, Fred W. 1971. "Bureaucrats and Political Development: A Paradoxical View." In Jason L. Finkle and Richard W. Gable, eds., *Political Development and Social Change*. New York: John Wiley and Sons.

Robinson, Kenneth. 1955. "Political Development in French West Africa." In Calvin Stillman, ed., *Africa in the Modern World*. Chicago: University of Chicago Press.

Rokkan, Stein. 1970. *Citizens, Elections, Parties*. New York: David McKay Company.

Rokkan, Stein, and Jean Meyriat. 1969. *International Guide to Electoral Statistics*. The Hague: Mouton.

Ronen, Dov. 1975. *Dahomey: Between Tradition and Modernity*. Ithaca, N.Y.: Cornell University Press.

Rose, Richard, and Harve Mossawir. 1967. "Voting and Elections: A Functional Analysis." *Political Studies* 15, no. 2 (June): 173–201.

Ross, Marc Howard. 1970. "Urbanization and Political Participation: The Effect of Increasing Scale in Nairobi." Paper delivered at the annual meeting of the African Studies Association, Boston.

Rotberg, Robert I. 1965. *The Rise of Nationalism in Central Africa: The Making of Malawi and Zambia, 1873–1964*. Cambridge, Mass.: Harvard University Press.

————. 1966. "The Rise of African Nationalism: The Case of East and Central Africa." In Immanuel Wallerstein, ed., *Social Change: The Colonial Situation*. New York: John Wiley and Sons.

Rothchild, Donald, and Michael Rogin. 1966. "Uganda." In Gwendolen M. Carter, ed., *National Unity and Regionalism in Eight African States*. Ithaca, N.Y.: Cornell University Press.

Rowland, H. R. 1967. "Nyasaland General Election of 1964." *Journal of Local Administration Overseas* 3 (October): 227–243.

Rubin, Neville. 1971. *Cameroun: An African Federation*. New York: Frederick A. Praeger.

Rudolph, Lloyd I., and Susanne Hoeber Rudolph. 1967. *The Modernity of Tradition*. Chicago: University of Chicago Press.

Rustow, Dankwart A. 1967. *A World of Nations*. Washington, D.C.: The Brookings Institution.

Sanger, Clyde, and John Nottingham. 1964. "The Kenya General Election of 1963." *Journal of Modern African Studies* 2, no. 1 (March): 1–40.

Sartori, Giovanni. 1968. "Democracy." *International Encyclopedia of the Social Sciences.* New York: Macmillan and Free Press.

———. 1976. *Parties and Party Systems: A Framework for Analysis.* Cambridge, England: Cambridge University Press.

Saul, John S. 1972. "The Nature of Tanzania's Political System: Issues Raised by the 1965 and 1970 Elections." Parts 1 and 2. *Journal of Commonwealth Political Studies* 10, no. 2 (July): 113–129; no. 3 (November): 198–242.

———. 1974. "Elections and the Politics of Socialism in Tanzania, 1965–1970." In University of Dar es Salaam, Election Study Committee, *Socialism and Participation: Tanzania's 1970 National Elections.* Dar es Salaam: Tanzania Publishing House.

Scarritt, James A. 1969. "The Zambian Election—Triumph or Tragedy?" *Africa Today* 15, no. 1 (February–March): 4–5.

Schachter [Morgenthau], R. 1961. "Single-Party Systems in West Africa." *American Political Science Review* 55 (June): 294–307.

Schaffer, B. B. 1965. "The Concept of Preparation: Some Questions about the Transfer of Systems of Government." *World Politics* 18 (October): 42–67.

Schattschneider, E. E. 1942. *Party Government.* New York: Holt, Rinehart and Winston.

Schmitter, Philippe. 1974. "Still the Century of Corporatism?" *Review of Politics* 36, no. 1 (January): 85–131.

———. 1977. "Modes of Interest Intermediation and Models of Societal Change in Western Europe." *Comparative Political Studies* 10, no. 1 (April): 7–38.

———. 1978. "The Impact and Meaning of 'Non-Competitive, Non-Free, and Insignificant' Elections in Authoritarian Portugal, 1933–1974." In Guy Hermet, Richard Rose, and Alain Rouquié, eds., *Elections without Choice.* New York: John Wiley.

Schumacher, Edward J. 1975. *Politics, Bureaucracy, and Rural Development in Senegal.* Berkeley and Los Angeles: University of California Press.

Scott, Ian, and Robert Molteno. 1969. "The Zambian General Elections." *Africa Report* 14, no. 1 (January): 42–47.

———. 1978. "Middle Class Politics in Zambia." *African Affairs* 67, no. 308 (July): 321–334.

Segal, Ronald. 1961. *Political Africa.* London: Stevens and Sons.

Shils, Edward. 1965. *Political Development in the New States.* The Hague: Mouton.

Sigmund, Paul E., ed. 1964. *The Ideologies of the Developing Nations.* New York: Frederick A. Praeger.

Sklar, Richard L. 1963. *Nigerian Political Parties.* Princeton: Princeton University Press.

————. 1979. "The Nature of Class Domination in Africa." *Journal of Modern African Studies* 17, no. 4 (December): 531–552.

Sklar, Richard L., and C. S. Whitaker, Jr. 1966. "The Federal Republic of Nigeria." In Gwendolen M. Carter, ed., *National Unity and Regionalism in Eight African States*. Ithaca, N.Y.: Cornell University Press.

Skurnik, W. A. E. 1970. "The Military and Politics: Dahomey and Upper Volta." In Claude E. Welch, Jr., ed., *Soldier and State in Africa: A Comparative Analysis of Military Intervention and Political Change*. Evanston: Northwestern University Press.

Smith, T. E. 1960. *Elections and Developing Countries*. London: Macmillan.

Smith, Tony. 1978. "A Comparative Study of French and British Decolonization." *Comparative Studies in Society and History* 20, no. 1 (January): 70–102.

Snyder, Frank Gregory. 1965. *One-Party Government in Mali: Transition toward Control*. New Haven: Yale University Press.

Staniland, Martin. 1969. "Single-Party Regimes and Political Change: The P.D.C.I. and Ivory Coast Politics." In Colin Leys, ed., *Politics and Change in Developing Countries*. Cambridge, England: Cambridge University Press.

Stevens, Evelyn P. 1977. "Mexico's PRI: The Institutionalization of Corporatism?" In James M. Malloy, ed., *Authoritarianism and Corporatism in Latin America*. Pittsburgh: University of Pittsburgh Press.

Stultz, Newell M. 1970. "Parliaments in Former British Black Africa." In Marion E. Doro and Newell M. Stultz, eds., *Governing in Black Africa*. Englewood Cliffs, N.J.: Prentice-Hall.

Suret-Canale, Jean. 1971. *French Colonialism in Tropical Africa 1900–1945*. Translated by Till Gottheiner. New York: Pica Press.

Swearer, Howard R. 1961. "The Functions of Soviet Local Elections." *Midwest Journal of Political Science* 5 (May): 129–149.

Tamarkin, M. 1978. "The Roots of Political Stability in Kenya." *African Affairs* 67, no. 308 (July): 297–319.

Tamuno, Tekena N. 1966. *Nigeria and Elective Representation, 1923–1947*. London: Heinemann Educational Books.

Taylor, Sidney, ed. 1957. *The New Africans: Guide to the Contemporary History of Emergent Africa and Its Leaders*. New York: G. P. Putnam's Sons.

Therborn, Goran. 1977. "The Rule of Capital and the Rise of Democracy." *New Left Review*, no. 103 (May–June): 3–41.

Thomas, Keith. 1978. "The United Kingdom." in Raymond Grew, ed., *Crises of Political Development in Europe and the United States*. Princeton: Princeton University Press.

Thompson, Virginia. 1962. "The Ivory Coast." In Gwendolen M. Carter, ed., *African One-Party States*. Ithaca, N.Y.: Cornell University Press.

———. 1963. "Dahomey." In Gwendolen M. Carter, ed., *Five African States*. Ithaca, N.Y.: Cornell University Press.

———. 1966. "Niger." In Gwendolen M. Carter, ed., *National Unity and Regionalism in Eight African States*. Ithaca, N.Y.: Cornell University Press.

———. 1972. *West Africa's Council of the Entente*. Ithaca, N.Y.: Cornell University Press.

Thompson, Virginia, and Richard Adloff. 1957. *French West Africa*. Stanford: Stanford University Press.

———. 1960. *The Emerging States of French Equatorial Africa*. Stanford: Stanford University Press.

———. 1974. *African Historical Dictionary: The Congo (Brazzaville)*. Metuchen, N.J.: Scarecrow Press.

Thompson, William R. 1975. "Regime Vulnerability and the Military Coup." *Comparative Politics* 7, no. 4 (July): 459–488.

Tilly, Charles. 1975. "Western State-Making and Theories of Political Transformation." In Charles Tilly, ed., *The Formation of National States in Western Europe*. Princeton: Princeton University Press.

Tordoff, William. 1966. "The General Election in Tanzania." *Journal of Commonwealth Political Studies* 4 (March): 47–64.

United Kingdom, Royal Commission on Population. 1950. *Reports and Selected Papers of the Statistics Committee*. London: Her Majesty's Stationery Office.

United Nations. 1948. *Demographic Yearbook*. New York.

United Nations, Department of Social Affairs, Population Division. 1953. *The Determinates and Consequences of Population Trends*. Population Studies, no. 17. New York.

University of Dar es Salaam, Election Study Committee. 1974. *Socialism and Participation: Tanzania's 1970 National Elections*. Dar es Salaam: Tanzania Publishing House.

Van De Walle, Etienne. 1968. "Characteristics of African Demographic Data." In William Brass et al., eds., *The Demography of Tropical Africa*. Princeton: Princeton University Press.

van Doorn, Jacques, ed. 1969. *Military Profession and Military Regimes*. The Hague: Mouton.

Veblen, Thorstein. 1961. "On the Merits of Borrowing" and "On the Penalty of Taking the Lead." In Max Lerner, ed., *The Portable Veblen*. New York: Viking Press.

Verba, Sidney, and Norman H. Nie. 1972. *Participation in America: Political Democracy and Social Equality*. New York: Harper and Row.

———. 1978. *Participation and Political Equality: A Seven Nation Comparison*. New York: Cambridge University Press.

Verba, Sidney, Norman H. Nie, and Jae-on Kim. 1971. *The Modes of Democratic Participation: A Cross-National Comparison*. Sage Professional Papers in Comparative Politics, no. 01–013. Beverly Hills: Sage Publications.

Von der Mehden, Fred R. 1964. *Politics of the Developing Nations*. Englewood Cliffs, N.J.: Prentice-Hall.

Wahl, Nicholas. 1962. "The French Political System." In Samuel H. Beer and Adam B. Ulam, eds., *Patterns of Government: The Major Political Systems of Europe*. Second edition. New York: Random House.

Wallerstein, Immanuel. 1961. *Africa: The Politics of Independence*. New York: Vintage Books.

———. 1966. "The Decline of the Party in Single-Party African States." In Joseph LaPalombara and Myron Weiner, eds., *Political Parties and Political Development*. Princeton: Princeton University Press.

———. 1967. "Class, Tribe, and Party in West African Politics." In Seymour M. Lipset and Stein Rokkan, eds., *Party Systems and Voter Alignments: Cross-National Perspectives*. New York: Free Press.

———. 1970. "The Colonial Era in Africa: Changes in the Social Structure." In L. H. Gann and Peter Duignan, eds., *Colonialism in Africa 1870–1960*. Vol. 2. *The History and Politics of Colonialism 1914–1960*. Cambridge, England: Cambridge University Press.

———. 1971. "The Range of Choice: Constraints on the Policies of Governments of Contemporary African Independent States." In Michael F. Lofchie, ed., *The State of the Nations: Constraints on Development in Independent Africa*. Berkeley and Los Angeles: University of California Press.

Wasserman, Gary. 1973. "The Independence Bargain: Kenya Europeans and the Land Issue, 1960–1962." *Journal of Commonwealth Political Studies* 11, no. 2 (July): 99–120.

———. 1976. *Politics of Decolonization: Kenya Europeans and the Land Issue 1960–1965*. New York: Cambridge University Press.

Webb, R. K. 1969. *Modern England*. New York: Dodd, Mead.

Webster, John B. 1966. *The Political Development of Rwanda and Burundi*. Maxwell Graduate School of Citizenship and Public Affairs, Program of Eastern African Studies, Occasional Paper no. 16. Syracuse, N.Y.

Weiner, Myron. 1971. "Political Participation: Crisis of the Political Process." In Leonard Binder et al., *Crises and Sequences in Political Development*. Princeton: Princeton University Press.

Weinstein, Brian. 1966. *Gabon: Nation-Building on the Ogooué*. Cambridge, Mass.: M.I.T. Press.

Weinstein, Warren. 1976. *African Historical Dictionary: Burundi*. Metuchen, N.J.: Scarecrow Press.

Welch, Claude E., Jr. 1970a. "Soldier and State in Africa." In Marion E. Doro and Newell M. Stultz, eds., *Governing in Black Africa*. Englewood Cliffs, N.J.: Prentice-Hall.

———, ed. 1970b. *Soldier and State in Africa: A Comparative Analysis of Military Intervention and Political Change*. Evanston: Northwestern University Press.

———. 1970c. "The Roots and Implications of Military Intervention." In Claude E. Welch, Jr., ed., *Soldier and State in Africa: A Comparative Analysis of Military Intervention and Political Change*. Evanston: Northwestern University Press.

———. 1971. "Cincinnatus in Africa: The Possibility of Military Withdrawal from Politics." In Michael F. Lofchie, ed., *The State of the Nations: Constraints on Development in Independent Africa*. Berkeley and Los Angeles: University of California Press.

Welfling, Mary B. 1971. "Political Institutionalization: The Development of a Concept and Its Empirical Application to African Party Systems." Doctoral dissertation, Northwestern University.

———. 1973. *Political Institutionalization: Comparative Analysis of African Party Systems*. Sage Professional Papers in Comparative Politics, no. 01–041. Beverly Hills: Sage Publications.

Wells, Alan. 1974. "The Coup d'Etat in Theory and Practice: Independent Black Africa in the 1960's." *American Journal of Sociology* 79 (January): 871–887.

———. 1976. "The Practice and Explanation of Coups d'Etat: Measurement or Artifact?" *American Journal of Sociology* 82, no. 3 (November): 674–687.

Wesolowski, Wlodzimierz. 1967. "Marx's Theory of Class Domination: An Attempt at Systemization." In Nicholas Lobkowicz, ed., *Marx and the Western World*. Notre Dame, Ind.: University of Notre Dame Press.

West African Directory, 1967–68. 1968. London: Thomas Skinner and Co.

Williams, Gavin, and Terisa Turner. 1978. "Nigeria." In John Dunn, ed., *West African States: Failure and Promise*. Cambridge, England: Cambridge University Press.

Wilson, Francis G. 1936. "The Inactive Electorate and Social Revolution." *Southwestern Social Science Quarterly* 16 (March): 73–84.

Wolfe, Alan. 1977. *The Limits of Legitimacy: Political Contradictions of Contemporary Capitalism*. New York: Free Press.

Wriggins, W. Howard. 1969. *The Ruler's Imperative: Strategies for Political Survival in Asia and Africa*. New York: Columbia University Press.

Yannopoulos, Tatiana, and Denis Martin. 1972. "Régimes militaires et classes sociales en Afrique Noire." *Revue Française de Science Politique* 22, no. 4 (August): 847–882.

Young, Crawford. 1965. *Politics in the Congo*. Princeton: Princeton University Press.

————. 1970a. "Decolonization in Africa." In L. H. Gann and Peter Duignan, eds., *Colonialism in Africa 1870–1960*. Vol. 2. *The History and Politics of Colonialism, 1914–1960*. Cambridge, England: Cambridge University Press.

————. 1970b. "Rebellion and the Congo." In Robert I. Rotberg and Ali Mazrui, eds., *Protest and Power in Black Africa*. New York: Oxford University Press.

Young, Oran R. 1969. "Professor Russett: Industrious Tailor to Naked Emperor." *World Politics* 21, no. 3 (April): 880–899.

Zambia. 1978. *Official Verbatim Report of the Parliamentary Debates of the 5th Session of the Third National Assembly*. 12 January–8 April, 1978. No. 48, Part I. Lusaka: The Government Printer.

Zeldin, Theodore. 1958. *The Political System of Napoleon III*. London: Macmillan.

Zolberg, Aristide. 1963. "Mass Parties and National Integration: The Case of the Ivory Coast." *Journal of Politics* 25 (February): 36–48.

————. 1964. *One-Party Government in the Ivory Coast*. Princeton: Princeton University Press.

————. 1966a. *Creating Political Order: The Party-States of West Africa*. Chicago: Rand McNally.

————. 1966b. "A View from the Congo." *World Politics* 19 (October): 137–149.

————. 1968a. "Military Intervention in the New States of Tropical Africa: Elements of Comparative Analysis." In Henry Bienen, ed., *The Military Intervenes: Case Studies in Political Development*. New York: Russell Sage Foundation.

————. 1968b. "The Structure of Political Conflict in the New States of Tropical Africa." *American Political Science Review* 62 (March): 70–87.

————. 1969. "Military Rule and Political Development in Tropical Africa: A Preliminary Report." In Jacques van Doorn, ed., *Military Profession and Military Regimes*. The Hague: Mouton.

Periodicals and Serials Consulted

Africa Confidential
Africa Contemporary Record
Africa Diary
Africa Digest
Africa Report
Africa Research Bulletin (Political, Social and Cultural Series)
Africa South of the Sahara
African Index
African Recorder

L'Afrique Française
Afrique Nouvelle
L'Année Politique, Economique, Sociale et Diplomatique en France
Countries of the World and Their Leaders
Daily Nation (Nairobi)
Daily Times (Blantyre)
Europa Year Book
Facts on File
Le Guid'Ouest Africain (Paris)
Jeune Afrique
Keesing's Contemporary Archives
New African
Outre-mer
A Political Handbook and Atlas of the World
A Review of Elections of the World (London: Institute of Electoral
   Research)
Rwanda Carrefour d'Afrique
Standard (Nairobi)
Statesman's Year Book
Times (London)
Times of Zambia (Lusaka)
West Africa
West Africa Annual
Zambian Daily Mail (Lusaka)

Index

Almond, Gabriel A., and Sidney
   Verba, 147
Althusser, Louis, 11, 146
Amin, Idi, 127, 161, 164, 165
Amin, Samir, 164
Anglophone Africa. *See* British
   Africa, post-independence
Anticolonialism, 32–33, 86
Apithy, Sourou-Migan, 107
Assemblies: territorial, 37;
   national, 123–127
Authoritarian regimes, 20, 130;
   establishment of, 2, 22,
   26–28, 168; types of,
   22–23, 27; and continuity
   of political economy, 34.
   See also Military regimes;
   One-party regimes;
   One-party competitive
   regimes; One-party
   plebiscitary regimes

Bandwagon effect, 89–91, 92,
   153
Barkan, Joel, 133, 138
Barrows, Walter L., 70
Bayart, Jean-François, 30, 127

Belgian Africa, post-
   independence: regime
   change in, 96, 101, 154,
   160–161; multi-party
   regimes in, 110; military
   regimes in, 141
Belgian Africa, pre-
   independence: introduction
   of elections in, 42–44,
   47–48; electoral
   participation in, 48, 49
Belgian Congo. *See* Congo
   (Zaire); Zaire
Belgium. *See* Decolonization;
   Europe; Institutional
   transfer
Bendix, Reinhard, 12, 16, 168
Benin (Dahomey):
   post-independence electoral
   policy in, 105, 106;
   unsuccessful party merger
   in, 107; regime change in,
   143, 157, 161–162, 163.
   See also Dahomey
Bienen, Henry, 71
Birmingham, W. B., and G.
   Jahoda, 90

Designer: Al Burkhardt
Compositor: Interactive Composition Corp.
Printer: Braun-Brumfield, Inc.
Binder: Braun-Brumfield, Inc.
Text: 10/12 Sabon
Display: Sabon